THE WOUNDED HEART

Dr. Dan B. Allender

CWR, Waverley Abbey House, Waverley Lane, Farnham, Surrey GU9 8EP

NATIONAL DISTRIBUTORS

Australia: Christian Marketing Pty Ltd., PO Box 154, North Geelong, Victoria 3215. Tel: (052) 786100

Malaysia: Salvation Book Centre, (M) Sdn. Bhd., 23 Jalan SS2/64, 47300 Petaling Jaya, Selangor.

New Zealand: CWR (NZ), PO Box 4108, Mount Maunganui 3030. Tel: (075) 757412

Nigeria: F.B.F.M., No.2 Mbu Close, S/W Ikoyi, Lagos

Republic of Ireland: Scripture Union Book & Music Centre, 40 Talbot Street, Dublin1. Tel & Fax: 363764

Singapore: Alby Commercial Enterprises Pte Ltd., Garden Hotel, 14 Balmoral Road, Singapore 1025.

Southern Africa: CWR (Southern Africa), PO Box 43, Kenilworth 7745, South Africa Tel: (021) 7612560

The Wounded Heart © 1990 by Dan B. Allender

Published 1991 by CWR.
Reprinted 1992.

Originally published 1990 in USA by NavPress, a ministry of The Navigators, USA. This edition issued by special arrangement with NavPress

Printed in England by Clays Ltd. St Ives plc

ISBN 1 - 85345 - 045 - 6

Contents

Foreword   9
Prologue: The Quest for a Cure   13

PART 1: THE DYNAMICS OF ABUSE
Chapter 1   The Reality of a War: Facing the Battle   25
Chapter 2   The Enemy: Sin and Shame   39
Chapter 3   Deflection: The Clash with Contempt   59
Chapter 4   The War Zone: Strategies for Abuse   73

PART 2: THE DAMAGE OF ABUSE
Chapter 5   Powerlessness   97
Chapter 6   Betrayal   111
Chapter 7   Ambivalence   127
Chapter 8   Secondary Symptoms   141
Chapter 9   Style of Relating   155

PART 3: PREREQUISITES FOR GROWTH
Chapter 10   The Unlikely Route to Joy   173
Chapter 11   Honesty   183
Chapter 12   Repentance   199
Chapter 13   Bold Love   219

Epilogue: Words to the Wise   241
Notes   249
Bibliography   251

Author

Dr. Dan B. Allender received his M.Div. from Westminster Theological Seminary and his Ph.D. in Counseling Psychology from Michigan State University. Dr. Allender has been an associate of Dr. Larry Crabb for over ten years and taught with him in the Biblical Counseling Department at Grace Theological Seminary for seven years. He currently teaches and counsels with Dr. Crabb at Colorado Christian University near Denver and travels extensively to present his unique perspective on sexual-abuse recovery issues to both victims and professionals. Dr. Allender and his wife, Rebecca, live in Littleton, Colorado, with their three children, Anna, Amanda, and Andrew.

Acknowledgments

My eight-year-old daughter once asked me: "Daddy, why are you interested in sexual abuse?" Thankfully, before I could answer she asked another question: "Daddy, do abused people have walls in their hearts that keep them from being happy, and will they have less bricks in their walls after reading your book?" I wept. Her simple questions expressed the heart of my personal calling (why am I interested in abuse?) and my professional task (will this book help?) and opened the door to deep gratitude. Those questions, calling, and tasks could not be addressed without the community of clients, friends, mentor, and family who have given me the freedom to ask difficult questions and formulate answers that have not always (or even yet) been clear, accurate, or helpful, without fear of rejection or retribution. That is unique in the Christian community.

The faces of countless men and women have been before me as I wrote this book. Their lives instructed me, broke my heart, and deepened my conviction that a good God does work, albeit in odd and surprising ways. I cannot mention their names, but many will hear in the pages of this book echoes of our conversations, with sorrow and joy. I cannot thank you enough.

The many friends who have taken time to read the manuscript and comment or interact with the material have offered profound encouragement. I mention those whose involvement has been long-term, sure, and life-giving: Al and Nita Andrews, Sandy Burdick, Karla Denlinger, Sandy Edwards, Lottie Hillard, Nancy Lodwick, Tremper Longman, III, Shannon Rainey, Robin Reisert, Melissa Trevathon, Tom Varney, and Lori Wheeler. A woman who has literally transformed the material by her wisdom, kindness, and humor has been my editor, Traci Mullins. I would never have endured the process without her competent ministration and light-hearted muse. Her heart unobtrusively shows itself on every page.

In even more dramatic form, the heart and soul of my colleague, mentor, and best friend, Larry Crabb, is transcribed in the life of this work. His probing, relentless personal honesty and his passionate hunger for God are the impetus that propelled my desire to move into the damaged soul with the hope for deep, eternal transformation. My debt and love are equally deep.

Finally, my wife, Rebecca, is my North Star. Her sensitivity and powerful voice of advocacy for those with a wounded heart has impassioned this work, and her heart for me is a gift of unsurpassing joy. Rebecca, gratitude to you will never be adequately expressed even if I were to take a lifetime to thank you for your love. The years in preparation for this work would never have been possible without your gentle heart.

Foreword

I wish things were simple. I wish that difficult problems could all be easily resolved through sincere determination to obey God, regular time in His Word, and fervent prayer.

In a sense, they can. The heart that is single-minded in its commitment to follow Christ will learn to unself-consciously love, to be so consumed with the wonder of God and promoting joy in others that personal concerns retreat to a well-deserved lower priority.

But our hearts are deceitful. A simple decision to surrender everything to Jesus may start a good process, but there are a host of hard, ugly things to deal with that we prefer to overlook as we keep on surrendering.

We sometimes manage to persuade ourselves that God is as pleased as we are with our developing maturity, while in fact His Spirit is gently pushing open doors into the darker regions of our hearts that we pretend don't exist.

Christians who have the courage to follow the Spirit into the unfriendly parts of their souls have a harder time pretending that the maturing process is coming along nicely. They face the fact that living in a fallen world sometimes exposes people to experiences that no bearer of God's image was ever meant to endure and that our reactions to those experiences are deeply stained with our own fallenness.

When people — through absolutely no fault of their own — are subjected to terrible crimes against God and against their souls, like sexual abuse, powerful forces are set in motion within them that make it especially frightening to give themselves to others. Exhorting them to "just trust God" tends to generate frustration and provoke angry questions about the reality of Christian truth.

One of the great needs in the church today is to replace a model for simplistic sanctification with an understanding of the gospel that is both simple and penetrating, reaching with power into the realities of sinful, damaged souls. That shift requires pioneer work in thinking hard about tough problems like childhood sexual abuse. Problems that, because they do not yield easily to our current ideas about victory in Christ, tend to be ignored.

If that pioneering effort is to be biblical, it must insist that the image of God is central to developing a solid view of personality; that our sinfulness, not how we've been sinned against, is our biggest problem; that forgiveness, not wholeness, is our greatest need; that repentance, not insight, is the dynamic in all real change.

The Wounded Heart is a remarkable book. It goes far beyond shallow ideas about change but remains firmly fixed on biblical foundations as it explores the depths of damage inflicted by sexual abuse. I regard it as a truly pioneer work. It doesn't offer the last word in defining a biblical approach to helping victims of abuse, but it offers far more than merely a first word. The carefully reasoned and extraordinarily poignant discussions of how sexual abuse damages the soul and what the victim must overcome in order to heal will bring first pain, then perhaps resistance, but always hope to the sincere reader, whether a victim or a caring person who wants to help victims.

Dr. Allender has managed to write graphically about an easily sensationalized topic without crossing the line of decency, and he keeps the focus on the gospel by passionately proclaiming his confidence in its power to restore victims of abuse to their dignity as forgiven people, who can now forgive and boldly love from sad yet joyfully alive hearts.

Reading the book will perhaps give some hint of the price that its author has paid in order to understand the problems of abuse with discerning passion. I've been with Dan during the several years while he has immersed himself in the details, sometimes unspeakably grotesque, of hundreds of instances of sexual abuse. I've seen him suffer. He has read widely, thought deeply, dialogued openly, cared passionately, and stayed involved when it required more than he had, in order to help victims of sexual abuse. This book represents his faithfulness to an unsolicited call from his God.

I make no effort to write an unbiased foreword. I can't. I love the man. I have been a part of his life since God began changing him from a bright seminary graduate with more natural boldness than restrained wisdom to a seasoned psychologist with the powerful combination of penetrating insight and gentle patience that comes from a rich awareness of being forgiven. Dan and I are knit together by a mutual loyalty, affection, and respect, developed through hard times and good, that defines the word *friendship*.

But don't assume for a moment that my strong endorsement of his book reflects only my bias. With as much objectivity as I can muster (and I'm a critical friend), I've concluded that *The Wounded Heart* not only is the most profoundly helpful book about childhood sexual abuse available, but also is a stimulating illustration of how to think biblically about topics not directly addressed in Scripture.

Nothing matters more than seeing clearly that the gospel of Christ speaks with heart-mending compassion and life-changing power to every struggle in life. This book has helped me to more clearly see that truth. And I believe it will do the same for you.

—DR. LARRY CRABB

Prologue:
The Quest for a Cure

Anyone who picks up a book on sexual abuse has a definite purpose in mind. Few would bother picking up a painful, deeply distressing book for recreational reading. In most cases this book will be read by those who are struggling to understand their own abuse. Others may read for the purpose of understanding their abused parishioner, client, or spouse. Whatever the reason may be for reading on this subject, I think that it is fair for the reader to ask a central question: *Why another book on this topic?*

An obvious answer is to offer hope to those who have experienced sexual abuse and guidance to those who work with abuse victims. One of the central messages of most books on abuse, this one included, is freedom from the guilt of the past abuse. What occurred is not your fault!

Unfortunately, that message is at first heard as good news but often does not endure over time. I've heard many victims of sexual abuse argue: "Others are excused, but not me. My abuse is different. If you knew the facts, you would understand that I am at least partially at fault. I led him on. I didn't tell anyone, and I know I should have found a way to stop his advances." For some reason the blanket amnesty of forgiveness offered to sexual abuse victims fades after the initial relief. This fading does not invalidate the good news. It simply implies that more must be done than affirm abused people and implore them to forgive themselves.

What is the enemy? What are the factors that make past sexual abuse so shameful and the basis of such grievous self-contempt? What must be done to lift the shroud of shame and contempt? The answer involves a strategy that seems to intensify the problem: *peer deeply into the wounded heart*. The first great enemy to lasting change is the propensity to turn our eyes away from the wound and pretend things are fine. The work of restoration cannot begin until a problem is fully faced.

This is a book about damage, the damage done to the soul by sexual abuse. It is also a book about hope, but hope that loves only after the harm of abuse has been throughly faced. If there is a central reason for this book it is found in the need to thoroughly explore the damage done to the soul as a consequence of past sexual abuse.

There is a natural reluctance to face the problem. Christians seem to despise reality. We tend to be squeamish when looking at the destructive effects of sin. It is unpleasant to face the consequences of sin—our own and others'. To do so seems to discount the finished and sufficient work of our Savior. And so we pretend we're fine, when, in fact, we know that something is troubling our soul. A dull ache occasionally floats to the surface, or stalking memories return in dreams or in odd thoughts during the day. But why bother about such strange feelings when our salvation is guaranteed and life's task is clear: trust and obey?

The unbelieving culture is not so dishonest. Our society faces realities that other eras chose to avoid. Unfortunately, however, it offers solutions that lead to even greater denial. The secular path for change seems to involve some form of self-assertion, setting one's own boundaries and choosing to act on the basis of one's own personal value system. Invariably, the result is a stronger, more self-centered humanist, who lives less for the sake of loving others than for his perceived advantage and benefits.

The solution the secular path offers is in fact filling a leaky cup with lukewarm water. It leaves the soul empty and unsatisfied. It never admits that the deepest damage is never what someone has done to me but what I have done regarding the Creator of the universe. The damage done through abuse is awful and heinous, but minor compared to the dynamics that distort the victim's relationship with God and rob her of the joy of loving and being loved by others.

This process is the end of secular solutions, but many so-called Christian alternatives are even worse. Several paths offered to the abuse victim often increase the burden and lead to revictimization: denial-based forgiveness, pressured demands to love, and quick relief from pain through dramatic spiritual interventions.

DENIAL-BASED FORGIVENESS

Forgiveness built on "forgetfulness" is a Christian version of a frontal lobotomy. An abused woman was told by her pastor that she was to forget the past and stop pitying herself, because many people have had a lot worse things happen to them than being abused by their father. This advice made any reflection on the effects of the abuse selfish and illegitimate. His comment felt as painful to her as the original abuse.

To be told, "The past is the past and we are new creatures in Christ, so don't worry about what you can't change," at first relieves the need to face the unsightly reality of the destructive past. After a time, however, the unclaimed pain of the past presses for resolution, and the only solution is to continue to deny. The result is either a sense of deep personal contempt for one's inability to forgive and forget, or a deepened sense of betrayal toward those who desired to silence the pain of the abuse in a way that feels similar to the perpetrator's desire to mute the victim. *Hiding the past always involves denial; denial of the past is always a denial of God.* To forget your personal history is tantamount to trying to forget yourself and the journey that God has called you to live.

What might be the motivation of the forgive-and-forgetters? The answer may be found in a deep and legitimate desire to protect the honor of God. A central question in the mind of the abused person, "Where was God?" compels many to answer by denying the influence of past events on present-day functioning. If the past is insignificant, then I don't need to ponder the question: Why did God not intervene? The unbelieving world is willing to see the damage of abuse, because it feels no need to defend the God who could have intervened to stop it. The Christian community, however, feels disposed to deny any data that casts doubt on God's presence or willingness to act for the sake of His children.

"Where was God?" is a legitimate cry of the soul to understand what it means to trust God. Irrespective of the answers, the question is not to be avoided. If God is trustworthy, He can be trusted without our efforts to distort and deny the past.

Another factor may be involved in the desire to "forget" the past. Christians believe in the possibility of healing or deep personal change. Change—or better said, the fruit of the Spirit—is the result of God's working in the person. This work enables us to love as Christ loved, to serve as He served, and to be of one mind with others as He is with the Father. These are high claims. The results are seldom, if ever, close to the ideal. One need only to observe our penchant for easy believism, materialism, superficiality, and hypercriticalness toward those who differ with our favorite doctrinal positions to call into question the work of the Holy Spirit in the change process. A secularist could easily sue us for false claims in advertising. Does the gospel really work to transform lives? The data is at times questionable. Therefore the Christian community feels disposed to deny any data that points to the thorns and thistles in the lives of those who claim to be filled with the power of God.

The unbelieving world acknowledges the effects of sin but offers incomplete solutions; the believing world is, at times, unwilling to face the current effects of sin, but has solutions that can provide substantial healing. The answer is quite simple. Let us as Christians acknowledge without shame that regeneration does not alleviate, or in fact diminish, the effects of sin quickly or permanently in this life. If we accept that, we are free to face the parts of our souls that remain scarred and damaged by the effects of sexual abuse without feeling that we are denying the gospel. Facing the reality of the Fall and beginning the process of reclaiming the land covered with weeds is the marvelous work of the God-ordained Kingdom gardener. It is labor eminently worthy of every believer to reclaim the parts of one's soul that remain untilled and unproductive for bearing fruit. And the denial of the past hinders this work of reclamation.

PRESSURED DEMANDS TO LOVE

A woman was told by her friends that she was tempting the judgment of God because she was taking her abuser to court. She was told that her desire to bring him to justice was unloving and vengeful. She wryly remarked that a friend had recently received a sizable out-of-court settlement for an accident, and no one batted an eye. It appeared to be acceptable to use the court system for a damaged car, but not for a damaged soul.

Another man refuses to visit, receive phone calls, or open mail from the father who raped him from age seven to ten. His father, an upstanding church member, is irritated by his son's unwillingness to interact, but flatly denies his son's abuse and has gone so far as to question his son's sanity and salvation.

What does it mean to love one's enemies? Does it mean to simply do good, regardless of what you feel? If the answer is yes, then what in the world does it mean to do good to a father whose unwillingness to face the past abuse is tantamont to living an evil-hearted lie? How is one to hate what is evil and cling to what is good while at the same time loving one's enemy?

There are answers to these questions, but the typical pressured-love solution involves being nice, not causing conflict, and pretending relationships are fine as the evil charade unfolds. Under this version of Christianity, the abused person feels secure and dead. There is safety in soul-numbing rigidity that does not require thought, reflection, or risk. But the honest person knows that *soulless conformity never leads to life-giving change.*

Love is not easily defined, nor is it quickly executed with a slight twist of the will. Loving one's enemy, in particular, requires that the heart be caught up in the freedom and power that God instills in the one who is willing to extend grace to an enemy. Love can be commanded, but is its fulfillment the exercise of right-doing, in spite of the absence of passion, desire, or authenticity toward the person who did harm?

Far too often the abused person is commanded to do good or to love their abuser without exploring the complexities of what it means to love or what may be blocking the God-given desire to love. The result is often a greater deadening of the soul in order to accomplish the burdensome task, or a backlash of rage toward God or anyone who would so insensitively encourage such a painful path.

The assumption taught in many Christian groups is that emotions will follow in accord with your choice of will. If you feel angry, then do good, because in doing good you will eventually not be angry. Even better, if you do good long enough, then you will actually feel loving emotions toward the person who did you harm. This is not the place to debate the interlacing intricacies of choice, thought, emotion, and longing, but an obvious point can be made. All the effort in the world expended to arrive at the "right" location will be of little avail if the traveler is moving in the wrong direction or has known or unknown reasons for not wanting to arrive at the destination. More must be done than shouting commands to love.

Love is at the core of change. But as love is defined by some, it lacks purpose, passion, and strength. In reaction to a culture that sees love as whim based on the unpredictability of emotion, some Christians have opted for a decision-based, emotionless act of the will to be nice and unoffensive. *Love is many things, but it is never weak or lacking in passion.* Simply telling an abused person to love his or her abuser is unhelpful, even if love is an essential component of the change process.

DRAMATIC SPIRITUAL INTERVENTIONS

I recently worked with a woman who was part of a charismatic church connected to a national healing and miracle ministry, which makes an assumption that sexually abused persons are demon-oppressed. The memories may be the concoction of the demons, thus discounting the validity of the past abuse; or the memories may be actual events that are kept in the mind by the evil host that inhabit the victim. In either case, the strategy is to cast the demons out through the ritual of exorcism.

The woman I worked with had learned through years of abuse to keep her mouth shut. If she disagreed with anyone, she assumed she must be wrong. The abused person often looks for someone who is strong, authoritative, and convinced that the damage can be quickly and painlessly resolved. This church provided that hope. She eventually endured several exorcisms where she experienced her handlers as abusive and demeaning, though for a time she felt relief and rest. That period ended when she required constant assurance and drug-like jolts of emotional enthusiasm to keep her wavering and transient faith stable.

Quick cures never resolve the deep damage. Instead, they offer change that requires little more than lying on a gurney before surgery: be still and let the experts do their work. Trust is defined as allowing the process to occur without creating obstacles that would hinder the work. Holy passivity is the key to most quick-cure solutions. The woman had enough integrity to acknowledge that the healing had not occurred, and that the healers were abusive and blind to the real damage in her soul. Once a "magical cure" has occurred, few are willing to admit that much is left to be dealt with.

Quick cures are not unique to any one group. Many offer healing from damaged emotions or memories by attempting to place a "positive" perspective around the painful event in the midst of a deep, flowing expression of pent-up emotions. The result is often a refreshing reclamation of lost parts of the past. It's as if the painful events can be safely looked at without fearing retribution or destruction.

My fear is that many stop at the point of deep initial relief without delving further into the damage. The initial washing of the wound will not be sufficient if the infection is not treated by even stronger medicine. The hunger for a quick cure is as deep as the desire for heaven. The tragedy is that many take the cheap cure and miss the path to a lasting taste of heaven.

THE BETTER PATH

There are many options available to the Christian for dealing with past abuse, but the outcome is unappealing: forgive and forget—denial; pressured love—passionless conformity; quick cures—irresponsible passivity. It is not difficult to understand why the Christian who has been abused often chooses either to seek help outside the church or to learn to handle the damage by pretending it does not exist. I strongly believe the Scriptures offer better ways of hope and change.

What is the better path? The argument of this book is that *the best path is through the valley of the shadow of death.* The crags of doubt and the valleys of despair offer a proving ground of God that no other terrain can provide. God does show Himself faithful; but the geography is often desert-dry and mountainous-demanding, to the point that the path seems too dangerous to face the journey ahead. Who wants to travel with the paltry amount of supplies that we possess or the outdated map we seem to be following, when so many more-modern guides are readily available?

The journey involves bringing our wounded heart before God, a heart that is full of rage, overwhelmed with doubt, blood-ied but unbroken, rebellious, stained, and lonely. It does not seem possible that anyone can handle, let alone embrace, our wounded and sinful heart. But the path involves the risk of put-ting into words the condition of our inner being and placing those words before God for His response. The Lord has promised He will not put out the smoldering flax or break the broken reed (Isaiah 42:3). But promises have been made before by a suppos-edly trustworthy person, and we swore the betrayal was the last we would ever allow our soul to experience. *The obstacle to life is the conviction that God will damage us and destroy us.* The problem is that the path does involve His hurting us, but only in order to heal us.

Why does abuse make it so hard to come to the Lord for the succor and life that our souls crave? What is the enemy to the healing process? In brief, the answer is shame and contempt. The damage of past abuse sets in motion a complex scheme of self-protective defenses that operate largely outside of our awareness, guiding our interactions with others, determining the spouse we select, the jobs we pursue, the theologies we embrace, and the fabric of our entire lives. This book takes a look at the inner workings of these dynamics with the hope that a clearer picture of the damage will enable us to make more conscious, godly decisions in dealing with others and with ourselves.

There are limits to what can be addressed in one book. The reader will quickly note the focus is not on how to deal with children or adolescents who have been abused. There is application of the material to children and adolescents, but I have not focused on those issues. Equally, the majority of my illustrations involve women. By inference it could be assumed that abuse of boys is either limited in extent or limited in its damaging consequences; neither conclusion is accurate or represents my view. There are two reasons for my focus on female abuse victims. One, at this point, women are far more likely than men to pursue counseling and education on the issues of abuse; therefore, my focus represents the audience that is most likely to read this book. Two, the focus of the book is on the damage that every victim will experience, regardless of gender and nature of the abuse; therefore, the illustrations reveal the core issues common to all victims, laying a theoretical framework that I hope will offer guidance for specific applications in individual lives.

There is another reason for writing this book. Every book is an odyssey. Some are theoretical; others are personal quests for the answers that elude our grasp. This odyssey is both. First, it is a theoretical quest that attempts to put words to the experiences of many friends who have entrusted their lives and stories to my care. A counselor is a memorial to the past suffering and future hope of his friends, a memorial—like the Holocaust museum in Jerusalem—that calls others to face the damage of living in a fallen, often diabolical world. The stories of my friends cry out for healing, for justice, for the day when all tears will be wiped away and all wrongs avenged. My prayer is that I will do justice to the words that have been spoken.

This book is also an intensely personal discussion of sexual abuse. Both my wife and I share histories of past abuse. The fact that I have a personal history with sexual abuse, and therefore a bias, does not ensure the validity of my reflections or the helpfulness of the material. It does require, however, that I take the journey of understanding sexual abuse for those whose stories I am telling and for myself. My prayer is to not only do justice to their words, but to offer a perspective on the One whose story is the central word of life, the One whose abuse on the cross gives perspective and direction for dealing with all the lesser abuses that each of us face in a fallen world. Then, indeed, I will have done well in telling the stories of us all.

With sadness and joy I invite you to join this quest for perspective.

PART ONE

THE DYNAMICS OF ABUSE

ONE

The Reality of a War: Facing the Battle

At times, I wonder if every person in the world, male and female, young and old, has been sexually abused. No doubt the nature of my work biases my perspective, perhaps severely. As a psychologist and a counselor trainer, I'm invited to enter into the lives of countless individuals: people who are your next-door neighbor, your kid's Sunday school teacher, your pastor, your physician and — this one will hurt — your wife or husband. For so many of them, a history of sexual abuse lingers like a chronic toothache, so familiar that it is no longer recognized, dulling the senses but not interfering with the capacity to perform the routine tasks of life. In most cases, you would never suspect who has been abused. If asked directly, many would not recall past abuse; others would lie to avoid the shame of admitting that they were victims of one of the few crimes where the victim feels more shunned and rejected than the criminal.

Sexual abuse is a difficult subject. More than most subjects, it provokes a horribly uncomfortable sense of shame, in both speaker and listener. In many groups, the person who admits to a history of past abuse becomes a lightning rod for the fear and rage of those with similar but unadmitted struggles. It is really easier for abused persons to deny the past, ignoring the memories, the pain, and the current struggles that may be related to the abuse.

I recall the plaintive words of a young woman who was facing memories of abuse perpetrated by her father, a respected pastor: "I'd rather be dead than face the truth of the memories. If I admit the memories are true, I'll be totally abandoned by my parents, family, and church. If I continue to live a lie, I'll slowly rot from the inside out, pretending all is well when I know I'm a zombie." Her choices were clear: lie, and die slowly; or talk, and be immediately cut off. It sounds tragic to put it this way, but in her mind, living (that is, admitting all that was true) required that she forget her only hope of life: the support of family and friends.

Her plight is not uncommon. It seems that whenever a woman or man who has been abused enters into the horror of his or her past, a terrible price must be paid. This situation is like that of a friend of mine whose wrist was broken when he was a young child. Due to the neglect of his parents the bone was never properly healed, but it did mend. The bone attached itself in a manner that allows him to function adequately until he attempts to bend his wrist. It is healed, but at the cost of his never being able to play any racquet sport in the way it was intended to be played. He copes well, but the effects of his parents' neglect are ever with him. If he wanted to restore his wrist, he would need to have the bone rebroken and endure a lengthy recuperative process, putting a sizable burden on his family for a time. *Why bother when he has learned so effectively to cope with the wound?* A similar question rages in the minds of many abuse victims.

The process of entering the past will disrupt life or, at least, the existence that masquerades as life. The ease of quiet denial that allows the person to be a pleasant but vacuous doormat or an articulate but driven Bible-study leader will be replaced by tumult, fear, confusion, anger, and change. Marriages will need to be reshaped; sexual relations may be postponed while the partners devote themselves to prayer and fasting. The fabric of life will need to be unraveled piece by piece as the Master reweaves the cloth to His design. The process would be difficult even in an ideal world with supportive partners, friends, and churches. In many cases, the external battle is dramatically difficult because others would prefer the nice woman remain sweet, the competent woman remain in control, and the happy-go-lucky woman remain the life of the party. When change is bumpy and messy, particularly if it impels others to change, it is viewed with suspicion and rancor usually reserved for the worst heretics. But what is viewed as the greatest heresy is usually the thing that calls those committed to comfort to deepest change.

One might wish that the process of sanctification was merely a stroll down a gentle country lane. In fact, the path is through the dark valleys and into the seemingly impenetrable darkness that eclipses the light of the Son of God. The horror of change is that it appears to involve a death that resurrection cannot restore. Therefore, the only apparent hope is to live in denial and to believe that God wants us to be complacent, spiritualized automatons. I view this as a diabolical coverup, a lie of such proportion and feasibility that it seems eminently reasonable. After all, what can be done about a pain of titanic dimension that seems to only get worse to the degree it is touched on, let alone plumbed to its depths? The litany of voices that clamor to sing, "leave well enough alone," are legion, and their degrees, life experience, and cautious reason serve as a numbing influence that dulls the throb in the soul and the pounding of the heart.

What is the point in pursuing firm hope and lively joy? The answer is simple: to live out the gospel. The reason for entering the struggle is *a desire for more, a taste of what life and love could be if freed from the dark memories and deep shame.* No one leaves the lethargy of denial unless there is a spark of discontent that pierces the darkness of daily numbness. To live significantly less than what one was made to be is as severe a betrayal of the soul as the original abuse.

Our motivation to change, however, is more than just dissatisfaction with an empty life; we are motivated by the goal that draws all believers. The apostle Paul talked about the end point as a crown of righteousness (2 Timothy 4:8). Paul was willing to be poured out like a drink offering, to fight the good fight, and to finish the race, because he knew his hunger for the Lord's appearing would be rewarded with the prize of the Lord's commendation. To be greeted by the Lord with the prize of His "well done" embrace was a reward that supplanted the ordinary concerns for comfort.

The person who desires to deal with the wounds of past abuse will not feel courageous, nor will there be the immediate exaltation of starting out on a new journey; the bonds on the soul will not be quickly freed or broken. What, then, is the reason for moving toward the goal of God's embrace? Again, the answer is *a hunger for more*. God has made us with a natural desire to be as He is: alive, righteous, pure, passionate, loving. *To honor what God has called us to be is the reason a man or woman chooses the path of change.*

The tragedy is that the adult who wants to deal with his or her past sexual abuse must be willing to confront an internally and externally fierce battle fought by Christians against other Christians. This sad state of affairs makes change, when it occurs, a supernatural victory of no small proportion. It is imperative that the man or woman who has been abused enters into the battle armed with both *an awareness of the cost* and *a deep conviction that life lived in the mire of denial is not life at all*. If the Lord Jesus came to give life, and life abundant, then a life of pretense involves a clear denial of the gospel, no matter how moral, virtuous, or appealing that life may seem.

What needs to be faced, if one is to enter the fray with the hope of change? In simple terms one must face that there is a war, one must recognize the enemy, and one needs to know why the battle is to be fought. There is a war. One enters it when one acknowledges the reality of the past abuse.

THE REALITY OF A WAR

A problem cannot be resolved until it has been faced. A major shift occurs when words are given to what is known or suspected to be true: *I have been sexually abused*. The enormous battle in labeling the truth is difficult to imagine.

A woman I worked with for over a year recently joined an incest survivors' group. She was reluctant to do so even though our work had concentrated on the effects of the abuse. She confessed that the difficulty was in admitting to herself that her only reason for joining the group was because she had been abused. Even though our conversations over the past year were largely about her past abuse, she had avoided fully acknowledging that she had been abused.

I had always been amazed at the reluctance to face the data head on until I had an encounter with a good friend. I had been involved in working with abused people for over a year when I conducted a seminar on the topic. At the seminar I was asked by several people if I had ever been abused. My answer was always no. The good friend who heard me teach asked the same question. I answered in the same manner. He probed and asked if I had ever been in a situation where I felt sexually uncomfortable, awkward, or debased. My answer was so quick it surprised me: "Well, of course." He asked me the details, and in moments, I had a stream of memories return about forced masturbation at a camp I had attended as an adolescent, of a homosexual invitation I turned down in Boy Scouts, and a sexual assault that occurred at a football camp. He looked at me with stunned sorrow and said: "Doesn't that fit your definition of sexual abuse?" I was dumbfounded. It was not that I had entirely forgotten those events, but I would never have allowed them to be labeled with a word that might open the door to further exploration. *There is a deep reluctance to begin the process of change by admitting that damage has occurred.*

A woman recently came to see me for the sole purpose of determining whether she had been sexually abused. She was well-educated, bright, and competent. Many knew her as a no-nonsense, reasonable woman. She shyly informed me, after explaining her purpose in seeking help, that for fourteen years she had been taken to a nudist colony by her parents. Each summer the clothed community was invited to attend a nude beauty pageant. During the pageant she was forced to pose in various positions, some pornographic, for an entire evening. Her soul died. She was mortified in being associated with her parents' nudity at home and at the colony, but even worse, she despised that annual evening when hundreds of men would gawk and slobber over the sight of her developing body. Again, I was stunned. Could she really be asking if she had been abused? Was the record not a thousand percent clear?

A woman who was sexually abused by her father, uncle, and grandfather agreed she was harmed by their behavior, but was reluctant to call it sexual abuse. Her father and uncle forced her to have oral sex with them. Her grandfather would exhibit himself in front of her. She said with great sincerity, "If I had been raped, I would call it abuse, but all they did was what a dozen other men have done to me over the years, so why should I call it abuse?"

What is sexual abuse? It seems that many people operate on the principle that whatever happened to them is not abuse, but if it had happened to someone else or if it had been a bit more extreme, then it would have been abusive. One man literally said, "My mother was always parading around the house without any clothes. She would often ask me to fasten her bra or check her legs for bruises. I know it was inappropriate, but how could that be abuse?" Because of this kind of confusion about what constitutes sexual abuse, it is imperative to have a clear definition:

> Sexual abuse is any contact or interaction (visual,
> verbal, or psychological) between a child/adolescent
> and an adult when the child/adolescent is being used
> for the sexual stimulation of the perpetrator or any other
> person.

Sexual abuse may be committed by a person under the age of eighteen when that person is either significantly older than the victim or when the perpetrator is in a position of power or control over the victimized child/adolescent. When the sexual abuse is perpetrated by an adult or older child who is a blood or legal relative, it constitutes incest, or intrafamilial sexual abuse.

There are two broad categories of abuse: sexual contact and

sexual interactions. *Sexual contact* involves any type of physical touch that is designed to arouse sexual desire (physical or psychological) in the victim and/or the perpetrator. Physical touch can include at the most severe level forced or nonforced intercourse, oral or anal sex (24% of victims); at the severe level forced or nonforced manual vaginal stimulation or penetration, breast fondling, or any form of simulated intercourse (40%); and at the least severe level, forced or nonforced sexual kissing, touch of clothed breasts, buttocks, thighs, or genitals (36%). The categories imply a continuum of severity, but *all inappropriate sexual contact is damaging and soul-distorting*. Seventy-four percent of the least-severely abused victims report severe damage later in life.

Sexual interactions are far harder to acknowledge because they do not involve physical touch and therefore do not seem as severe. Many times they involve a subtle sexual invasion that leaves the victim wondering if it occurred or if it is a byproduct of her own distorted imagination. Interactions can be categorized as visual, verbal, or psychological. Visual sexual abuse involves interactions where the child is forced or invited to watch sexually arousing scenes or pictures or is observed by the perpetrator in a state of undress that is arousing to the adult.

One client's father used to leave pornographic literature in the bathroom before she would take a shower. After she had begun to bathe, he would enter the room and retrieve his magazine, lingering for a moment to observe his daughter's teenage form silhouetted behind the shower door. This was not an inadvertent mistake; the pattern was confirmed in other visual intrusions.

One young teenage boy returned home each day with a mixture of trepidation and excitement, wondering if his alchoholic mother would be drunk and naked or partially unclothed, lying on the living room couch. Each time he swore he would not look, but his teenage curiosity and growing sexual responsiveness to visual cues betrayed him.

A parent or adult who finds arousal in watching a naked

child or introducing a child to sexual stimuli (through pornography or exhibitionistic sexual exposure) has without a doubt sexually victimized that child.

Sexual verbal interactions can be equally abusive. A good friend of mine casually discussed her father's lifelong habit of talking about her body as if he were expressing interest in her grades. Every day he visually scanned her developing body as if he were looking for evidence of head lice. He measured her skirt, checked out her hair, evaluated and judged her boyfriends, and most embarrassingly, commented on her body in front of her dates. His vilely endearing term for her was T.T. No one knew what it meant for years, but she knew he was referring to her breasts. Such repeated verbal degrading obviously constitutes emotional abuse, but it should not be ignored as it also violates the young girl's sexual identity.

Verbal sexual abuse can also come in the form of suggestive or seductive interactions. A woman recalled her disgust in being around her grandfather. Every time he saw her, he would wink and chuckle. Her internal discomfort was viewed as disrespectful by her parents and as a symptom of craziness in the young girl. That lasted for thirty years until I probed for other interactions with her grandfather. It finally came to light that he would wait until no one else was around and then say, "You are so sweet I could eat you. Come here, honey, and let me taste your lips." Was he a silly old man, innocent but slightly inappropriate? Or was he a sexually suggestive abuser who used words as the stimulant that increased his perverse sexual arousal? One indication is that he spoke like that only when he was alone with his granddaughter. His other grandfatherly embraces went unnoticed, because they were innocent enough apart from his suggestive remarks that highlighted his lengthy hugs or kisses. Nevertheless, every time he touched her, she felt disgust and tightness.

Actual seductive verbal interactions are easier, in most cases, to discern. To be invited to take a shower with dad, or to go down in the cellar with your brother, or take a long walk in the woods with your uncle when sexual cues are emitted or past sexual abuse has occurred clearly are abusive encounters. Verbal abuse is a power-ful and deep wound. *Sexually abusive words produce the same damage as sexually abusive contact.* Yet the potential for minimization or feeling weird for being damaged makes the potential for change even more difficult for those more subtly abused than for those more severely abused.

A final category of interaction is psychological sexual abuse. There is an obvious overlap between visual and verbal sexual abuse and psychological abuse. Psychological sexual abuse will occur through verbal or visual means (usually both) but will involve more subtle (nonspecific, more mood-generating) communication that erodes the appropriate role boundaries between a child and an adult. For example, a mother who seeks advice or solace from a teenage son about her sexual struggles with his father has stepped across the line between honest sharing and pandering. To pander is to act as a go-between in love intrigues, to act as a pimp. A pimp solicits sexual involve-ment for his own benefit. A father who uses his daughter as a surrogate wife or confidante has bound his daughter's heart to him in a subtly sexual way. The damage may not be overt, and in fact the daughter may feel so special that she would defend to her death the appropriateness of her father's interactions. It is nevertheless abusive. In the same way a mother who talks about her son as being her "man," her "companion," or her surrogate "husband" has set up a dynamic of competition with her adult husband and a sense of sexually bonded uniqueness for the son that violates the natural boundaries between mother and son.

Whenever a parent or caregiver uses a child to fulfill overt sexual desires or more subtle longings related to the adult's sexual identity, abusive dynamics will be unleashed in that child's soul. *The fact that sexual abuse can be subtle ought not cloud our perspective that it is equally abusive and damaging.* The very nature of satanic harm is that it is perpetrated by the father of lies who masquerades as an angel of light. Whether the perpetrator is acting under direct satanic sway or indirectly in the way that all sin can be ultimately tied to Satan's province, a certain degree of deceit and subtlety can be assumed in all sexual abuse.

TYPES OF SEXUAL ABUSE: CONTACT AND INTERACTION

CONTACT

Very Severe: Genital intercourse (forcible or nonforcible); oral or anal sex (forcible or nonforcible)

Severe: Unclothed genital contact, including manual touching or penetration (forcible or nonforcible); unclothed breast contact (forcible or nonforcible); simulated intercourse

Least Severe: Sexual kissing (forcible or nonforcible); sexual touching of buttocks, thighs, legs, or clothed breasts or genitals

INTERACTIONS

Verbal: Direct solicitation for sexual purposes; seductive (subtle) solicitation or innuendo; description of sexual practices; repeated use of sexual language and sexual terms as personal names

Visual: Exposure to or use for pornography; intentional (repeated) exposure to sexual acts, sexual organs, and/or sexually provocative attire (bra, nighties, slip, underwear); inappropriate attention (scrutiny) directed toward body (clothed or unclothed) or clothing for purpose of sexual stimulation

Psychological: Physical/sexual boundary violation: Intrusive interest in menstruation, clothing, pubic development; repeated use of enemas;
    Sexual/relational boundary violation: Intrusive interest in child's sexual activity, use of child as a spouse surrogate (confidant, intimate companion, protector, or counselor)

WHO ARE ABUSERS?

The abuser can be anyone. He can be your father, your pastor, your brother, your seventy-year-old next-door neighbor. Often a victim has had so many abusers that it seems as if he or she sent a serial letter inviting them to join in the debauchery of abuse. It is not unusual to see a client who has been abused by several family members, a neighbor, boyfriends, teacher, counselor, or employer.

The abuser may be a man or a woman. It is far more common for a young girl to be abused by an adolescent or adult male, but it is inaccurate to presume that men do not abuse boys or women do not abuse girls and boys.

The abuser may be decades older or the same age. He or she may have an honored role in your family or may not be known to you or anyone in your family. In any case, the perpetrator will have a face, a voice, a smell. Even if you cannot recall any details about him, he will be like a faded picture you carry in your wallet. Though you may not have seen him in thirty years or you may have eaten lunch with him yesterday, he still plays a significant part in your daily life, and likely an even greater role in every dream and nightmare.

A great deal of research has been done about the perpetrator and the effects of his abuse. The focus of this book is not on the abuser, nor on the variance in damage caused by different kinds of perpetrators. This book explores the nature of the damage done to the soul of the victim by any kind of sexual abuse, irrespective of the perpetrator. The abuse victim, however, often defends or ignores the perpetrator, especially if the abuser was a family member. It is important to understand how this is done.

Many who have been sexually abused tend to make excuses for the perpetrator or minimize the damage. The most typical way is to find comfort in the fact that at least the perpetrator was not one's closest, most intimate caregiver or friend. Betrayal by an intimate, deeply trusted companion is almost too much for the soul to endure. The victim does not want to face that the perpetrator may have been a person with access to the deepest recesses of his or her soul, a bearer of a key that no one else possessed. For this reason, many who have been abused by an uncle will say, "At least it was not my brother or, even worse, my father." Or if the abuse was perpetrated by someone outside the family, the relief centers around the fact that it was not a relative. The fearful and fallen heart does not want to anguish over the loss of safety and nurturance; therefore, the damage is seemingly diminished in the relief that the perpetrator was not someone closer or that the damage could have been more severe.

The second tendency is to put the abuser in a category that explains away the harm. The damage will be faced to the extent the abuser is seen as the perpetrator of a crime—if not a civil infraction, then certainly a violation of God's law. The battle will not be entered if one makes excuses for the abuser and his or her crime.

The excuses are legion. The abuser was abused as a child. He had a hard background that would have made anyone a little crazy. He was going through a terrible time with his wife and was so lonely. He drank to the point that he just didn't know what he was doing, so how could he be held accountable? He did so many wonderful things for people, how can I be angry for just one failure? All excuses should be silenced; the perpetrator committed a crime against the abused person's body and soul.

A central point needs to be highlighted again: Sexual abuse is damaging no matter how the victim's body is violated. At first, many will doubt the veracity of that claim; it does not immediately stand to reason that being violently raped by one's father can be compared to being lightly touched through the clothing by a gentle, grandfatherly next-door neighbor. No one would question that being raped by one's father will be far more difficult to deal with than handling the nuisance of a pawing dirty old man. The degree of trauma associated with abuse will be related to many factors, including the relationship with the perpetrator, the severity of the intrusion, use of violence, age of the perpetrator, and the duration of abuse. But in every case of abuse, the dignity and beauty of the soul have been violated. Therefore, damage will be present whether one has been struck by a Mack truck traveling 50 miles per hour, or "merely" hit by a tricycle rolling at the same speed.

Obviously, there are certain abusive relationships that are more damaging than others. An assumption can be made about sexual abuse: With all other factors being equal, damage will be *in direct proportion to the degree that it disrupts the protection and nurturance of the parental bond.* There are two issues related to the potential disruption: the abuse and the revelation of the abuse. When abuse is perpetrated, it sets into motion the tremors of an internal earthquake that requires a strong and nurturant environment to quell. If that environment is unavailable, or worse yet, if the environment is hostile, cold, and/or insensitive to the resultant damage, then a victim will set aside the internal process of healing to ensure his or her own survival.

For this reason, incest is usually more devastating than extrafamilial abuse. A sexual relationship with an older cousin will not be as traumatic as the same sexual experience with one's father. A father is called to be a secure, trustworthy, and life-generating surrogate for God until the child develops the capacity to see his or her heavenly Father as the only perfectly trustworthy Source of life. *The victim's struggle to trust will be proportionately related to the extent her parent(s) failed to protect and nurture her as a child.*

Intrafamilial abuse will almost always be more devastating except when the revelation of extrafamilial abuse threatens to damage the relationship with the victim's parents or other family members. If a child were to report to his parents that a neighbor was fondling him several times a week, he might fear being doubted or, worse, blamed for the abuse. He might have a hundred other reasons to fear his parents' response, therefore he fears the repurcussions of the revelation. To the degree that confidence in the love and respect of one's parents is disturbed, the damage of intra- or extrafamilial abuse will be more traumatic.

To summarize, the first task in entering the battle is facing the fact that a battle exists. There are many who will read this chapter and label for the first time the awful experiences at home, school, or church as sexual abuse. Facing the reality of past abuse is a process. It does not happen quickly or in one climactic moment of honesty. It usually occurs over a lengthy period of time when sudden memories or vague, dreamlike glimpses of a nightmare creep into view. Many times the memories are accompanied with little emotion other than disbelief or incredulity. Doubt of the truth of the memory or of oneself serves as a guard that protects a fragile soul from the growing terror. It is not unusual for a person to store the first wave of memories in a deep, icy locker for an interminable period of time. The frozen memories, like ice statues, can now be controlled without fear of retribution. The arctic portions of our minds, however, are continually tempted to thaw by the warmth of the longings of our soul. Every pleasant interchange is an invitation to life; every deep sorrow stirs the passion of grief. Those daily temptations to life are viewed by the person who has been sexually abused, at best, as a two-day vacation to a warm climate and, at worst, as the melting of the polar ice cap. A total meltdown spells disaster; therefore, the icy soul must remain frozen and hidden.

The sexually abused person often denies the abuse, mislabels it, or at least minimizes the damage. The enemy goes unrecognized or misunderstood, so the victim cannot fight the battle. Once the war is avoided, then something must be done with the wounded heart that cries out for solace and hope. The cry must be heard or squelched. Sadly, the choice is usually to stifle the groan. What normally mutes the cry is the internal dynamic that promotes denial, mislabeling, or minimization. The dynamic involves the subtle workings of shame and contempt that serve to keep the soul frozen and the warmth of life at a distance. The next two chapters will explain the internal dynamic that unnecessarily deepens the wound.

TWO

The Enemy: Sin and Shame

The war has begun, but who is the enemy? The question seems too simple. Let me tell you why. Sometime ago I was inflicted with the male counterpart of childbirth: a kidney stone. If you had asked me to describe my enemy (assuming I could answer at all), I would have looked incredulous and shouted, "my pain," referring of course to the searing pain that was signaling the end of my existence. The effect of intense anguish is interesting: It dispels all thoughts other than the desire for relief. *The enemy is the pain and whatever is responsible for it.*

To ask an abused person, "Who is your enemy?" invites the same kind of response. The enemy is the pain of abuse and the person responsible for causing that pain! The pain would not be there if the abuser had not committed the crime. The enemy is obvious. *Or so it seems.* But notice what happens when the enemy is the abuser. The victim is caught in a vicious reactionary cycle of either fight or flight. To diminish the poison of the abuse, all that can be done is to forget, overcome, master, or retaliate against the abuser who brought the pain into the soul. It is not only an endless war, but a futile one. Imagine trying to forget someone. The effort itself focuses attention on the person you long to forget. The energy enlisted and expended in trying to forget dooms the enterprise before it begins.

Similarly, a commitment never to be hurt again by the abuser (or anyone else like him) creates a hard, inflexible exterior and, in turn, leads to the loneliness that the hardness was developed to avoid. The victim's defensive armor will add more pain to her soul and her pain will strengthen her resolve never to be hurt, inevitably increasing the wintery ice in her heart. The protection against pain, in fact, intensifies the pain that it was supposed to decrease.

If the enemy is the abuser, hated or excused, then he will continue to play out his heinous role, years later, by eliciting an endless, reactive response. There are two possible strategies to deal with the foe: fight or flight. The two options seem very different. One involves frontal attack and the other is face-saving retreat. The strategy of fight (angry, man-hating zeal) and the strategy of flight (quiet complacency) are in fact more alike than different; both are an attempt to avoid the internal battle. The energy that fuels the vindictive attack or stagnant submission is a desire to escape the wounded heart. Any battle fought against this enemy (and he does deserve to be called an enemy) will lead to hopeless despair. It is like fighting a phantom, a ghost that cannot be punched, stabbed, or otherwise killed. The abuser is a problem, but (this is good news) he is not the major one.

Who, then, or what, is the real foe? Simply put, *the problem is in the victim*, leading to broken relationships, loneliness, depression, eating disorders, promiscuity, sexual coldness, and frightening rage. Something is wrong inside. Nothing can quite manage to cover it up: smiles, busy schedules, successful Christian living—nothing soothes the battle raging deep within the soul.

I once asked a woman who was raped by her father and later by her husband to define the essence of her struggle in life. With a biting snarl and a caustic tone that communicated strong hatred (betrayed only by the sadness in her eyes), she said, "If I could only rid myself of my hunger for a man, I could be happy." Her words might be elaborated as follows: "If I could only find a way not to hunger for relationship, if I could deaden my soul to what I was made for—the longing to be pursued, embraced, known, and enjoyed—then I could live without sorrow." *Her enemy was her longings.*

Let me state an important observation: I have never worked with an abused man or woman who did not hate or mistrust the hunger for intimacy. In most victims, the essence of the battle is a hatred of their hunger for love and a strong distaste for any passion that might lead to a vulnerable expression of desire. The same woman, in tears, said, "I only wish I had not wanted my father's love. I could have found some way out, if I wasn't so weak and stupid." *The enemy, or so it feels, is the passion to be lovingly pursued and nourishingly touched by a person whose heart is utterly disposed to do us good.* Such people (if they exist at all) are rare; it is therefore easier to hate the hunger than to wait expectantly for the day of satisfaction.

The abused woman has plenty of reasons to despise her own passion. Hating her longings starts a self-annihilating civil war that kills her soul. But the enemy is not really the longings of her heart any more than it is the abuser. Neither is responsible for sabotaging life and love; yet something is deadening the soul. What is it?

Ultimately, the enemy is the prowling beast that attempts to devour and destroy the beauty of God's Kingdom. The enemy is *sin*, that fallen, autonomous striving for life that refuses to bow to God. *The enemy is the internal reality that will not cry out to God in humble, broken dependence.* It is the victim's subtle or blatant determination to make life work on her own by refusing to acknowledge or let God fulfill her deepest longings.

The enemy is the same for the abused person as it is for those who have not been sexually abused: a determined, reliable inclination to pursue false gods, to find life apart from dynamic, moment-by-moment relationship with the Lord of life. For the abused person, however, the past grievous violation of trust and intimacy even more dramatically inflames her determination to live without the pain of unmet longings—and thus without the raging thirst of a soul that pants for God alone.

The issues that are found in all our lives are more intensely and dramatically present in the struggles of those who have been sexually abused. An understanding of sexual abuse, therefore, will help make clear what happens to anyone's soul when he or she is sinned against, whether "normally" and inevitably, or severely when abuse occurs. Victimization provides a rich soil in which the issues of sin are intertwined with legitimate feelings of anger, hurt, and disappointment. When a person is victimized, her inherent commitment to depend on her own resources swings into action. The determination to make it against all odds begins a frightening cycle involving the elements of shame and contempt.

Shame and contempt are not well-understood terms, and their role in the experience of sexual abuse takes time to comprehend. This chapter will deal with shame, and the next chapter will examine contempt. To set the scene for an understanding of these concepts it is important to understand what it means to be a person, a sinful person, a fallen image bearer.

MAN: A PERSON OF DIGNITY AND DEPRAVITY

Man, as Francis Schaeffer has put it, is a glorious ruin, a stately castle, intricately and masterfully constructed by the hand of an Artisan who designed His work with no thought of expense or practicality. A proper concern for God's own glory and majesty was His only guiding force in creating a person. The castle, however, was given a life of its own, capable of rearranging itself. When man (speaking of both men and women) took it on himself to be as God, he ruined everything. Crumbling walls, rotten wood, and overgrown gardens: the decay became so extensive that only one with the eyes of a craftsman could see the structural beauty that remained underneath the overgrown foliage and overthrown walls. Nevertheless, it has glory in its form and composition. Man is an amalgamation of dignity and depravity, a glorious ruin.

Dignity
Man, bearing the image of God, was made to be like God in his capacity to relate and his capacity to rule. In these capacities lies his dignity.

God is a personal and relational being. He has existed forever in perfect relationship with Himself. Father, Son, and Holy Spirit have loved and honored one another from eternity to eternity. Man is like God in that he was made to be in relationship with God and God's creation. God has designed man to enjoy intimacy, to deeply desire to be known and to know. Man's capacity for enjoyment and the longing to realize his capacities draws man into deeper and deeper relationship with God and His creation.

God is the designer, creator, and owner of the cosmos. One need only consider the staggering array of creatures, their often bizzare form and blinding color, to be stunned by the mind of the Creator. And over this zoological kaleidoscope, man was put in charge to be God's manager and foreman. Man is not a creator who makes something out of nothing, but he was made to be an inventive, imaginative user of all that God made. The longing to see our life count or matter, the passion to make a dent in the world, to influence another person because of our presence, is a God-designed passion built into every man and woman. Man's person and position was indeed glorious and rich with dignity.

Depravity

Another aspect of man must be considered, however: depravity. The ruin of the glory was sin. The fall into sin was the most absurd, groundless, unexplainable violation of glory known to man. How could man who had all but one thing, absolute authority and knowledge, desire to own more? There is no answer, because words and logic can never capture something so patently crazy. The choice to abandon vulnerable dependence on the word of God brought man to ruin.

Through all the centuries since that day, we have maintained our commitment to strive for autonomous, independent control over life, supressing the knowledge of God in unrighteousness. This depravity shows itself in murder and immorality and in every endeavor of life, including witnessing to our neighbor, laughing with our friends, and kissing our spouse. To understand the depth and extent of sin is to comprehend that our motives, as fallen but regenerate beings, are stained by sin even as we attempt to honorably love God and others. The glory of the Cross is that in spite of every act, thought, or feeling being stained by the Fall, our regenerate deeds are cleansed under the righteousness of our Elder Brother's sacrifice.

Every person enjoys dignity and suffers from depravity. The structure of personality is a result of the interaction of these two dynamics. Dignity and depravity may be the raw elements of the human personality, but another reality serves as a driving force that motivates fallen man: *shame*. Shame lurks as another powerful enemy to the damaged soul that gasps for life.

SHAME: THE DREAD OF BEING KNOWN

For most people, shame is another word for embarrassment. Everyone knows that embarrassment is unpleasant, but hardly life threatening. Years of careful grooming and mastery have enabled us to avoid embarrassment, or if we are caught, to melt into our surroundings as adroitly as a chameleon. No wonder little is known about the experience of embarrassment, let alone its more hideous counterpart: shame.

Shame is a silent killer, much the way that high blood pressure is a quiet, symptom-free destroyer. Fortunately, shame has a set of symptoms that can be discerned, once the eyes are open to its presence and operation. But like heart disease, it is easy to ignore the problem or to mislabel it as heartburn or a minor chest pain.

Shame has the power to take our breath away and replace it with the stale air of condemnation and disgust. A section of a letter from a friend illustrates the point:

> Sharing the fact of my abuse with them [a small Bible study group] elicited a cold silence that violently rattled the chains of shame deep within me. It was almost as if my disclosure of the abuse produced a shame that reached out and swallowed us all. It was only grace that enabled me to cling tenaciously to the knowledge that I am not a lesbian and that there is no shame in deeply longing to be loved. As I reflect on that evening with my friends, I believe I understand how my shame in actuality deeply touched long-ignored wounds in the souls of my friends.

Unlike other feelings that relinquish some of their power by putting words to the inner sensation, shame has the propensity to increase in intensity when it is first acknowledged. The mere discussion of shame awakens the undealt-with shame in others. For that reason shame is a shameful topic, one that most people would prefer to ignore.

All of us have lived with the bitter taste of shame. Our memories need only return to grade school or junior high to recall at least a few stories of insufferable shame. I will never forget the boy in eighth grade who was sent to the drugstore to purchase paper napkins for the class float. He returned with a huge box of sanitary napkins. I recall the stunned look of horror on the face of the teacher and the snickering laughter and smirking eyes of the girls. I was as unaware of the ribald humor in the purchase as was the boy who made it. I didn't know what a sanitary napkin was, but I was sure of one thing: I would never volunteer for any service, if the result could be so devastating.

It was not my shame, but I borrowed it and swore I would never do anything so stupid. I knew I was just as dumb in the ways of the world, so I chose to never do anything that required a risk of exposure. During gym, I went out to the track confident that I would be picked in the first or second draft when a team was chosen for a sporting event. I was a good athlete. But at lunch I avoided the athletic track when boys were sizing up girls and girls were giggling about boys. I was shy and awkward. I learned in many situations that a girl could expose my sophomorish inexperience, and I would not knowingly walk into my own disgrace.

Shame is a potential reality at every stage of life. The pressure to perform, to do well, to succeed can alternately be looked at as a desire not to fail, because every failure lands in the rubble of shame. A major partner in a prestigious law firm remarked that he owed his entire career to shame. The hundreds of hours spent on a case were designed to ensure that no one knew more or was better prepared for a trial. What was the motivation? "I cannot handle being beaten. Whenever I lose, I feel as if someone took my pants off in front of all my peers." He was describing the experience of shame. The shame he felt at losing a case cannot be considered righteous and consistent with God's purpose for his life. The lawyer's shame at defeat implies that his real motive in doing well has little to do with serving Christ or using his abilities to their utmost; rather, he is compelled by a drive to win. His god is success, peer prestige, financial rewards, and more likely the thrill of conquering others.

WHAT IS SHAME?

Why are we so prone to feel shame over failure or making a mistake, when we rarely experience shame over yelling at our spouse or snubbing a friend? An answer to that question will help us begin to understand, to a degree, why a woman who has been sexually abused feels shame over something that was not her fault.

Shame has been called by Jean-Paul Sartre a hemorhage of the soul. It is an awful experience to be aware that we are seen as deficient and undesirable by someone whom we hope will deeply enjoy us. Shame seems to involve at least four important elements: exposure, revelation, dread of the consequences, and empowering trust.

The Exposure

Shame is an experience of the eyes. If I were to commit a normal but socially vulgar act in private, like nose picking, I would not feel shame; but if caught in that act by someone I know, I would likely feel shame. Shame is an interpersonal affect; it requires the presence of another, in fact or in imagination, for its blow to be felt.

Consider the account of the Fall in the third chapter of Genesis. We are told that Adam and Eve were naked and felt no shame (Genesis 2:25). Their nakedness, a description of their physical appearance, equally implies an absence of conflict and the presence of gentle, loving involvement. Then the Evil One tempted Eve to question God's right to require dependent, vulnerable trust; he persuaded her that she had the right to be as God, knowing good and evil. The man and woman ate, and they became self-conscious. They saw their nakedness and sought leaves to cover their raw shame and betrayal. They knew that their rebellion deserved death, and they fled from the presence of God.

Their capacity to feel shame did not lead to change or a return to the Creator. It led to the opposite attempt to hide behind a bush. God discovered their hideout by asking Adam a series of questions designed to expose their rebellion and shame. The exposure, however, led to an arrogant attack against God. Listen to the narrative:

> But the LORD God called to the man, "Where are you?"
> He answered, "I heard you in the garden, and I was afraid
> because I was naked; so I hid." And he said, "Who told you
> that you were naked? Have you eaten from the tree that
> I commanded you not to eat from?" The man said, "The
> woman you put here with me—she gave me some fruit
> from the tree, and I ate it." (Genesis 3:9-12)

Imagine telling the Lord God: "Don't blame me. It's not my fault; You made her. If You had not created this woman, then I would not be in this mess. It's ultimately a failure of Your creation. You, God, and the woman You made are the cause of the Fall."

Exposure, more often than not, leads to shame. The natural response of an autonomous (independent and self-reliant) heart is to hide behind fig leaves or any convenient bush. If that does not work and if we are discovered again, we will resort to vicious condemnation of the Creator or His creation. As children of Adam and Eve, we bear not only their likeness to God as image bearers, but also their desire to be autonomous and their propensity to hide, blame, and attack when caught. As a result of the Fall we despise standing vulnerable before God and others; therefore we find countless ways to flee from His presence and avoid being seen.

Shame is a dreaded, deep-seated, long-held terror come true: what we have feared has actually come about. We've been found out. The dark secret—and their are many in every life—that may involve a past sexual indiscretion, thought or behavior, a past disloyalty, a failure of conscience, a violent act, a cruel outburst, or a personal failure is known. All our elaborate defenses, disguises, and personality traits are held in bondage to the goal of not being known, because to be known is to be caught naked and defenseless.

Sexually abused people often feel marked for life. The exposure of the past abuse sets them apart from normal, supposedly unstained, undamaged people. (It is not unlike the segregation that minority groups feel when they are set apart because of a difference in appearance or in the color of their skin.) The stain of the abuse seems to color the perspective of anyone who learns of the victims' past. Therefore, to avoid the awkwardness of other peoples' discomfort, the patronizing support of those who do not understand the internal damage, and worse, the subtle implication that it was their fault, it seems better to hide behind the cloak of denial.

The Revelation
Shame exposes pretense and subterfuge; like a play, the curtain parts and on center stage for all to see is a sight that provokes condemnation and disgust: *I am naked and I am mortified.* What is seen in the revelation? It depends on whether the experience causes legitimate or illegitimate shame.

Shame is not an easy topic. It involves a universal experience most people would like to ignore, but it is also a complex concept. Shame can be a result of the exposure of sin, therefore legitimate and desirable. However, even the exposure of sin may provoke an experience of shame that is too intense and self-absorbing to be from God. On the other hand, much of the shame we experience is not due to the exposure of our sin, but the revelation of some deficiency (or better said, perceived deficiency) in our dignity. The difference between illegitimate and legitimate shame is found in the object of the exposure. *Legitimate shame exposes depravity, and illegitimate shame shines a light on some element of dignity.*

A man who feels shame when he trips in front of a group

of people has been seen as clumsy. His longing (an aspect of his dignity) to be viewed as competent and in control has been disappointed because of his deficiency. Now exactly why would he feel shame at something as inadvertant as tripping over a step? The answer involves an obvious observation: We blame wounds to our dignity, by others and ourselves, for most of the pain in life. We were called lazy when we forgot to make our beds, ugly when we failed to get a date, stupid when we did not excel in school. Each attack ignored our depravity and zeroed in on some aspect of our dignity. Now when our dignity is ignored or demeaned, we will feel exposed as undesirable, and we will likely hate whatever part of us has caused the pain. If it is our nose, then we will hate our face; if it is our ethnic name or culture, then we will want to blend with the light-skinned and blond people who are most highly valued. *But the part of ourselves we hate the most is our longing to be wanted and enjoyed.* If we didn't want, then we would not care. If we did not care, then we could not be shamed by others' rejection.

This will help us begin to understand why shame is such a significant part of sexual abuse. Consider the damage done to the soul when the abuse is fused with the legitimate longings of the heart. The flower of deep longing for love is somehow hideously intertwined with the weed of abuse. Longings are wed to abuse, abuse begets shame, and shame is inextricably related to a hatred for one's own hungry soul. Any significant abuse causes the victim to despise the way he or she's been made: a person wired for deep, satisfying, eternal involvement with others and God.

A young woman I worked with felt nausea every time her boyfriend embraced her and showed any signs of physical warmth. When she was fourteen, she was forced to engage in oral sex with her older brother. She did not believe that her past sexual abuse had anything to do with her sick stomach; she saw it as a quirk in her personality, but one that was not a big deal. Her reason for seeing me was a ten-year bout with depression. The depression seemed more severe when anything positive happened in her life.

One event will help set the scene. Her boss gave her an unexpected raise because of her significant contribution to the company. After she left work, she was filled with dread. She began to wonder if he was setting her up for an affair. She spun from those thoughts to a terror about several projects that she knew she had yet to complete. Soon she was in a maelstrom of doubt and despair. She was surely going to be found out. Her peers at work would laugh at the thought that she had been rewarded for work that others did as a normal part of their day. Before the day was over she was in a full-blown depression. The route to understanding her despair became clear many months after this event.

This woman could not bear praise or success. Good events set off a hunger for what she knew she would eventually lose. She later recalled praying for hours that her brother would not come into her room, demanding oral sex. Many evenings would pass, and she would relax and enjoy the stillness of the night, only to hear her brother's door open and the creaking of his footsteps that signaled a night of horror.

One night she begged him to leave her alone. Never before had she allowed the full weight of her longing for a clean, loving relationship to grip her, and she wept. That night he raped her. After that sickening violation, she decided never to pray or want or hope again for anything. Her longings for relief were shattered. Her dignity was assaulted, and the horror of the abuse was intertwined with the hunger for an advocate who would tenderly wash her wounds and comfort her.

In a deeply sad and perverse way, the only relief she found was in destroying her desire for escape. Now, years later, whenever some delightful event occurred, she felt herself tighten and flee from the rising desire for more. Whenever the desire to be loved and to be enjoyed was aroused in any setting, she experienced a wave of nausea and shame. Longings and shame were wed to her sense of being a woman whose only worth was in being used for someone else's pleasure.

A good rule of thumb can summarize the major point of the story: *We ignore the issue of depravity and feel shame about our*

longing for what God intended us to enjoy. It should be so different. We should feel shame when we have verbally, emotionally,
or physically demeaned or slighted another human being, thus
violating our relationship with them and the Lord. We should
be heartbroken, humbled, shamed, when we do not worship the
Lord our God with our whole heart, soul, mind, and strength.
But instead we often ignore our failure toward others and others' failure toward us. We feel shame when our longings surface
and we are failed or we fail. A godly response in the face of
abuse is to grieve—for the perpetrator's sin and for the damage
done to our soul; but the natural response is to cower in shame,
condemning our own soul for being so foolish as to hope, want,
or risk.

Illegitimate shame comes when we have failed to achieve
what our heart craves (the longings that reflect our dignity) and
we feel we are at fault, because if we had not done ____, or if we
had only done ____, then we would not be empty, alone, and
exposed. Legitimate shame involves the exposure of depravity.
If our heart does not flee to self-justification or denial, and the
Spirit of God lives within us, then we will be nudged into the
light of His presence and seared by His penetrating eyes. It is
God's kindness to orchestrate the events of our life so that our
heart will be tested and then humbled, so that our heart will
hunger for the kind of bread that comes only from the mouth
of God (Deuteronomy 8:2-7,15-18). Legitimate shame is the same
inner experience as biblical humbling. It is the recognition of our
state as desperate and our response to our rebellious condition as
deplorable, deserving condemnation and death.

The story of the prodigal son is a picture of biblical humbling (Luke 15:11-32). He was forced to see his desperate condition through God's testing and orchestration of events. His belly
ached, and he knew his condition was deplorable. He was eating
food given to unclean animals that his people would not eat. He
humbled himself and returned to his father. He took the risk that
he would be sent away or mocked. What he found was the riches
of mercy that must have undone the remaining remnants of pride.
Legitimate shame, in other words, always leads to a sense of being

lifted up by God to possess what is surprising, unnerving, and undeserved (James 4:9-10).

One of the best descriptions of the power of shame is found in C. S. Lewis's *The Great Divorce*. One of the shadowy bus travelers from a type of hell suffered from an overriding commitment to hide from the sight of others. The dialogue between this shadowy ghost and an angel spirit is worthy of reflection:

"How can I go out like this among a lot of people with real solid bodies? It's far worse than going out with nothing on would have been on earth. Have everyone staring at me."

"Oh, I see. But we were all a bit ghostly when we first arrived, you know. That'll wear off. Just come out and try."

"But they'll see me."

"What does it matter if they do?"

"I'd rather die."

"But you've died already. There's no good in trying to go back on that."

The ghost made a sound something between a sob and a snarl.

"I wish I'd never been born," it said, "what are we born for?"

"For infinite happiness," said the spirit. "You can step out into it at any moment. . . ."

"But I tell you, they'll see me."

"An hour hence and you will not care. A day hence and you will laugh at it. Don't you remember on earth—there were things too hot to touch with your fingers, but you could drink them all right? Shame is like that. If you will accept it—if you will drink the cup to the bottom—you will find it very nourishing; but try to do anything else with it and it scalds."[1]

The ghost battled with the shame of being seen and known. The spirit offered life, but the process involved embracing shame—in fact, drinking the hot liquid so that it would transform the soul from death to life. If it was handled without being embraced, it would destroy; if consumed, it would harm, but eventually bring perspective and relief.

Shame is an excellent path to exposing how we really feel about ourselves, what we demand of ourselves and others, and where we believe life can be found. It unearths the strategies we use to deal with a world that is not under our control.

The Dread of the Consequences

Another element involved in shame is the anticipated outcome of being found out: *rejection*. Rejection is almost always a byproduct of being seen as deficient, even when the exposure involves a failure of minor proportions. A friend I know ruminated in shame all day over a failure to respond to an invitation on time. She saw it as a blunder that would be remembered for years by the mavens of the social circle she so desperately desired to join. Her blunder was not a sin; nevertheless, her soiled dignity would be like a mark of Cain, haunting her all over the earth.

If life and continued relationship with our false god depends on the quality of our sacrifice, then performance is required for life. The tension to keep up the pretense will be overwhelming. If we are found lacking in whatever is required, then we will pay the exacting cost of failure. The cost can be our life or reason for living; therefore, it is often not that great a sacrifice to give up our family, health, or relationship with God in order to achieve momentary relief from the pressure.

The dread in being found out is sufficient to fuel radical denial, workaholism, perfectionism, revictimization, and a host of other ills. But the fear is greater than simply losing relationship. It is the terror that if our dark soul is discovered, we will never be enjoyed, nor desired, nor pursued by anyone. Let me illustrate. A fight I had with my wife ended in sharp words and angry accusations. I turned away from Becky in fury. Though she was only on the other side of the bed, she might as well have been on the other side of the universe. After a time, I knew my barbs were absurd, unfounded, and cruel. I could not imagine how she could ever talk with me again. I wanted to say I was sorry, but it seemed as empty as apologizing for murder. How could I have been so mean? What was she thinking? Would she even accept my apology? Shame filled my being like cold water rushing through the hull of a sinking ship. As irrational as it may be, given my godly wife, I could not imagine her wanting to be in relationship with me.

The triggering event and resulting shame is worse than being rejected, because rejection assumes a path by which to return to acceptability. The fear involved in shame is of permanent abandonment, or exile. Those who see our reprehensible core will be so disgusted and sickened that we will be a leper and an outcast forever.

Empowering Trust

The three elements of shame—exposure, revelation, and consequences—are relatively complex, but what complicates shame even more is the final aspect: *trust*. Shame is the outcome of a failure in trust. Trust is a giving of our soul to another with the hope that we will not be harmfully used. Such trust invests in another the power to determine whether or not we are acceptable and desirable. When trust, defined as *an empowering of another to determine our desirablity and worth*, is absent, shame is usually not experienced, even with exposure of our dignity or depravity.

For example, I likely would not feel shame when I am caught performing a vulgar act, unless I cared about your opinion of me. If I wanted to offend you, then to be caught doing something vulgar would delight me. Shame is experienced before the one I've entitled or given the right to judge me. Ultimately, that is the prerogative of God alone. To give that privilege—in essence, the opportunity to bestow or retract life—to anyone other than God is idolatry. This concept helps clarify further the difference between legitimate and illegitimate shame.

Idolatry is placing our longings for what only God can provide in the hands of a creature instead of the Creator. When I live for my work, or my wife, then I have made them my false god. When I am failed (and I can be absolutely sure that a false god will be impotent at the point of my greatest need), then I will experience the shame of failure and misplaced trust. The writers of Scripture are crystal clear that dependence on a false god will inevitably result in loss, pain, and shame (Isaiah 42:17, 44:9-11). A false god will disappoint.

A friend recalled waiting for her father in an airport where she had a two-hour layover. Two days before her scheduled flight, they had planned on this meeting at the airport. As she waited for him, she was aware of a slight fear that he might forget and she cautioned herself against putting too much hope in her father, a bundle of energy who has time for everyone and everything but her. She waited with keen anticipation, rehearsing in her mind the things she wanted to share with him. Time passed; he did not appear. After an hour she quit looking and began to read a book. Every time she would look up to see if he was finally coming, she would feel a wave of self-hatred and shame. Her hope of connection with a man who was her false god—the one who could bestow or retract life—failed her, and she was ashamed.

Of what was she ashamed? The answer involves two inter-related forces: the ache of *disappointed longing* and *misplaced trust.* "I am alone and it is my/your fault. I should never have wanted you to come. If I could pretend that you are dead, then I could live without pain." Longings that are raw and exposed make a person feel naked and shamefully alone.

The second aspect, misplaced trust, involves an exposure of folly. How could I be so foolish to think that a freshly cut tree, half used for firewood and the other for my family idol, could ever rescue me from the hardships of life? How could I believe that an idol I fashion with my own hands can save my soul? A. W. Tozer says it well: "God's gifts now take the place of God, and the whole course of nature is upset by the monstrous substitution."[2]

The shame of folly is involved whenever our false god remains deaf and dumb, impotent to heal the wound of our heart. For example, the sexually abused man often puts his trust in his own strength after he has been violated. He develops a mind-set of invulnerability to compensate for the frightening time when he felt extremely powerless. A number of my male abuse clients were long-distance runners, avid weight lifters, and macho risk takers. They often expressed the same attitude of control and invulnerability by refusing to feel any emotion that reflected weakness or to feel intimate (other than sexually) with any other person. Their demeanor was often cool, tough, and in control. The message was clear: "I've been violated once, and I will never again feel myself lose control. I will never feel that powerless again in the presence of another person."

A policeman who had been raped by an older cousin literally trembled with anticipation every time he pulled a car over for a speeding offense. He wanted the person to resist him or challenge him so he could conquer his adversary. Whenever he was reprimanded by a superior or confronted by a peer, he felt an overwhelming urge to destroy them in a violent rage. His quiet demeanor—albeit slightly cocky and self-assured—covered over intense shame whenever someone belittled him. The false god of total control over others mocked him when he failed to perform well.

False gods are a diverse lot. They can include people, objects, or ideals. Central to a false god is the assurance that we will be protected by their ministrations, and when they fail us or we perceive that we have disappointed them, the combined shame of rebellious independence and naked aloneness floods our soul.

Legitimate shame is very different. If we have acknowledged God as the One, and the only One, who has the power to determine our acceptability, then we will feel only grief, not shame over loss or disappointment. The prophet Isaiah, speaking of the Suffering Servant, reflects that hope in a statement that is a foundation for dealing with injustice and wicked misuse:

> "I offered my back to those who beat me, my cheeks to those who pulled out my beard; I did not hide my face from mocking and spitting. Because the Soverign LORD helps me, I will not be disgraced. Therefore have I set my face like flint, and I know I will not be put to shame. He who vindicates me is near. Who then will bring charges against me? Let us face each other! Who is my accuser? Let him confront me! It is the Soverign LORD who helps me. Who is he that will condemn me?" (Isaiah 50:6-9)

The Servant of God understood that faith was not a protective shield against the brutality of those who beat Him or the ignominy of those who pulled out His beard. In that culture, nothing could have been more shameful than having one's beard plucked. Nevertheless, no one could stand as His accuser and bring His soul to shame because the Father stood as His advocate and judge.

Legitimate shame (that is, facing our failure to trust God) is the basis of our return to the Father. For most, trusting God means relying on Him to keep our body or our world intact. But that is not biblical trust at its essential core. Trust involves relying on Him for what is most essential to our being: the intactness of our soul. A return to the Father ensures that no one can shame or disgrace or possess our soul—that quintessential core of who we are that will live eternally with Him—no matter what is done to our body, reputation, or temporal security.

All of these factors make shame an experience that we avoid as readily as a room full of venomous snakes. Snakes can be avoided, but the potential for shame lingers like a dark cloud over every human encounter. The strategies devised to deal with our dread of exposure are as varied, complex, and idiosyncratic as the number of human beings. But one common denominator surfaces in every strategy: deflection of our sin through the use of contempt or, perhaps in more familiar language, blame shifting.

In Genesis 3, Adam felt shame and used fig leaves to cover his nakedness. When he was discovered, he did not repent; instead, he blamed God and Eve for his fatal decision to eat of the fruit. He condemned God for His creation. *He poured his shame-based rage on God and through contempt nullified the need for humble repentance.* As Adam's children, we can discount our need for humbling by the same deflection. The abused person, facing deeper shame than most people, is even more apt to resort to radical deflection to hide her wound and her commitment to self-protection.

We now will turn to the role of contempt in deflecting the work of God.

THREE

Deflection:
The Clash with Contempt

The sexually abused person is in a war. The enemy is ultimately the Evil One and the path of loyalty to Satan's vision: rebellion, autonomy, or in other words, sin. The dilemma is that Satan is crafty and his path is often subtle. All sin is felt to be reasonable and justifiable, given the situation, and rarely experienced as malicious or God-dishonoring in its intention. The unkind word or the forgetful lapse of sensitivity appear to be either a minimal offense given what we may be capable of, or actually acceptable if one were to see the world from our vantage point. Even the more severe expressions of sin—adultery, dishonesty, slander, or greed—seem less heinous when their context is brought into perspective. An affair may be wrong, but if you only knew how unhappy I am, or what kind of marriage I've endured, then I may not be vindicated, but at least I'd be understood and eventually forgiven. Sin, in fact, seems like the most reasonable, rational, common-sense response to a fallen, frightening, and potentially dangerous world.

God's perspective and path, at least at first, and often for the duration, seem entirely absurd. The call to give up life in order to find it, the promise that the poor in spirit will be blessed, turn our world upside down and violate our natural, though fallen, understanding. If sin is subtle and appears eminently reasonable, and godliness is paradoxical and seems absurdly impractical, then it stands to reason that what we consider to be normal may, in fact, be insanity. And what we consider to be acceptable or even godly may be prideful arrogance and rebellion against the Creator. The categories we consider sin in many cases exclude other elements that equally embody the commitment to find life apart from relationship with God. That commitment involves subtle and noxious interplay of shame and contempt.

WHAT IS CONTEMPT?

Contempt is best understood in its operation. Consider how you handle the loss of your car keys or cope with forgetting an important date. What are the words that you utter when you realize you've done something stupid or silly? A friend of mine describes those events as "self-bashing opportunities": "How could you have been so stupid, you fool!" "Why don't you keep better control of your schedule, you idiot!" Few would consider the internal dialogue as a problem or as a sign of arrogant sin. At worst, it would be seen as a result of a poor self-image. Is there a possibility of something more pernicious in this self-bashing?

Or consider what our internal response often is to negative feedback. We may say, "Thank you for your thoughts. I will seriously consider your feedback as we work on the project," while internally challenging the messenger: "How arrogant! How can you presume to critique our approach when you're not even an expert in your own field!" The feedback is not considered, because the character or competence of the messenger is scrutinized under the microscope of condemnation. Both the reaction to the loss of our keys and the critical thoughts regarding a colleague involve the use of contempt to diminish the potential for shame.

Legitimate shame has the power to expose sin. It pierces the seemingly impenetrable masquerade of idolatry and cuts open the heart to reveal a person's basis for life and hope. But the light is often found to be too bright and disturbing; therefore fallen man quickly resorts to a shield that seems to deflect the intrusion of God: the power of contempt. Contempt is absurd in that it inevitably increases man's vulnerability while it enables him to regain a semblance of control that protects him against dependence on God. Contempt is a major weapon against the humbling work of God. To understand the effects of living in a fallen world in general or the damage of sexual abuse in particular, a thorough understanding of contempt is required.

Contempt is condemnation, an attack against the perceived cause of the shame. The attack is laced with hatred, venom, and icy cruelty, though it can be as insidious as a warm smile and gentle rebuke. The condemnation can be against the person whose eyes are penetrating our facade or against the element of our being that is the cause of the shameful revelation.

Shame is a phenomenon of the eyes. The eyes usually drop and the shoulders slump when one feels shame. More than anything in the world the shamed person wants to be invisible or small so that the focus will be removed, the hemorhage of the soul stopped. How can the shamed person accomplish this? Somehow the eyes of the one who sees him must be deflected or destroyed. And there are two options. The shamed person can turn his eyes away from the penetrating gaze and focus on the element in his own being that is the cause of the shame. Or he can attack his "enemy's" eyes directly with the poison of his hatred, blinding those eyes so their power is nullified. The first option, self-contempt, and the second, other-centered contempt, though different in form, are similar in function. Both the form and function of contempt have profound implications for those who have been sexually abused.

THE FORMS OF CONTEMPT

Contempt is poorly understood. At best, self-contempt is associated with a poor self-image, and other-centered contempt is seen as haughty disregard of another. That perception may be accurate, but it is woefully incomplete. Contempt, in either orientation, comes in many different forms. It is best to think of the possible variations of contempt on a continuum from very severe to least severe.

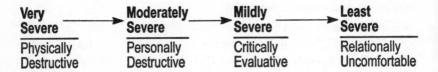

Very Severe	Moderately Severe	Mildly Severe	Least Severe
Physically Destructive	Personally Destructive	Critically Evaluative	Relationally Uncomfortable

Very Severe Contempt

A woman who was abused by a babysitter over several years began to consult me regarding her sexual abuse. She had worked with a number of counselors before, so our work progressed quickly and she made significant progress in dealing with her life. As we began to address her relationship with men, however, she became seized with terror. Our work was painful but productive. In one significant session we discussed a number of events that revealed an enormous hatred of her longing for an intimate relationship with a man. She had gone to awful lengths to undermine her beauty of body and soul. As I listened and reflected with her, I was overwhelmed by the sadness of her hatred, and I wept. She was overcome with terror. A look of overwhelming fear covered her face, and I was confused. She was unable to put words to her experience, and the hour ended.

The following session she reported an intense desire to do physical harm to herself after our last visit. She had left my office and driven home at frightening speeds. She later took a walk in a section of town that is known as "rape alley." She slept little, ate poorly, and drove herself unmercifully at work. She was tempted to pick her fingernails, scratch her skin until she bled, and resume past patterns of bulimia. She also dreamt of my death in a violent car accident. Needless to say, it was not one of the best weeks of her life. She was flooded with extreme self- and other-centered contempt.

Very severe contempt is seen in a desire to do physical harm to oneself or another. It is the desire to destroy, or at least damage through wanton disregard, the physical needs and limits of the human frame. It may be blatant like suicide or subtle like binging on junk food. In either case, *the body is punished for existing and wanting*. In other cases, there is a desire to actively or passively destroy the person who has provoked the hunger of the soul.

Moderately Severe Contempt

A conservatively dressed woman, meek in disposition with a Sunday school demeanor, told me of her fantasy to be physically beaten and raped by a gang of ruthless men. The replay of the violent fantasy during intercourse was the only means by which she could achieve an orgasm with her husband. The same woman would occasionally fantasize hanging a faceless man from a tree by his genitals or verbally humiliating a man for some minimal offense. The essence of her fantasy was degradation and abuse.

Violent thoughts, words, or images are like a slashing knife that bleeds the soul of life. The titillation found in violent images serves as an anesthetic that dulls the ravages of overwhelming loss.

Moderately severe contempt can also be seen in elaborate fantasies of revenge. The frustrated employee who dreams of finding some way to vindicate his worth to the company by saving millions of dollars that his idiotic boss would have lost due to negligence and incompetence is utilizing other-centered contempt to regain face and control.

Mildly Severe Contempt

Mildly severe contempt is probably the most common and easy to recognize, therefore it often operates without being seen as contemptuous. It involves a comparative evaluation of oneself or another in which the loser of the analysis is rebuked or angrily exhorted to perform more adequately.

Imagine your response as a teenager to a new crop of skin blemishes, or as an adult to spilling a drink in your lap. The acrimonious inner dialogue may be severe, the names used unsightly, but the result often appears to be greater energy to make a change.

A friend of mine cannot play tennis without haranguing himself on his performance. He analyzes and critiques every shot as he works himself into a frenzy of desire. He claims his play improves as he maligns his performance. He feels energized to play better so that he won't suffer the bitter sting of his own flagellation. In a similar way, the Christian community often encourages self-contempt as a means of increasing holiness. For instance, if you chastise yourself harshly enough for masturbating, then you will be less likely to engage in that activity with impunity.

Other-centered contempt is evident whenever fault is found with another and the motivation is not love. It is used to diminish some inner struggle that is almost invariably linked to a sense of being exposed as inadequate or undesirable. Quiet or public condemnation of another keeps them in a place that is manageable and secure and diminishes whatever threat they may pose.

The sexually abused woman often finds ample opportunity to destroy her enjoyment of being a woman through negative evaluations of her face, body, clothing, or manner of relating — especially in light of comparisons to other women. An attractive woman may harbor deep hatred for her own body and still be critically evaluating the beauty of rivals.

Least Severe Contempt

A friend of mine could not receive a compliment, even if her life depended on it. She cannot bear the relational intensity she feels when someone enjoys her. If you enjoyed her cooking, she would decry her inadequate preparation. If you were to thank her for her friendship, she would confess to being a poor servant. If you were to point out her unwillingness to receive a compliment, she would feel awful for hours. It is difficult to enjoy giving to a person who undermines her own beauty, kindness, and abilities, because she is always faster than the eye in pulling the rug out from under your compliment. She may appear to be humble; there is, however, a profound arrogance in never receiving the gift of another's kindness.

At times, the discomfort in receiving a compliment is due to a keen sense of unworthiness (self-contempt) or doubt about the sincerity of the kind word (other-centered contempt). The attitude projected, in either case, is that she will not be touched by the other's movement toward her, nor will she allow the other to enjoy the reciprocal interplay of giver and receiver enjoying each other's pleasure. For a person who fears that deepening spiral of relational enjoyment, any intimacy must be headed off before it is intensified.

The sexually abused person often carries contempt as an anti-dote to the bite of pleasure. The first stirring of aliveness or passion in contact with another feels like a venom that may take both parties into a destructive spiral of lust or revenge. One woman informed me, "You don't know what I might do if I were to think that someone really liked me. I'm so afraid that I would do any-thing, including something immoral, to keep their approval. It's better for us both if I ignore or doubt your warmth." Contempt, in any form, operates for a purpose: almost always to protect the user from damaging others or replicating the past abuse that wounded her soul. A more detailed look at the function of contempt will help explain its usefulness to the victim of sexual abuse.

THE FUNCTIONS OF CONTEMPT

Most of us feel confused by what we do. Some things come out of our mouths without much thought. Why did I mock my wife's new Bohemian outfit? Why, because it seemed silly, and I don't really know. For that matter, who cares? What difference does it make that I know the purpose behind my remark?

The answer is complex: To know *the why* opens the door to the possibility of seeing the enormity of the problem and the need for something more than mere behavioral alteration. At best, aware-ness of the motivation behind behavior reveals the web of our fallen desire and creates a desperate need for God's intervention to rescue us from such a dark maze.

Insight alone does not provide the impetus to change destruc-tive behavior; it only creates a context for more fervent repentance. At its worst, an understanding of motivation may lead to fascinat-ing intrigue, self-absorptive introspection, and a focus away from issues of sin, salvation, and sanctification. The solution, of course, resides in the heart of the explorer. The person who plaintively cries out from her core, "Lord, see if there be any secret, harmful way in me," will eventually be blessed with a picture of her sin and God's nurturant provision of grace. The one who explores human motivation out of an ultimate desire to explain away the horror of sin or the profound need for a Savior will pleasantly ruminate about motivation without conviction or change. It is my desire to explain the function of contempt in a way that leads to clarity about sin and path to change.

Why would anyone use contempt? In simple terms, the motivation involved in contempt is similar to Adam's attack on God: deflection of the eyes of the Creator. If we can avoid His look, then perhaps we will be able to flee from the consequences of our sin. Contempt serves us in at least four ways: it diminishes our shame, it deadens our longings, it makes us feel in control, and it distorts the real problem.

Diminishes Shame

Contempt either blinds the eyes of the observer (other-centered contempt) or turns the eyes of the one shamed away from the one who has observed (self-contempt). In either case, the effect is the same: The intense experience of shame has been diminished. Both forms of contempt may be used alternately, attacking self and then attacking the other. Though, in most cases, an individual will be more comfortable and predisposed to utilize one style of contempt more consistently than the other.

Shame always includes an aspect of anxiety. What will happen when I am found out: Will I be abandoned or mocked? Behavioral psychologists discovered that relaxation, sexual arousal, and anger are incompatible with anxiety. It is not possible to simultaneously feel both the gnawing uncertainty of anxiety and the pulsating energy of rage. One will win out. In most cases, rage will prevail. So it is in the case of contempt. Contempt uses rage—sometimes loud and violent, and other times quiet and insidious—as a means of chasing away the uncertainty of shame. As long as contempt is present, shame will not stop a person in her tracks, but will energize action and movement away from the dreaded exposure.

Deadens Longings

In the midst of shame, longing for what the heart craves intensifies the anguish of the soul. Most of us, therefore, are committed to avoid or, if possible, to destroy whatever increases sorrow in our unpredictable and dangerous world. *For the woman or man who has been abused, one of the greatest enemies of the soul is the longing for intimacy.* To feel, particularly to feel alive, passionate and hungry of heart for what God made man for invites the memory of past abuse to stir again. The past abuse—drowned in a sea of denial or ever-present as a living nightmare—threatens to overwhelm the victim if she relaxes her vigil and lets down her defenses. To feel good in relationship with another, like no other experience, opens the door to past horror and future terror.

I've worked with a number of single women who've been abused. In the midst of significant personal change, a softening and freeing of their souls occurs that increases their beauty of body and soul. Several have had dating relationships turn more serious at this point. The potential realization of a hidden desire—to be married—often triggers a return to the memories of past abuse, an exacerbation of the presenting problem, and a strong ambivalence about the future; on one hand, wanting the relationship to work and on the other, sabotaging the outcome.

Proverbs 12:12 says, "Hope deferred [lost] makes the heart sick" (NASB). The abused person has lost hope and in many cases is leery about regaining a rich desire for intimacy or justice. It seems so convoluted. The person who might offer hope and life is viewed as an enemy; the one who ignores, uses, or harms is embraced as a lost friend and lover. Many women who have been abused end up in tragic relationships in which they are revictimized. One factor involved in that choice is the unconscious commitment to find people who will guarantee loss, so that hope is never deeply stirred.

Contempt is a cruel anesthetic to longing. As long as I turn my condemnation against myself, I block the potential of your movement toward me and my longing for you to care. When I turn my condemnation against you, I am free from believing that I want anything from you. In either case, *contempt kills longing.*

Provides the Illusion of Control
Fallen man works tenaciously, at times to psychotic lengths, to gain magical control over life by generating reasons that explain

the why and what for of that which seems beyond his understanding. Have you ever noticed the penchant to explain God when difficult events occur in our life? There is an overwhelming desire to find the "reason" for the suffering. There may be a perspective that will comfort and instruct, but many are unwilling to accept the uncontrollable and mysterious until they've found an explanation that makes sense.

This is particularly the case when the struggle involves deep personal loss. Why am I not married? Why did my husband leave me? Why did my father abuse me? Questions about human suffering tear the soul away from the pleasant pretense of fairness. Is life just? Is it fair? Or does inequity and inequality expose the well-manicured yards of our lives to reveal the sordid underbrush and squalid weeds of the Fall? For many the raw reality of life in a fallen world is too much to endure; therefore, more acceptable, more controllable explanations must be found. Contempt provides a strange antidote for the struggle of confusion, terror, and helplessness.

Consider the usefulness of self-contempt in dealing with a past of sexual abuse. One woman told me that as a five-year-old she was apparently too sexy for her father to resist. She excused his heinous sin by blaming herself. As long as she was at fault, she did not have to face her sorrow. Perhaps, even more, the explanation gave her a means of organizing and controlling her life. If she was abused because she was too sexy, all she need do is to hide any part of her body or spirit that men might find appealing. Her dress was modest to a fault; her demeanor was boring to tears. Her contempt provided her an explanation for the past harm and a plan for living more safely in the world.

Another client lived out her self-contempt quite differently. She saw herself as a cheap, stained, seductive woman who loved to entrap helpless men. Her self-contempt was used as a weapon to violate the men who hopelessly fell to her charms. Her thrill was to entice and then frustrate her victim, until he reached a point of either whimpering or lashing out in rage. A number of times she was beaten or raped by her victims. In this example, we can see the frightening interworking of both kinds of contempt. She had a contemptuous plan for living that gave her a false sense of control over her longings: "I am a whore, so why should I long for a clean relationship with anyone? I am a conqueror who will make you pay if you want to use me."

The role of contempt is no different for a man. A male client told me how he was often sexually accosted by older boys as he came home from school. He learned to tolerate their roaming hands and the way they degraded him by making jokes about his sexual prowess and the size of his penis. He continued to mock himself in the same way throughout his adulthood. He expressed his other-centered contempt by never approaching his wife for sexual involvement. He always made her approach him. His seeming lack of interest was a deep wound to his wife. He explained his self-contemptuous joking as a safety valve that released pent-up anguish and rage that he could not face directly.

This pattern of explanation and control is found in less extreme situations as well. If I blame my looks for my being single, then I not only have an explanation for why I am alone, but I can also have the illusion of doing away with my deficit by buying better clothes or working on my weight. *As long as I believe there is something I can do about my problem, then I am not constrained to feel hopeless.* A contemptuous explanation provides a direction to pursue to regain control over my emptiness.

Distorts the Real Problem

Contempt distorts the fact that the central human problem is sin. Other-centered contempt is the easiest to comprehend. It ignores one's own depravity and centers the blame on another person's failure. The classic paradigm is Adam's shifting of contemptuous blame on God and then on Eve. It was their fault, their responsibility. If they had only done their jobs better, Adam would never have been in that mess.

Those who are good at other-centered contempt are perceptive and usually accurate in their analysis of wrong. God had certainly made the woman, and Eve had clearly given Adam the fruit. The issue was not whether Adam was accurate in his analysis, but whether he was willing to accept the consequences of his rebellion. Other-centered contempt involves analysis for the aim of exploitation, feedback for the purpose of control. Self-contempt, though no less distorting, is more subtle in its effect.

Contempt can be called the Great Masquerade. Self-contempt in particular is Satan's counterfeit for conviction over sin. When I feel bad about myself, angry that I said something insensitive to my wife, it can look like sorrow over sin. In actuality, it is usually a denigration of some element of my dignity, rather than a sorrow over my depravity.

A client told me about a fight with his wife. She vehemently attacked him for being uninvolved; her words were full of bitterness and rage. I asked him what he said to her, and he told me that he put his head down on the pillow and wept. He felt overwhelmed. He hated himself for being so unloving and uninvolved. At one level that sounds biblical and repentant; however, he was blaming himself for being a poor communicator, unable to really listen to his wife's pain. He saw his problem as a failure of concentration, communication skills, and empathy. Those deficiencies do not get to the heart of his radical selfishness that protected him from responding to her rage.

His contempt did not bring about sorrow unto life. Instead, his pain was consistent with what Paul called sorrow unto death, a death due to self-absorbed self-protection. His deep sense of failure did not touch his wife, nor give him the energy to move toward her. In fact, his contempt simply turned his eyes away from her, dulled his pain, explained why the marriage was so bad, and offered him a strategy to be nicer, but not more involved with his wife.

If he were under conviction of sin, he would have admitted to himself what a wretched woman she was, faced the ungodliness of his withdrawal, and moved toward her with sorrow, passion, and love. I am not sure what it would have meant for him to have loved her at that point; it might have involved a willingness to enter into battle, or hear out her complaint. But in either case, conviction would have freed him to move toward her with an energy that was other-focused and perseverant.

Contempt is complex and often hard to see. It sometimes

masquerades as conviction; other times it seems like righteous indignation. At one point, it appears as a poor self-image, and at another, as a bad attitude toward others. Whatever its form or function, one thing can be assumed: *Contempt hinders the work of God.* It directs our sight away from our deepest longings and deflects the focus from our depravity and need for a Savior to an attack against our own or another's dignity.

The struggle with shame and contempt—a common experience for everyone—is an intensely felt battle for the man or woman who has been sexually abused. There are many reasons for the significant struggle. The primary factor has to do with what is triggered in the human soul when a deep route to intimacy, whether physical contact or psychological interaction, is used to ensnare and enslave the young heart of the victim in a polluted and perverse relationship.

We turn next to what happens to the human soul when abuse occurs.

FOUR

The War Zone: Strategies for Abuse

Sexual abuse exacts a terrible price in the victim's life in terms of shame, contempt, and denial. The sins of the perpetrator continue to color the victim's life through an inability to enjoy relationship, intimacy, and hope. The victim's soul feels bound to denial; the heart feels wounded and alone. Longing for more or delighting in what is available equally stir and endanger the soul; therefore, the person feels it is better to live without awareness of passion, hunger, or pain.

This ache cannot be acknowledged, but neither can it be entirely silenced. The silent scream deepens the paradox of living life without feeling in order to keep the threads of hope intact. The complex web of desire and defense, of longing and contempt, are often hidden below a socially competent exterior that does not look wounded or confused. The outwardly pleasant layer functions to control both the inner emptiness and shame and the risk in being deeply involved in relationship.

How is one to enter the chambers of the wounded heart that struggles below the guise of competence and congeniality? Like a labrinyth, the twisted pathway will not reveal its secrets to one who does not understand the complexity or pitfalls of the process. The wounded heart must be gently and accurately understood if it is to reveal the heartache it has stored for years. A grasp of the internal pain begins with an idea of how abuse occurs and what abuse does to the perspective of the victim.

THE STAGES OF ABUSE

There is a common process involved in many cases of abuse, whether perpetrated by a relative or by a known non-family member. Abusers usually have a fairly clear strategy for ensnaring their victims. But a warning needs to be highlighted before considering the typical stages of abuse. At first glance, there are so many variations and exceptions to the rule that it almost invalidates the presumption of a pattern. The fact is, the details differ in every case; each person is uniquely abused. So what is the point in discussing a common pattern if there is so much variation? The reason is the same as learning the rules of English grammar. There may be more exceptions to the rule than not, but if the rule is learned, the exceptions can be handled. The rule provides clarity to the process, so that exceptions are viewed from a unified perspective, rather than seen as a mass of disorganized particulars.

In most cases, sexual abuse is not an event that occurs out of the blue, suddenly and capriciously, by someone who lurks in the bushes and waits for an unsuspecting child to walk into his lair. In fact only 11% of all sexual abuse is perpetrated by a stranger. The vast majority of sexually abusive events occur in relationship with a family member (29%) or with someone else known by the victim (60%).

All abuse is a violation of the sanctity and wholeness of the human soul, but when sexual abuse is perpetrated by a member of one's family or by someone who has gained one's trust, the loss is even more severe. Sexual abuse is always a violation of relationship. The violation always damages the soul, irrespective of the severity, nature of the relationship with the perpetrator, use or nonuse of violence, or duration of the abuse.

Sexual abuse is an event or a series of related events that occur in a context. The context is an important part of understanding the first stage. Few abuse victims come from happy, so-called normal homes, even if the appearance is enviable to outsiders who do not know the inner workings of the family. The typical home where abuse occurs is relationally distant and empty. The variations of the pattern are many, but the fact remains that legitimate, healthy intimacy is rare or nonexistent in abusive homes. The environment is a breeding ground for deep soul hunger.

Many abuse victims are prone to deny the shortcomings of their own homes. The most obvious reason is that whatever was typical is viewed as normal. Chances are, however, that the two factors that are essential to a happy home were absent in the victim's. The first factor is a sense of being enjoyed for who one is rather than for what one does. Many abuse victims were enjoyed for being the adultified child, but that kind of appreciation leaves the hungry heart untouched. A second factor is a respect of one's being that permits the opportunity to develop uniqueness and separateness from other members of the family.

It is typical for the abused daughter to be singled out, often before the abuse, as the one who is expected to function as a "little adult." The parentified child may be expected to do the shopping and cooking, and handle the family finances. One woman, abused by a friend of the family, was expected to be the source of solace and strength for her mother and sisters. She was the family bulwark and was severely criticized when she wept or showed any weakness. She knew that she could not ask her mother for help because she would upset her mother, potentially provoking another stupefying depression. When asked why she did not tell her mother, she quietly sighed, "It would have meant months of picking up the pieces. I felt as if I had enough to cope with in saying no to the abuser."

A man who was abused by his mother was regularly expected to rub her feet and read to her when she had severe migraine headaches. Her expectation that he would provide comfort and nurturance were inappropriate for a nine-year-old boy; the mother gave him the role of a husband.

The role distortion tears away a child's childhood and replaces it with adult burdens that are too heavy to lift, but must be carried if the child is to enjoy any benefits of life or love in the dysfunctional home. The forsaking of childhood begins the long process of giving up the soul in order to taste a few crumbs of life.

The role confusion is further complicated by repeated violations of the child's boundaries and individual rights. Boundaries are appropriate lines that rightfully separate one's inner and outer world from the domain of others. They provide a sense of uniqueness and independence and help a person orient who he or she is in contrast to who others are.

A common boundary is the right to privacy while performing hygienic practices. Many abused individuals were never granted privacy of space, let alone thought or feeling. To be walked in on by family members while showering is an intrusion that implies that one's body is not one's own. One client had to go to her father to ask for sanitary napkins. Each time she asked, she was subjected to his leering eyes and suggestive questions. Another woman's father intensely scrutinized her clothing and makeup every time she got ready to leave the house. His scrutiny went far beyond a caring father's concern for his daughter's propriety; his near obsession with her appearance functioned as a guise for him to peer more deeply at her sexuality and violate her boundaries. The cases described are examples of sexual abuse that, although they did not involve physical contact, were severely intrusive and damaging.

We make hundreds of choices every day that reflect a sense of legitimate ownership of our body and our being. These choices require a sense of separateness and individuality that begins with an idea of what is rightfully ours and what is reasonable for others to expect of us. A person who has been abused will likely have grave difficulty comprehending the boundary issues that many of us take for granted. The right to decide within limits what we wear to work or school, where we worship, or whether we have the freedom to say no to a request are issues that are often confusing for those who have not been allowed to form and experiment with their own boundary choices.

Other boundary violations occur when a parent tells a child that her feelings are wrong, crazy, or nonexistent. One mother used to tell her daughter: "You are *not* afraid of going to school.

Are you crazy? No normal kid is scared of going to school! You are not afraid." The denial or rejection of emotions or thoughts violate the privacy and sanctity of a child's inner world. A child likely will question the validity of her perception, making the cost of trusting her intuition exorbitantly high.

So far the home of the victim has produced relational hunger, a sense of being needed but nevertheless demeaned, while making it difficult for the child to trust her perceptions and feelings. The atmosphere is also demanding, conservative, and rule-bound. The highest family value is loyalty: always faithful, no matter the cost, to protect the family from attack and shame. The hook is often put deep into the child's psyche: "No one will love you but me. If you tell anyone what goes on in this home, I will die, or you will lose all opportunity to find love. You won't be believed. People will hate you, doubt you, and blame you for hurting your parents." Seldom are the words spoken so clearly. The unstated rule is assumed and infused into the family psyche like fluoride in the public water system.

The scene is set for abuse. The child is (to some degree) empty, alone, committed to pleasing, boundary-less, burdened, and bound to a family or a parent whose desire becomes the bread of hope for the hungry child. The two key words are *empty* and *dependent*. The child is dependent on the parent's physical provisions for life; therefore, in most situations, she cannot economically provide for her own wants unless she resorts to prostitution or crime. The child is also psychologically intertwined in the push and pull of the parent's every offer or refusal to provide nurturance and support.

Usually, the future victim has learned at a very young age how to survive, how to maximize pleasure and minimize pain, through a series of trial and error experiments. The repeated opportunities to learn an effective style of relating secures for the child a stable pattern of behaviors that we call personality. Many factors influence personality, but the central organizing theme in a dysfunctional family will be how to deaden the pain of soul hunger, while remaining sufficiently alert and predisposed to act in one's own best interest. Soul deadness—or a heart dulled to its own pain—and a hypervigilant, poised alertness are not compatible partners in the dance of life. In order to live in the inherent contradiction, the child or adolescent must develop a split between the two (or more) antithetical positions, thus existing as two different people: an inner person who quietly and unobtrusively stores what is most precious away from the sight of a dangerous world; and a public person who adopts the manner, dress, voice, and face that others who distribute the bounty of life expect to be displayed. If Dad expects me to be a good student, I will perform to his desire (if possible); the reward will be an occasional smile, or perhaps a free night to spend with my friends, rather than waiting for him to plod to my room after a night of drinking to play his little games under the covers.

The child is caught in a wretched dilemma. Survival requires fitting in, and to fit in means to live a life of torment. *The experience of being profoundly used and let down by someone we trusted and relied on sears the hope that relationship can be purely enjoyed.* What makes the abuse even more sickeningly painful is that the trust placed in one's father, brother, neighbor, pastor, teacher, or older friend was used by the abuser to gain an uninformed, naive, innocent compliance from the victim. Such compliance falsely implicates her as a willing participant in her own demise. The advantage in understanding the process of abuse is that it frees the abused person from unnecessary guilt for compliance and offers categories for understanding events that evoked confusion and contempt.

Sexual abuse often follows a typical sequence of stages: (1) development of intimacy and secrecy, (2) enjoyment of physical touch that appears appropriate, (3) sexual abuse proper (physical contact *or* psychological interaction), and (4) maintenance of the abuse and the shameful secret through threats and privileges.

Although this is a general pattern, there are countless exceptions. For instance, a child might be raped without being set up or seduced. Once the rape has occurred, however, silence or ongoing sexual exploitation will likely be purchased through threats or the offer of privileges. Stage 4, in this scenario, is very similar to Stage 1.

Stage 1: Development of Intimacy and Secrecy

The first stage of abuse can be considered a conscious, intentional setup that opens the refrigerator doors to the sight and taste of the hungry child. Often the details of the abuse indicate that the perpetrator began the seductive setup months and even years before any actual physical abuse occurred. Even in cases that involved forced intercourse or violent attack, the perpetrator often pursued an intimate relationship with the victim prior to the assault. The essence of Stage 1 is the offer of relationship, intimacy, special privilege, and rewards. It can be viewed as the offer of water to a person dying of thirst.

A thirteen-year-old girl was invited to her seventy-year-old neighbor's barn to see his new bunnies. She was a Christian, from a conservatively religious home. She told me that she could not recall ever being touched, hugged, or held by anyone in her family. Her parents were cold and austere. The invitation delighted her, and she readily responded. The neighbor seated her on a bale of hay and put several bunnies on her lap. He stood behind her and told her about their birth and the reproductive habits of rabbits, using words and phrases that were sexually provocative and suggestive. He began to massage her shoulders as she held the rabbits, and after a few moments he slipped his hand down her blouse and touched her breast. She was stunned and unsure of what to do. After what seemed to be an eternity, she stood up and ran out of the barn. She never told her parents what occurred. His offer was a taste of heaven; his touch, frightening and strangely warming. The setup in this case took less than ten minutes before he moved to Stage 2, physical touch that appears appropriate, and then to Stage 3, sexual contact.

Other situations may take several years to set up. A woman who was abused by her pastor began having private meetings with him when she was twelve. For several years, they shared secrets and quiet, knowing looks. He would often invite her to stop in after church for a theological discussion, prayer, or a snack. When she was thirteen, he began to confide to her some of his relational struggles with his wife and would ask for a "woman's perspective" in coping with her moods. Soon he began to share some of their sexual struggles and doubts about his own virility. The precocious, adultified child often affirmed his maleness and flirted with him when he was particularly depressed.

How conscious was his seduction? Did he know a year or two in advance what was to occur? In this case, there is no conclusive data that would indicate without a shadow of a doubt that his intention was to abuse her from the beginning of their relationship. However, the steady, unrelenting, and inappropriate pursuit of a young girl—progressively building trust and intimacy, slowly exposing her to his heart and sexual struggles—implies conscious intentionality far in advance of the first physically abusive episode. It must be remembered that the setup itself, even if the abuser never moves beyond Stage 1 (though it is rare for him not to), is severely damaging to the victim's soul.

Stage 1 sets the hook. The hungry fish takes the bait, and the adroit fisherman waits until he feels the tug and then he jerks his pole back, implanting the sharp steel in the soul of his unwary victim. The kindness is cruelty; the warmth, violating. But the unsuspecting child or adolescent feels relationally alive and nourished, as he or she has never been before.

The abuser offers the very thing he has withheld from the child to gain trust and access to her heart. After years of neglect a child may be wary, but underlying the suspicion is a desire for involvement that brims with passion. She craves to be wanted, even if what she's wanted for deprives her of her dignity. As the adult or older young person offers warmth and intimacy, or its symbolic counterpart (a ride in a boat, a new comic book, the privilege of staying up late), age-old barriers are dropped in anticipation and desire.

For many, the first gift is followed by no expectations or demand, other than secrecy: "Don't tell your brothers we stopped for ice cream. If they know, I'll have to bring them next time!" Secrecy, at least at first, is confined to the privileges of intimacy and deepens the "special" relationship that is beginning. Consequently, the victim tastes the first luscious bite of grace, a free gift of life with no obligation to perform. The result will be increased hope and hunger, a dropping of ancient defenses, a spritely responsiveness that brings to the soul the first sense of femininity or masculinity.

One woman described this period as the glory days of her life. Whenever she daydreams, she recollects the time when she was six and her father bought her a new dress and allowed her to parade around the home to his oohs and ahs. She was for a day his princess, his delight and dream. The day ended several weeks later when he masturbated her for the first time.

Stage 1 produces *a desire for more*, a hope that spring is ahead. Maybe, just maybe, the dead tree that has languished in the child's soul for years will see verdant green leaves cover the brown, decaying branches. Essentially, this stage involves the development of intimacy through the offer of relationship. *Relational pleasure* is enhanced through the bonding of secrecy and privilege.

Stage 2: Physical Contact that Appears Appropriate

This stage logically follows the introduction of relational intimacy and secretiveness. During the first stage, physical touch (handholding, back massages, scratching the head, hugs) may be present. In all likelihood, there will be a separation of time between the two stages. The time may be minutes, days, or even years.

The essence of Stage 2 is the beginning of physical and sensual bonding. A special physical connection is made during periods of heightened relational intimacy that increases the child's affective response to the adult's care. As a snowball picks up momentum as it rolls down a hill, so does relational intimacy as it includes physical touch. Touch enhances the pleasure of relational bonding, and relational intimacy gives meaning and vibrancy to physical contact. Intimate involvement and some form of physical touch are correlates of love. The child or adolescent in Stage 1 feels loved and longs for the fatherly or motherly touch of the adult who is bonding with her.

An important distinction needs to be understood at this point. The child or adolescent's desire for physical touch is not in any shape or form sexual, unless the child has been conditioned to interpret sexual contact as the essence of and legitimate expression of relational intimacy. A child, as well as an adult, however, experiences physical touch through sense receptors that produce an arousal that is pleasurable. It is impossible to consciously experience a hug or a back rub as anything but sensual. Perhaps because of other factors, the experience may be unenjoyable but nonetheless physically arousing.

A dilemma in this discussion is that our culture, which is so heavily attached to sexual images and stimulation, cannot conceive of sensual-physical touch that is not an invitation to sexual arousal. Sensual and sexual, in our day, are seen as the same thing. The fact is, however, a back rub can be physically arousing—that is, sensually pleasurable—without bearing a trace of sexual pleasure. This introduces the possibility that a child, as young as a few hours old, can experience sensual physical arousal that is both soothing and stimulating and under normal circumstances not sexual.

When I cuddle with my daughters or son, they are aware of a sensual pleasure that is not available when we are roughhousing or working on a tennis stroke. Each involves touch and physical contact, but cuddling nourishes their young souls in a different way than play or normal physical contact. The gentle, relational touch quiets the soul and invites the recipient to relax in the warm strength of another; pleasure, comfort, nourishment, and trust are wedded together in a delightful mixture that deepens and sweetens the taste of life and passion.

The effect of sensual contact on the child or adolescent who has lived much of his or her life without nourishing touch is equivalent to watering a flower that has been left without water for days. The drooping stem straightens and the closed bud opens; the lifeless plant brightens into the glory that it was meant to reveal. So with the heart of the hungry child: the warmth lifts her face, and the nourishment brings hope to her eyes. The memories of this stage are hard for the abuse victim to recall without an awful combination of shame and confusion. A child isn't as sure as an adult when touch by another is inappropriate, but she does sense that something is "weird." Her sense of discomfort, however, is clouded by the thrill of feeling cared for. Seduction desensitizes a child over time so that she doesn't recognize the abusive progression.

A good friend of mine told me of the terrible rape perpetrated by her father when she was four years old. The event was very difficult for her to describe, her memories were vague and her emotions constrained. She was able to describe the awful event with her eyes directly looking into mine. When I asked what happened after the rape, her eyes dropped and her mood changed from factual reporting to convulsive shame. After a long period of silence, she whispered these words: "He held me. And rocked me. And sang me a lullaby." In rage she looked up and nearly shouted: "I hated him, but I allowed myself to relax in his arms and be soothed by his touch."

Whether the tender touch occurred before or after the physical abuse, in many cases the effect will be the same: comfort and enjoyment. And the questions remain: "Why did I allow myself to trust? Why did I allow myself to want a man who would (or did) abuse me?"

The questions still persist even when the victim knows full well there was no way to discern the deceitful intentions of the perpetrator. A fourteen-year-old girl was invited by her uncle to go for a drive in his new car. On the drive he offered her opportunity to steer the car. She enjoyed the privilege (Intimacy—Stage 1) so much that he asked her if she would like to learn how to drive a car. Since she was underage, he cautioned her not to tell her parents, because they might forbid her the opportunity (Secrecy—Stage 1). He was her uncle, an adult, a man with authority and power, and he allowed her an opportunity for relationship that her angry and cold parents seldom, if ever, provided. The setup was in place.

On the first drive he told her to sit close to him as she steered the car. Several times later he had her sit on his lap as he operated the pedals. Soon he occasionally ran his hand down her leg; the process was slow and steady over time as he conditioned her to his touch. The physical touch was pleasurable and apparently innocent for weeks. Then he began to cross the border to "accidentally" touch her thighs or breast. She was awkward and uncomfortable when he touched her, but was too tense to speak, fearing that she might lose the opportunity to drive the car if she offended him. Her intuitive sense of discomfort was clouded by the thrill of feeling cared for and attended to. Their conversations revolved around "adult" talk and language, and she felt relieved to be away from her parents' stodgy fundamentalism and honored that she was being treated like an adult. When the overt sexual abuse occurred, she was already silenced by her sense of complicity. Didn't she enjoy the privilege? Hadn't she responded to the closeness of the nonsexual touch? She was framed, and she accepted the penalty of her supposed crime.

In summary, Stage 2 can be called the process of silencing the victim and sealing his or her fate. To a six-year-old, the difference between having one's head rubbed and being masturbated is only a matter of degree. If one is accepted and enjoyed, why not the other? For a fourteen-year-old, the difference may be clear: one is acceptable and the other is not. But an adolescent, no matter how sophisticated, will not impute the same meaning to a sexual act as an adult. The adolescent will not see the touch as a choice, as clearly as an adult might, especially if she has been locked in sensual isolation for years, hungry of soul for contact, unsure of her own right to boundaries, and doubtful of her own intuitive judgment.

Stage 3: Sexual Abuse Proper

Abuse comes in so many different forms and from so many different sources that it is dangerous to speak about this stage without certain cautions. There are clearly different levels of severity that intensify the damage of abuse. The nature of the relationship, especially degree of role closeness (father versus neighbor), and degree of prior intimacy play a part in the extent of the damage. The degree to which physical or psychological violence was used or threatened to be used also effects the nature of the short- and long-term results of abuse. All of these factors cannot easily be put into an equation to ascertain the extent of the damage. Therefore, I will discuss sexual abuse in generic, common-denominator terms, rather than looking at the distinct consequences that arise due to the variations in each component.

A second caution concerns the dilemma of discussing sexual abuse in graphic language. By accurately describing what has occurred, I run the danger of titillating the reader. It is almost impossible to describe sexual events, even perverse, heinous events, without provoking morbid curiosity. It is the same dynamic that occurs when people drive by an accident and want to look but also want to turn their eyes away. Yet the risk in being vague is that abuse is potentially sugar-coated, and the terrible nature of the damage quietly ignored behind a guise of civility. I hope to make neither error.

Sexual abuse occurs in a context of emptiness, confusion, and loneliness, a context that sets up the victim for a baffling interplay of betrayal, ambivalence, and powerlessness as the adult moves the victim from one stage of abuse to the next. The initial involvement feels like nourishment to the soul (Stage 1), and when physical touch is offered (Stage 2), the senses are intertwined with the thrill of relationship and the arousal of aliveness. To be alive is to feel passion, a blood-tingling, intoxicating passion that opens the door to the soul with a breath of fresh spring air. *Sexual abuse is the final blow that sabotages the soul in a climactic betrayal, mocking the enjoyment of relationship and pouring contempt on the thrill of passion.*

The betrayal involves more than relational sabotage. It is also intensely personal and physical. This is a very difficult concept to understand and accept, especially for those who have been abused. When a little boy or girl, adolescent young man or woman, is abused in an overt, physical manner, he or she often will experience sexual arousal. It is nearly impossible for the victim to not experience physical arousal when the primary or secondary sexual organs are touched. God has built the human body with more nerve endings in the head of the penis and the clitoris than anywhere else in the body other than the taste buds. God is concerned with our pleasure; otherwise it would be difficult to understand

His choice to have so created male and female. His plan for arousal is perversely misused by sexual abuse, but the arousal experienced is neither sinful or abnormal. *The tragedy of abuse is that the enjoyment of one's body becomes the basis of a hatred of one's soul.* Abuse arouses within the victim a taste of legitimate pleasure in a context that makes the enjoyment a poison that destroys.

The thirteen-year-old girl who was abused by her pastor went from intimate and meaningful theological discussions to holding hands while they prayed. Hugs were common and often longer than legitimate. She recalled feeling both guilty and special, but the powerful drive to keep the relationship intact kept her from facing either her discomfort or her growing pleasure in their physical contact. By the time overt sexual abuse began, she felt extremely ambivalent about their relationship. On one hand, she enjoyed the closeness and intimacy, and on the other, she felt scarred and guilty. She felt sexually aroused by his touch, but equally she felt used and cheap. Her commitment to stop the abusive relationship would always falter when she was lonely; her resolution to avoid sexual arousal melted when he tenderly touched her. She felt weak and overwhelmed; she felt like a traitor every time they met together.

It is difficult to describe the paradoxical experience of ambivalence. To have one strong emotion (terror) and another equally powerful feeling (desire) seems inconceivable. The apparent contradiction adds to the confusion. How can one hate and want the same person? How can one equally enjoy and despise the sexual pleasure experienced during the abuse? The confluence of antithetical emotional currents makes the victim feel powerless, crazy, and ashamed.

To add to the complexity, there are times when the child literally will feel betrayed by his own body, because he is powerless to stop the abuse or even his physiological response to it. A man told me about the times he was masturbated by his mother. She came to his bed late at night, long after he had gone to sleep. She would rearrange the covers and scratch his back. If he was lying on his side, she would stroke his penis. Many nights he would feign to be asleep and turn on his side when she entered the room. He hated himself for feeling aroused and would occasionally feel overwhelming guilt and then turn away from her touch. Other times he allowed himself to be aroused to orgasm. Afterward, he would hate himself for his "sick" response and failure of resolve. Sensual arousal, sexual pleasure, and even orgasm may occur when a child or adolescent is abused, even if there was a strong effort to avoid the sensation.

Sexual arousal will not be experienced every time abuse occurs. Sometimes fear will block arousal; other times, physical pain is so severe, arousal is impossible. It is also common for the victim to effectively dissociate her thoughts and feelings from her physical experience so that no conscious arousal occurs. This state is akin to what is referred to as an out-of-body experience or self-induced hypnotic trance. In psychological jargon, the experience of dissociation is called splitting. Human beings have the ability to separate or split off their feelings from their thoughts or, at times, to even ignore the sense data that is being perceived so that the mind is not permitted to translate what is being seen, heard, felt, or tasted into familiar categories. It is as if the mind knows what the soul can endure. When the data is too overwhelming, a fuse is blown so that the entire electrical-wiring system does not burn out. It is not uncommon for the victim to entirely block out her feelings of rage, or alternately to be so aware of her anger that she cannot even recall feeling relational, sensual, or sexual pleasure. The movement between rage and pleasure may be erratic and severe, resulting in significant personality changes in a matter of moments. The combination of powerlessness, betrayal, and ambivalence make splitting a natural option to the overwhelming internal flood of traumatic emotions.

Betrayal		Relational
Powerlessness	→ Rage ∿∿∿ Pleasure ←	Sensual
Ambivalence		Sexual

It is important to point out that not all Stage 3 abuse involves physical violation. Sexual abuse proper also includes psychological interactions that are just as soul-wrenching as rape. For example, even if the uncle referred to earlier had never touched or overtly violated his niece as he taught her to drive, his seductive heart had already invited a response from her that asked her to give parts of herself that she could not give without feeling used and perverse. In other words, his involvement with her, even if it had remained at the level of psychological interaction, was Stage 3 abuse.

To give another example of nonphysical Stage 3 abuse, a young man who was being guided through the rigors of a gymnastic routine by his trainer was severely rebuked or praised by him according to his performance. The trainer's effusive feedback created a powerful bond between the two of them that left the young man hungry for more special attention (Stage 1). After he executed a difficult maneuver, his trainer often touched the back of his head or gently squeezed his shoulder (Stage 2). Occasionally, the trainer commented on the grace and strength of his developing body (Stage 3).

As this man told me about his experience, he blushed, remembering how desired he felt by his trainer at those seemingly innocent but intimate moments. As an adult, he could acknowledge that his trainer's interest had been more than aesthetic. He had invited the boy to respond to him not as a student, but as a lover. His invitation was abusive. The horror of Stage 3 psychological interaction is its wicked subtlety. It oftens lingers quietly in the mind of the victim as a gift rather than a violation.

In summary, sexual abuse proper triggers a mess of emotions. In many cases, some degree of sexual arousal will be part of the experience of sexual abuse. Ambivalence — the intertwining of hate and desire, pleasure and shame — activates a strong desire to dissociate or separate the two opposing emotions, so that a deep chasm is created in the soul between pleasure and rage, often with both components entirely obliterated from memory.

Ambivalence is further intensified by the rage of betrayal and the terror of losing relationship with the abuser and others in one's family. The inability to change the abuser or the internal cross-currents of emotion should make it clear why the victim would prefer to feel nothing at all.

Stage 4: Maintenance of the Abuse and Secrecy Through Threats and Privileges

The final stage of abuse is in many ways similar to the first stage: the development of intimacy and secrecy. Unlike the first stage, however, the glory days are gone forever. The abuser will use whatever leverage he or she can to instill loyalty and fear in the heart of the victim to ensure silence and compliance. Fear is infused through threats and loyalty through privileges.

Fear is usually based on physical or psychological threats or actual use of violent force. Physical threats include the threat to bodily harm the victim or someone dear to her. One abusive brother used to hold his sister's rabbit over a fire until she took her clothes off. He once killed a pet in her presence to warn her to keep quiet. I have had a number of clients who were physically tortured by their perpetrators and lived with a deep and legitimate fear of death.

Psychological threats are equally powerful. One woman was told that if she did not continue to service her father, he would send her mother to an insane asylum. Another woman was threatened with the responsibility of her uncle's suicide if she told on him. The variety of ways that men and women have been coerced into silence and compliance is numbing to the mind. The essence of the attack is the threat to destroy the body and soul. The body is threatened by death, and the soul through shame.

Privileges also run the gamut of physical and psychological benefits. One woman, in tears, told me that her brother gave her a comic book every time they had intercourse. The value of her soul was precisely twenty-five cents, the cost of one book. Others have received money, new clothes, and cars. Many times the privileges are not material but psychological, such as the right to be the judge and jury of the other children, or the one who gets to accompany

Dad on his business trips. In one family, the child who sat at the head of the table was the one who was clearly favored. The material advantage was in having first access to the food, but the relational benefit was in the warning to the other siblings to avoid conflict with the favored child. This points to another tragedy in the abusive family. The child that is set apart for abuse is usually hated for his or her privileges by the other siblings. The child who feels different because of the abuse is then even further alienated due to the sibling jealousy.

STAGES OF SEXUAL ABUSE

Typical Sexual Contact:
High School Teacher and Thirteen-Year-Old Student

Stage 1: Intimacy and Secrecy
Builds relationship through granting study-hall leave and sharing secrets about struggles with his dominant mother.

Stage 2: Physical Touch that Appears Appropriate
Hugs that linger a little too long after an academic achievement, hair tousling, and playful pinches.

Stage 3: Sexual Abuse Proper
Sexual kissing, contact with clothed breasts, and eventually rape.

Stage 4: Securing of Silence and/or Maintenance of Sexual Abuse Through Threat and/or Privilege
Pleads for forgiveness, states the consequences of exposure (jail, loss of career, and public humiliation), offers greater privileges.

Atypical Sexual Contact:
Uncle and Niece

Stage 1: Intimacy and Secrecy
Buys her a gift and offers to take her to a show. She refuses and is blamed for being ungrateful. Eventually she gives in to avoid family criticism.

Stage 2: Physical Touch that Appears Appropriate
Hug at the doorway after the family reunion and friendly kiss.

(continued on page 91)

STAGES OF SEXUAL ABUSE, continued

Stage 3: Sexual Abuse Proper
After a family reunion, he finds her in the cellar and lifts up her skirt, squeezes pubic area, and touches clothed breast.

Stage 4: Securing Silence and/or Maintenance of Sexual Abuse Through Threat and/or Privilege
Reminds her of his good reputation with the family and threatens her with the disbelief and horror of others, which would result in her shame and ostracism.

Typical Sexual Interaction:
High School Teacher and Thirteen-Year-Old Student

Stage 1: Intimacy and Secrecy
Builds relationship through granting study-hall leave and sharing secrets about struggles with his dominant mother.

Stage 2: Physical Touch that Appears Appropriate
Hugs that linger a little too long after an academic achievement, hair tousling, and playful pinches.

Stage 3: Sexual Abuse Proper
Shares story of first sexual experience, invites her to talk about her first experience.

Stage 4: Securing of Silence and/or Maintenance of Sexual Abuse Through Threat and/or Privilege
Talks about how uptight, rigid busybodies might use their conversation against them if it were ever told to anyone else; promises to share even more incredible experiences at another time.

Atypical Sexual Interaction:
Uncle and Niece

Stage 1: Intimacy and Secrecy.
Buys her a gift and offers to take her to a show. She refuses and is , blamed for being ungrateful. Eventually she gives in to avoid family criticism.

Stage 2: Physical Touch that Appears Appropriate
Hug at the doorway and friendly kiss, which she spurns—more family criticism.

Stage 3: Sexual Abuse Proper
After seeing her in a swimming suit, he begins to visually undress her

(continued on page 92)

STAGES OF SEXUAL ABUSE, continued

---

and makes leering comments about how he wishes he were a few years younger and not her uncle because she has such a nice body.

Stage 4: Securing Silence and/or Maintenance of Sexual Abuse Through Threat and/or Privilege

Reminds her of his good reputation with the family and threatens her with the disbelief and horror of others, which would result in her shame and ostracism.

The silence is rarely broken. Few children or adolescents tell a parent, friend, or teacher about the abuse. It remains a dark secret for years, if not forever. The abusive event may be a one-time occurrence or continue over several years. The silence and continued compliance intensifies the victim's resolve to deaden all feelings and find some way to endure, to survive the assault of his or her soul. The ambivalence fluctuates between rage and occasional experiences of pleasure until the internal warfare has so wounded the heart that it simply gives up the fight. Usually, by that point, the abuse has ended or the victim has moved out of the home. A flight from the internal and external battle is the only relief that seems possible for the already devastated soul.

Escape to another life and world requires a new identity and history and a burial of the awful past. Victims often concoct an image of the past as tranquil and happy until it actually becomes true in their mind. The illusion of a good home and loving parents satisfies the curiosity of others and quiets the crippling pain of the past. The rage and the pleasure are deeply buried in the soul, with no marker or adequate opportunity for grief. The effects of the damage, however, continue to work their way through the human personality. *The streams of powerlessness, betrayal, and ambivalence continue to feed the river of rage that has been held back by the dam of denial.* In many cases, the dam is as ineffective as a sieve in holding back the water; rage pours out in torrents. In other cases, the rage is held back by rigid cement barriers, producing enormous supplies of energy for family, work, and ministry. The energy, however, is tainted with rage, barely concealed behind layers of self-contempt. The victim's effectiveness in the world doesn't compare to the power the Spirit of God could produce if her heart was His.

If change is to occur, the streams that supply the raging water must be discovered, understood, and eventually altered in their course. The next three chapters will focus on the internal damage caused by abuse: the streams of powerlessness, betrayal, and ambivalence.

PART TWO

THE DAMAGE OF ABUSE

FIVE

Powerlessness

As we scrutinize each element of the damage done to the soul by sexual abuse, a magnification may occur for a brief period, making the effect appear larger and hopelessly overwhelming. Two reminders are necessary before we proceed.

True hope never minimizes a problem in order to make it more palatable and easily managed. For the Christian, hope begins by recognizing the utter hopelessness of our condition and the necessity of divine intervention, if we are to experience true joy. Any personal change that can be achieved solely through human, in contrast to supernatural, intervention will neither satisfy nor change our heart. A proper focus on the deep wound is therefore neither negative nor does it promote despair. Rather, it sets the stage for the dramatic work of God.

A second reminder involves the danger of myopia. If one looks through a microscope too long at one group of cells, it is possible to develop tunnel vision. In this chapter we will focus on the experience of powerlessness, but there are other factors involved in the damage that include, but go beyond, the experience of feeling helpless. In focusing narrowly on one aspect we run the danger of limiting perspective and creating the illusion that one part of the damage is more severe or significant than another, or that one aspect of the damage functions in isolation from the other elements. In fact, the damage can be described in terms of powerlessness, betrayal, and ambivalence only if we understand that all three aspects of the damage function together in one tumultuous river that rages through the soul, tearing away hope, faith, and love. In order to take a close look at the river, we will travel further upstream to examine the source of each separate stream.

Our look at each stream will expose the abuse in terms of its cause, cost, consequence, and core image. In other words, how did the damage occur? What are the internal repercussions of the damage? What are its external results? And how will the victim see himself or herself as a result of the damage?

THE CAUSE OF POWERLESSNESS

It may be obvious, but to most abused people it is not clear: *Abuse strips a person of the freedom to choose.* Sexual abuse was never wanted nor invited; therefore, its occurrence was not a choice. If the abuse occurred one time or hundreds, the fact does not change; to the degree that choice was denied, powerlessness was experienced and dignity was assaulted. There are (at least) three forces that cause a sense of powerlessness: the inability to change the dysfunctional family, the inability to stop the abuse, and the inability to end the relentless pain in the soul.

The Emptiness of the Home

I am continually amazed how often someone who was abused will begin by telling me they had a happy childhood or how richly loved they felt by their mother and father, even though the history indicates that nothing could be further from the truth. A child would rather have a bad parent than no parent, and even more would rather be a bad kid than face the wickedness of the parent he is dependent upon. How is a child to survive if he fully admits that his life is in the hands of someone who will neither protect him against harm nor provide for his legitimate relational desires?

The denial of the emptiness is further fostered by an absence of comparison. How is a child to know what she is missing if she has nothing else to compare it to? In most cases, the relational emptiness is all the child ever knew, and so it is viewed as acceptable, if not normal. Proverbs 27:7 states the dilemma well: "A sated man loathes honey, but to a famished man any bitter thing is sweet" (NASB). For a child who is humiliated at the dinner table every night, to be merely ignored may be a relief, in fact a joy. Or when a child is often forced to participate in oral sex, to be merely fondled seems minor and expected.

The routine becomes a child's definition of normal, even if the "normal" is bizzare, abusive, or evil. For that reason, it may take years, if not decades, for a person to fully see her world from the vantage point of what could and should have transpired. We are so terribly reluctant to imagine the horror of an event, when it is so easy to cloud the pain by seeing it as "just the way it was." Consequently, many children and adults are not aware of how much energy they spent trying to change a world that was viewed as normal, but was internally experienced with dis-ease and emptiness.

Sexual abuse never begins at the point of the first sexual contact. It begins in the matrix of some level of emotional neglect, role distortion, harshness, coldness, rigidity, and fear-induced loyalty. In most cases, the family, prior to the abuse, was a festering sore where dis-ease and emptiness were a normal part of life. But the normal abnormalcy of the family is at odds with the child's innate, God-designed desire for stability, intimacy, and respect. The child may learn to accept the wretched harm of the abuse as normal, but a quiet inner voice will, at some point, begin to whisper strange, but true, words: "It's not right for Mom to let this occur. Dad should not be touching me this way. I wish our family was loving and happy like my friend's home." The seeds of discontent are the first fruits of awakened desire. Sadly, the seeds often fall on rocky soil and are eaten by the wolves of doubt and self-contempt. The initial seeds of discontented desire often stir a hunger for more and an equal pressure to find some means to perform well enough to see the dream of a happy family come true.

The desire for change is a mixed blessing. It both opens the door to a taste of hope and binds the child's soul to the pernicious whims of the family. The child becomes a prisoner to the hope that something can be done to lift Mom's spirits or keep Dad from being enraged. The passionate desire to see the family change energizes the child to pursue academic, athletic, social, or religious excellence. The result — irrespective of success or failure — is deeper disappointment that the mom or dad did not change. The reason for their lack of change is always assumed to be the failure of the child: "If only I had worked a little harder, maybe the coach would have let me play on the first team. If only I had a more outgoing smile, maybe I would have been invited to the prom by one of the wealthier boys. If I had succeeded well, then maybe Dad would not need to abuse me, or maybe Mom would be nicer to Dad, and life would be better." *The impossibility of being enough to change a dysfunctional family leads to the initial experience of powerlessness.*

The subtle demands of the needy parent, who has often assigned the child an adult role, adds to the sense of ill-fated child omnipotence. A child who has been labeled as "Mom's little helper" or "Dad's special girl" is trapped in an adult role that the child cannot possibly fulfill, but one that must be accomplished if hope is to be realized. What an awful bind! A child is given the keys to the kingdom, the power to please and bring change, and then at some point realizes she is not tall enough even to fit the key into the lock that towers above her. Slowly, the child faces the fact that no matter how good she is, how gifted, intelligent, musical, social, and competent, it is not enough to change the intractable emptiness of her family.

The Helplessness of Sexual Abuse

A second deep well that pours out water for the violent stream is the impossibility of stopping abuse once it has begun. Abuse is either an unplanned, sudden event that occurs because a person was in the wrong place at the wrong time, or a carefully constructed setup that was organized for optimum secrecy and ease. In either case, the victim could not have known what was going to occur. There was no way to stop the assault. The victim was not given an option, time to reflect, perspective on the issues involved in the abuse, or the opportunity to seek the help of another in making a choice about involvement. In other words, the assault, in either the sudden, unplanned attack or the well-orchestrated seduction, stole the opportunity to choose. Whether physical pain is experienced or not, the violation of the body and soul leads to a sense of being small, helpless, and alone.

Furthermore, once the abuse has occurred, the abuser often uses threat or shame to silence the victim. The fear of being burned to death or sent to an orphanage, would understandably, keep almost anyone mute. Violence, however, is not the only weapon used to weaken the victim's voice. Shame is just as effective a tool. The threat of even more exposure and humiliation increases a sense of hopelessness.

The Relentless Pain of the Soul

The two previous forces can be viewed as an inability to change a system (family) and an inability to stop the abuse (abuser). In both cases, the inability involves something outside the soul. The third factor, however, is not interpersonal and external, but personal and internal. It involves the victim's inability to stop his or her own soul from bleeding.

The absence of deep involvement is exponentially magnified by sexual abuse. The heart aches, and there is no immediate recourse for relief, except the soul-numbing choice to abandon a sense of being alive. What a terrible choice! *If the victim wants to live free of the pain, then she must choose to not be alive.* One woman said it was as if the abuse flushed rancid sewage into her home, which could not be tolerated unless she destroyed her sense of smell.

Although a victim may choose to kill the part of her soul that feels pain, the grace of God renders her unable to utterly destroy her own or anyone else's intuitive sense of being. She cannot entirely wipe out the pain, no matter if she opts for catatonia, multiple personalities, amnesiac forgetfulness, or hyperspiritual denial. The remnant of pain alternately mocks and soothes the victim's heart: "I am in pain, and I am not in control. I am alive, and I am not a mechanical automaton." The pain persists and cannot ultimately be altered by efforts to escape.

The essence of all three forces of powerlessness — the family, the abuser, and the pain — is the inability to escape or change the ravaging consequences of living in a fallen world. Every day we are assaulted by forces of evil, injustice, selfishness, and abuse as a normal course of living with sinful people in a fallen world. When the pretense that the good life is a matter of hard work and fair play is stripped away through victimization, we are faced with the awful fact of how little, if anything, is in our direct control. Powerlessness, the inability to redirect the family heartache, stop the physical touch of the abuser, or silence the hollow screams inside the heart, is a reality that is endemic to all humankind, but is faced by few. We are all helpless, but only those who have been radically deprived of the inherent freedom to choose and the legitimate desire to redirect that which is wrong will know how truly powerless we are in every endeavor that matters the most to us.

Powerlessness is no gift, but the consequences of facing our helplessness, as victims of abuse and even more as sojourners in a world that is not our own, can open the door to new vistas of power and a radical taste of what it means to be free.

THE COST OF BEING POWERLESS

The experience of powerlessness need not destroy or damage the soul. However, in most, if not all, cases, profound helplessness leads to deep scars and wounds. The internal damage follows the path of *doubt, despair,* and *deadness.*

Self-doubt is common when our efforts fail to bring results. Failure is a rock in our shoe that nags us until we find relief. At first, failure to achieve our desired end will elicit careful scrutiny (What can I do better?) and resumed commitment (How can I try harder?). Success may be achieved — straight As, an athletic scholarship, perfect Sunday school attendance — but the real goal — a happy family, an end to the abuse, or relief from the pain — is always out of reach. The natural result will be a severe (and likely contemptuous) question as to what is wrong with us. "Why can't I run faster, or sing better, or be more perfect?" The self-doubt opens the door to despair.

The result of continued, frustrated labor that fails to reach the carrot at the end of the stick is *learned helplessness.* Learned helplessness is an orchestrated retreat that has learned to give up before one even tries, because there is no point to pursue an objective that is doomed to failure before ever begun. Imagine being unjustly locked in a dark cell. After being put in the cell, you might shout, cry, plead, threaten, and beg until your voice gave out. After a time you might check to see if there is any way out. When it is clear there is no exit and no one will hear you or rescue you, all hope of change is abandoned. Hope deferred makes the heart sick, and we'd rather not feel ill; therefore, if we abandon hope, then, we can live without a nauseous heart. Despair is a protective blanket that shields the soul against the cold demands of harsh self-doubt; depression is the middle ground between the pressured energy to change and the total abandonment of hope.

Those who abandon hope deaden their soul by cutting off the parts of it that still feel rage, pain, and desire and exiting those parts to the furthest reaches of the unconscious. At times the choice is as conscious as the taking of an oath. One woman recalled a commitment she made during the time her uncle flirted with her: "If I don't feel anything, he will stop." He didn't stop, but only intensified his verbal intrusions by making comments about her developing body. She deepened her commitment: "If I never feel anything, at least he will never have the pleasure of seeing me respond." From that point on she became an ice maiden, an unfeeling automaton who exiled her soul into a subarctic region of denial. Her deadness was a hunger-induced commitment to lose her soul rather than hurt anymore. She described herself as a person who left her porch lights on, but was never at home. She smiled and feigned involvement, but no one was ever invited into her empty soul. She was never at home in herself.

Because of the way God has made us, it is impossible finally and completely to deaden the soul. The soul will resurrect, in spite of the cruelty used to destroy it. It will pop up and then be slain again, return and be shoved down through contempt. The power to destroy the soul is not in the hands of Satan, another human being, or even oneself. Nevertheless, when we manage to deaden our soul, even temporarily, we open the door to terrible consequences.

THE CONSEQUENCES OF BEING POWERLESS

The experience of powerlessness is almost always damaging. The external consequences of the doubt, despair, and deadness set into motion a process that eventuates most often in broken relationships and further revictimization. When we feel profoundly helpless, we can lose our sense of pain, which in turn leads to the loss of a sense of self, and inevitably results in a loss of judgment and wisdom. The process can be deadly.

Loss of a Sense of Pain
Pain is a gift. We may not welcome it when it intrudes in our life, but imagine what would occur if we never felt pain. Dr. Paul Brand, a renowned physician who studied and treated leprosy for many years, found that the disease destroyed its victims by numbing their nerve endings. The progressive deadening of the nerve sensations permitted the leper to put his hand or foot into dangerous situations of extreme heat, cold, or harm without awareness. The disease indirectly destroys a person by deadening his awareness of pain. The obvious parallel to our spiritual condition and life is a marvelous metaphor that brings perspective and honor to the experience of suffering.

A sexually abused person often forfeits the experience of pain by a process of splitting, denial, and loss of memory. Splitting involves an unconsious process of segmenting memories and feelings into separable categories of good or bad. The categorization of the self as all good or all bad is then intensified by the construction of a huge barricade between the two. It is not possible for the person to see errant motives in her "good self" or legitimate desire or even honorable intention in her "bad self." The two are separated by an iron curtain: on one side exists all the lust, vengeance, hate, and hunger of the soul; and on the other, all the love, forgiveness, and warmth. If feelings from the dark side are experienced, they must be either denied or embraced in an orgy of compulsion. The binge eater hates herself, but periodically "allows" for a break in her "good self" routine by a few minutes of oral debauchery. She knows she must pay the price of shame and contempt, but even that is a small price since the self-hatred adds another layer to the wall and more distance from the deeper pain inside. Splitting leads to a wall of denial. Denial separates the mind from the agony in the heart. It is the dividing wall between the "good" and "bad" selves.

Is it any wonder the internal struggle eventually leads to forgetfulness? The struggle of being powerless in the face of overwhelming evil and emptiness is a titanic battle that seems best forgotten. The energy required to keep the iron wall of denial intact is costly and time-consuming. Therefore, it is common for the memories and feeling to be lost to the soul, buried in deep storage, rather than anguished over in a world that offers no help.

As long as we're dead, we can't feel pain. If there's no one home to answer the door, then we don't have to feel disappointed when no one knocks for us. But what else happens when the experience of pain is lost? Simply stated, *when we abandon pain, we lose a sense of being intact and alive.*

Loss of a Sense of Self

The concept of the self is an intuitive rather than scientific notion. What is the self? How do we define the word *soul* or *self* or, for that matter, the idea of life? There is something inside us that provides continuity and cohesion to the divergent experiences of life. I can recall going on a Boy Scout field trip to the governor's office. I wore shorts, a T-shirt, and a Davy Crocket coonskin cap. All my peers wore a shirt, a tie, and a suit. I was mortified, especially when we had our picture taken with the governor. As I recall that event, nearly twenty-five years later, I can feel my face blush. I can see that awkward, pudgy, curly-haired boy as quite different than me, and yet I blush for him, because I know it is me.

But what is me? I have no idea. All I know is that I am connected to that boy, and he is connected to a man I can see twenty-five years from now who is the slow, overweight, balding man I will become as the years transpire. I am not my body, but my body is as much me as I know anything else to be. I am so much more than my body; nevertheless, I am at least the totality of all that I have experienced in my body. Confused? Maybe that is partly God's intention. My being can never be defined outside relationship with God. I am an orphaned child of Adam and an adopted child of the King. My identity and being find their beginning and end in something outside myself, but if I am numb to my hunger and thirst, I will never look outside of myself for meaning or life.

Hunger and thirst—or better said, longing for relationship and impact—is our subjective link between the soul and the body. If we lose a sense of hunger and thirst, we equally lose a sense of the person we are; consequently, the sense of selfhood that provides perspective and cohesion to life is lost.

Sexually abused persons often seem like strangers to their own soul and history. Many times the chronic patterns of lying or deceit common to abused persons arise because of a forsaken history that forces them to concoct a past and a present that has no connection to their abused soul. The consequence is not only a loss of the past, but also a loss of the ability to judge the present and plan for the future.

The Loss of a Sense of Judgment

All decisions involve the use of perspective. We cannot make a choice without the use of thought and feeling. What occurs when we make a choice without awareness of hunger and thirst, or a sense of self? We will continue to make decisions, but our energy will be defensive and self-serving (self-protective). Ultimately, all choices will be directly or subtly designed to keep our soul under wraps and the past hidden behind a veil of shame. The tone of our life will be rigid and distant, illusive and uninvolved, no matter how kind or sweet our dispostion. Careful scrutiny will show how a painless person's judgment is darkened by her lack of soul.

For example, a woman who visited a new gynecologist felt in his questions and clinical touch a level of familiarity that she deemed inappropriate. She managed to nullify her initial assessment, however, by viciously assaulting herself with contempt for so crudely misjudging her competent physician: "He's a good man. Whatever I'm feeling is typical of my crazy, perverse way of seeing things." Consequently, each subsequent appointment over the next six months only confirmed her wanton and despicable heart, because each time she felt his interest to be inappropriate. When he eventually raped her, she was only more convinced that she had led him on, rather than appalled that his initial warmth and tender touch were a setup for later overt abuse. Her lack of a sense of pain and self, and her refusal to trust her own intuition, made her unnecessarily vulnerable to a wicked man's physical attack.

Distorted judgment is seen more often than not in the arena of relationships. An abused woman may be a trial lawyer, run a huge corporation, or be your surgeon and make extremely competent judgments about her field of endeavor. In fact, in most cases, though it sounds macabre and cruel, I would prefer my lawyer to be obsessively perfectionistic. The hard-driving, extremely competent sexual-abuse victim makes a fine lawyer, surgeon, or CEO because all of her defensive energies are oriented to finding some domain that is under her control; *she will not be powerless again!* May she ever be on my side in the courtroom, but Lord help me if she is my neighbor, friend, or wife. Her deepest pain occurred in relationship, and it is in relationships that her judgment will most likely be distorted. Since she has played dead to her pain in the past, she doesn't learn what hurts her; therefore, she often unwittingly opens herself to further victimization in the future.

The cause of this relationship between abuse and revictimization is not entirely clear. There are at least two significant factors. First, an empty and unsure person is an easy mark for those who are looking for illicit pleasure and gain. Who is most likely to be gypped by the unscrupulous used-car dealer: the knowledgeable, savvy buyer or the frightened, innocent first-time shopper? Many abused persons seem to advertise their past victimization through naive, blind trust and through weakness that invites abuse. The unconscious signal sent is a loud invitation in an evil world that attracts wolves to an easy kill.

A second factor is more difficult to explain and understand. Abused men and women often entangle themselves in relationships with people who are not trustworthy, faithful, or loving. I've worked with a number of abused women who have been married and divorced several times, seduced, and cheated out of large sums of money by men who are cut out of the same pattern. It is not uncommon for an abused woman to be enmeshed with men who cannot make decisions, do not desire intimacy, and defend their weaknesses with a distant defensiveness that occasionally erupts in rage. Why would this be a result of a loss of judgment?

From the vantage point of shame, poor judgment can be understood as a result of not feeling worthy to be in relationship with a truly loving man. That seems easy and clear. It's from the side of contempt and self-hatred that the waters get murky. A woman who feels stripped of power in most of her important relationships feels out of control in relationships, particularly relationships in which her heart comes alive with the hope that love might touch her deadened soul. The ambivalence is great: "Do I allow myself to hope deeply and therefore make my soul vulnerable to being crushed again if I am robbed of the love I so crave? Or do I settle for a relationship that touches more shallow parts, feels good, excites and nourishes for a short time, but will likely end in expected disaster?" Who will provoke greater fear: a committed and loving man or an uncommitted and selfish man?

The man who might truly offer relationship will scare the abused woman far more than the unfaithful man. At least the uncommitted and uninvolved man is predictable, does not raise hopes too high, and hurts far less than the man who has the ability to deliver a quality relationship. The man capable of relationship not only provokes more fear but is far less easy to control. This is a terrible struggle for the abused woman. She longs for a man who will take hold of her. On the other hand, she is terrified to be in a position of being out of control. Her option is to find a strong man who is in control, competent, and aggressive in his career (external strength) and too busy to deeply involve himself in relationship with his family (no involvement), or to find a passive man who will give himself neither to his career (no strength) nor to his family (no involvement). In either case, the woman will not have to give up relational control.

A weak, undependable man seems the perfect choice for a boyfriend or mate. He does not arouse the deepest passion of the heart, but he provides a taste of relationship without ever requiring the woman to experience profound powerlessness. He provides evidence that she is not truly attractive and desirable (if she was, then why would he treat her so badly?), intensifying her contempt, thus serving her by being a hired mercenary to put to death her hungry heart. She also has free reign to vent her untapped rage toward a weak and uninvolved man. The rage of being powerless finds a ready target in a man who does not challenge or threaten her lonely isolation and wounded heart.

Poor judgment about relationships is common and predictable. The factors behind the loss of judgment involve a choice to forsake the soul, while still retaining a semblance of control over those who do not threaten the heart that is afraid to hunger and desire more. Powerlessness spawns a perspective about self, others, and God that is deeply entrenched and difficult to change.

CORE IMAGES RELATED TO POWERLESSNESS

When an abused person feels powerless, she internalizes an image of herself as profoundly inadequate. She deeply questions her ability, competence, and intelligence. The doubt that opened the door to despair and deadness centers on these questions: "Why could I not stop the family emptiness, abuse, and heartache? Why did I not get better grades? Why did Dad like my sister more than me? Why did Mom always find fault with me?" The questions of doubt center on the issue of *failure*.

Failure at a task seems to imply inability, incompetence, or lack of motivation. The abused woman will often see herself as mentally deficient. I have worked with men and women who have attained the highest level of proficiency in their field and yet view themselves as idiots. One woman always found a way of undercutting her academic achievements by blaming the ease of the exam. Later, when she was accepted at the Harvard Medical School, she excused her success as the result of a more lenient attitude toward women. Her election as chief resident at a prestigious hospital was rationalized as the result of her "adequate" organizational skills, which the other students never worked to achieve since they were too gifted and cerebral.

It is utterly useless to encourage such a person to evaluate her God-given assets more realistically, because the energy behind the deep doubt and hatred is not based on reality. The image of being talentless, mediocre, average, or worse is a self-serving, self-protective evaluation used for a purpose: it provides the victim with a contemptuous explanation for not being able to halt the pain. As long as she is unintelligent and mediocre in ability, she can explain both why she was powerless and hope that she can become more powerful (through studying, improving her speaking skills, or listening more attentively). The contemptuous evaluation of ability and intelligence also serves to deaden pain and refocus attention away from what the abused person feels most powerless to do anything about: her hatred and rage.

In summary, it is a good rule of thumb to listen to how people talk about their natural abilities, intelligence, and accomplishments to get an initial assessment of the nature and intensity of their contempt. Self-hatred in the area of intelligence or ability is often a result of an abusive past that the person was powerless to stop.

The damage of abuse is not limited to powerlessness. Another deep wound is the experience of betrayal, the awful reality of being set up and used by the abuser and being unprotected by the nonoffending parent or parents.

SIX

Betrayal

There is something odious about a person who betrays a sacred trust. Children may not know the name of the current vice-president or who was president when they were born, but most kids know the name of Benedict Arnold. A traitor etches his name in infamy. Why is betrayal so devastating that a traitor's name is as well, if not better, known than the names of many who drafted the Constitution of the United States? What kind of destruction is set off in the human soul by betrayal?

Honor is the opposite of betrayal. Trust and respect are the foundation of all human endeavor, including politics, business, marriage, and friendship. Can people count on your word? Is your heart directed toward honoring God in your relationships? Relationship cannot be endured—certainly cannot be enjoyed—unless the parties involved are honorable in intent and word. Failure will inevitably occur in all relationships, but trust is not built on the absence of failure as much as on the willingness of each party to own and rectify each harmful break in the relationship. Honor assumes the need for honesty and restitution. In the context of honor, failure opens the door to deepening trust as wrongs are righted and wounds are healed.

The antithesis of honor is hypocrisy. It turns any relationship from one of mutual support and consideration into an adversarial struggle for preeminence. The moment core trust is lost in a relationship, efforts to understand and nourish the other person are forgotten in a battle to control and minimize damage to oneself.

Let me illustrate this phenomenon by calling to mind a common experience. How do you feel when you walk into a showroom to make a major purchase? The salesman approaches with a smile and an outstretched hand. Is your heart warmed? Do you find yourself relaxing in his presence, knowing your best interest is being considered? Or do you sense that his keen interest in learning your name, his comment about your darling children, and his open ear regarding your reason for shopping in his store belie his primary intent: to sell his product at the highest possible price?

We are accustomed to casting a jaundiced eye on the merchant, the politician, the religious leader, the next-door neighbor—in fact, almost everyone but ourselves. Cynical humor becomes the badge of sophistication for those who know that man's heart is always evil. To trust is to be destroyed; to expect honor is to be deceived. In such an atmosphere, relationship is doomed.

In contrast to cynical sophistication, some people develop a naive, childish blindness that rejects the evidence of deceit and selfishness and wantonly assumes that all will work out well, without direct action or intervention. In that atmosphere, rich relationship is exchanged for superficial saccharine pleasantries. In either case, relationship is violated.

Violation of relationship opens a Pandora's box of suspicion and shame that exists in every person. The suspicion that we feel toward a world that has at times cavalierly ignored our longings and at other times abused our soul is like a tinder box of dry wood. Betrayal is the spark that ignites the explosive heap of mistrust in our soul. When paranoia flames, relationship is severed, hope is shattered, and belief in the other person is put on a prove-it-to-me basis with no opportunity for restitution. The human soul is left charred and empty, blown about by the vicious winds of loneliness and doubt.

Something deep inside us reacts to deception and betrayal. Betrayal not only inflames doubt and severs relationship with our neighbor, but also inevitably deepens hatred for ourselves. The person who is betrayed often laments: How could I have been so stupid? How could I have trusted someone who was so deceitful? The shame of being taken advantage of increases the fury of self-incrimination. *The one who was betrayed assumes that she could have prevented the betrayal if she was less needy or naive.* The attack she makes against her own soul is often more vicious than the original betrayal. The goal of her attack, as in all self-contempt, is to kill her hungry soul. She fears that if she stays open to her desire for relationship, she may foolishly open herself to repeated betrayal. Nobody can be trusted, especially herself. After all, her own desires (to be honored, valued, wanted, etc.) are what got her into trouble in the first place! Better to kill them off than live at risk of further betrayal and humiliation. Better to expect little from anyone and avoid the desire for more. Deadness is somehow more tolerable than fighting with personal doubt or loneliness. No wonder the victim ignores the wound or opts for cheap forgiveness to wash away the traitorous act.

What I have just described is the result of any betrayal, be it the deception of being sold an inferior product, or being told a lie by a close friend. Betrayal can be defined as *any disregard or harm done to the dignity of another as a result of one's commitment to find life apart from God.* Betrayal, thus defined, is a constant wound inflicted in all relationships. It is such a normal part of life that our attention is hardly drawn to the casual, innocuous betrayals of everyday interactions, that is, unless serious betrayal has occurred that predisposes a person toward vigilant scrutiny and jaundiced perception. Such is the case for those who have been sexually abused.

The remainder of the chapter will focus on the internal damage generated by the betrayal of sexual abuse. What are its cause, cost, and consequence, and what core image will a person internalize when he or she is betrayed on such a profound level?

THE CAUSE OF BETRAYAL

The betrayal of sexual abuse is so obvious and intuitively clear that a discussion of its origin may seem superfluous. Nothing could be further from the truth. The actual betrayal experienced in Stage 3 (sexual abuse proper) is only one part of the damage. Sexualization of the relationship is devastating, but its horror is given an even darker impact because of the setting in which it occurs.

The betrayal has three levels: the failure of the family to nourish the child prior to the abuse, the traitorous act of the perpetrator, and the lack of protection offered by the nonoffending parent(s). The lack of appropriate relational nourishment is the necessary soil in which the weeds of abuse may flourish. A healthy environment in which children are respected and treated with sensitivity and compassion rarely produces abuse. It is impossible to use someone you love. The desire to possess or subjugate — the hunger to repay or destroy — is the ground for abuse.

The home where abuse occurs, or where extrafamilial abuse is ignored, is a dangerous and unpredictable environment. The child does not have the intellectual understanding or the contrasting experience of a nourishing home to evaluate the inadequacies of his parents and siblings. Yet his inherent drive for relationship sets up a crosswind of confusion even for the preverbal child.

Look at the face of a one-year-old child who has been denied a pleasure that he deems desirable. Even if the child is dealt with tenderly and consistently, tears will often erupt and disappointment will contort his face. Imagine the face and the interior of the child if he is hit across the face when he explores the top of the kitchen table. Does that child learn anything from that experience? Even the less dramatic failures of an uninvolved, distorted environment teach the child to cower under the weight of potential neglect and harm, and alternately to assert and deny the burgeoning longings of his soul. The pre-sexually abusive home is often a place of great betrayal.

The overt sexual abuse is preceded by a period of setup. In most cases, the child is introduced to relational and physical pleasures that contradict the "norm" of living in the desert of neglect. Privileges and intimacy that were either nonexistent or carefully rationed are now available at more luxurious levels. One woman described this as a period of being invited to an oasis. For years she had been kept in a desert with only a subsistence level of water to slake her thirst. She never felt satisfied by the almost empty glass of lukewarm water she was offered, until her father put a tall, cold glass of liquid in front of her and offered her a chance to drink to her deepest satisfaction. She downed the liquid and felt the cool waves of relief. When she put the empty glass down, she realized in a moment of horror that she had just consumed urine, which would not kill her, but nevertheless, cheapened and stained her momentary sense of relief.

The graphic metaphor of drinking urine describes the betrayal of sexual abuse. *The victim of abuse is left thirsty and then is forced to participate in consuming something that both touches the legitimate thirst of her being, while also destroying the very aspect of her being that has been relationally aroused.* This catch-22 situation is awful. If she feels alive in the presence of the abuser, then she must want what he offers. If she doesn't want what he offers, then she must not be alive. The betrayal is not merely the abuse, but also the upheaval of living on an internal roller coaster that jolts the soul both toward death and life at the same moment. If that were not enough, there is another betrayal, which in most cases, is even more difficult to endure.

The Role of the Nonoffending Parent(s)

It is difficult for those who are unacquainted with the issues of sexual abuse to comprehend the anger and hurt experienced by the victim as she considers the role of her nonabusive parent(s). An illustration may shed some light on this betrayal. Years ago a woman was murdered in broad daylight in full view of twenty or thirty people. The woman's screams and savage death was ignored by some and watched by others. No one came to her aid, nor even bothered to make an anonymous call to the police. Society was shocked and enraged. The furor was less over the man who murdered the woman than over the disregard of the crowd. The act of murder was heinous; the refusal to intervene was viewed as cowardly and despicable.

That is the case of the parent, or in some cases both parents, who for various reasons choose not to intervene, or not to see the need for intervention. There are several different forms of betrayal that characterize the nonoffending parent(s).

One form of betrayal that is difficult to imagine, but occurs often enough to be mentioned, is *complicity*. A parent or relative who sets the child up for another adult or older child to abuse has committed a terrible crime. Complicity may involve direct solicitation in which a father may send his daughter into the bedroom of his own father with the instruction "obey your grandfather and do what he tells you to do."

One mother told her daughter to go play baseball with her father, uncles, and cousins. Not wanting to hear her mother's incessant nagging, the fourteen-year-old girl went out to play. A short time later her mother told her to take her blouse off so that her shirt would not be soiled. Again, the mother's harangue worked, and the girl took her blouse off. It should come as no surprise that both her cousin and father abused her shortly after the game. In that case, it should be clear that her mother set her up and gave permission to the other members of the family to abuse her daughter. She was an evil parent.

I've encountered a number of situations in which Christian parents — including full-time Christian workers — have clearly set up their children for harm. The reasons a parent might do such damage to a child are beyond the scope of this book; nevertheless, it is naive to think that it is impossible to live two lives: one of devout, sacrificial, other-centered kindness and another of evil, destructive, narcissistic abuse. Because it seems inconceivable that a man or woman may be a respected servant in the church by day and an abuser by night, such situations are even more possible.

A second form of betrayal involves *chosen neglect or denial*. I've talked to countless men and women whose parents discovered them in bed with another child or adult and said nothing, or at best barked a command to stop that behavior, without ever following up to find out what occurred. In other cases, a parent may not see the actual abuse occur, but sees enough signs to warrant concern and chooses to ignore or deny the evidence.

One mother took her daughter to her aunt's home every Saturday. When her daughter was eleven, she was fondled by her fifteen-year-old cousin. The next time she was dropped off at the house, she begged to be included in the shopping trip rather than be left with her cousin. The mother ignored her plea, and she was subsequently beaten for her request and was raped for the first time. Thereafter, she wept the entire twenty-minute trip to her cousin's home. The tears continued for two years. Her mother never once asked her why she did not want to go or why she convulsed in tears every time she was left with her cousin.

A parent does not need to know about or suspect sexual abuse to betray a child. A third form of nonoffending betrayal comes as a result of the victim *having no place to turn* once abuse has occurred, because of the parent's character weakness. Imagine telling an angry, potentially violent father that his son has abused his daughter. If you were the daughter, you would fear a catastrophic scene and the dissolution of your family. Or what if your mother was a high-strung, emotionally unstable worrier who might be thrown into a year-long depression? Is it likely that you would share with your mother details about how your uncle fondled you at the family picnic? Abuse victims rarely admit the near "impossibility" of securing help from their family of origin; rather they blame themselves for not seeking help.

In all three forms of nonoffending betrayal the parent(s) chose the route of personal comfort or self-protection over the parental privilege and responsibility of providing a safe environment for their child. The damage may vary due to the type and intensity of betrayal, but in all cases the damage will be profound.

THE COST OF BETRAYAL

What happens inside of a person who has been profoundly betrayed is difficult to separate from the other damaging factors. It would be safe to say that betrayal hardly ever occurs without some experience of powerlessness. The person who denies the freedom of choice has betrayed the other. Consequently, all that was argued as part of the cost of powerlessness will also be true of betrayal. What is added in the experience of betrayal? If powerlessness leads to an internal deadness, betrayal sets the stage for an intense, hypervigilant suspiciousness that often leads to a distortion or denial of accurate conclusions about oneself and others.

Hypervigilance

An abused man I worked with was constantly concerned with uncovering the ill intentions of neighbors, friends, and family. He saw the frowns on their faces or their awkward glances directed toward him. And he knew what they were thinking: they were against him. Signs that I would never have noticed in a million years, he regularly observed. It was no use to dispute his findings, because in most cases he was accurate about the details.

Other individuals, equally aware of their external world, live with a profound self-consciousness about how others may see them. In either case, life is centered on taking in as much evidence as possible. The goal is never to be surprised. If one knows the enemy and where he is at all times, a measure of control can be attained.

The dilemma with hypervigilance is at least twofold: myopia and exhaustion. Hypervigilance leads to missing more details than would come through intent but relaxed observation. The old phrase strikes home: seeing the trees but missing the forest. The data gained is over-scrutinized, analyzed, and dissected, and often the obvious detail or fact is missed in the frenzy to comprehend. The result is exhaustion. The human frame was not made for frenetic hypervigilance. After time, the senses dull, analytic faculties tire, and the conclusions reached are tainted by observing so much but seeing so little.

Suspiciousness

Hypervigilance often masks a deep strain of suspiciousness. It almost seems as if the person tries to discount or deny soul-damaging relationships while suspiciously distancing herself from soul-enhancing involvement.

Notice how a self-contemptuous woman handles a compliment about her attire. Very seldom will she warm to the remark; at times she may stiffen, or simply brush it off in a comical retort about her old outfit. In many cases, the past betrayal has inserted a filter that evaluates all kindness, warmth, and involvement in the light of the question: "What do you want? And, what am I required to lose to keep you happy?" The suspiciousness may be gentle and jocular ("Oh, I'm sure you say that to everyone") or vicious and full of rage ("I know what you're looking for"). In either case, the relational distance produced is the same.

Suspiciousness is not only directed against others, but can also be turned against the self. When an abused person feels warm toward another person, it is not uncommon for him or her to suspiciously evaluate the feeling as immoral and dangerous. If she feels anger she may fear that vicious rage will pour forth and destroy the object of her ire. *Both the fear of danger and of being dangerous to others coexist in the heart of the person who has been sexually abused.*

Distortion and Denial
A common experience for many abuse victims is living in a haze of distortion, partial truths, denial, and a lack of objectivity. I've worked with high-power executives who make competent and accurate decisions about multimillion-dollar projects, but cannot accurately read their thirteen-year-old daughter's moods or feelings. The haze distorts relational data.

There are two primary forms of this distortion: an inability to trust relational intuition and a bent toward conclusions of contempt. Sexual-abuse victims have learned to doubt their own feelings. Often their feelings have been guided by an abusive family or the perpetrator of abuse along convoluted and contradictory paths. One father repeatedly told his son that anal sex was not only normal, but made him more of a man. He felt debased, but his father told him he was feeling like a man. Which was it? A woman was told as a child that she was angry and needed to be spanked, flirtatious and needed to be isolated, guilty and needed to be forgiven. In fact, she never consciously felt anything but loneliness and fear. Repeated exposure to inaccurate information about internal realities leads to a mistrust of one's own feelings and intuition.

In addition, if intuition were acknowledged and trusted, the obvious would be even more horrible. A mature woman told me about the countless meals she had with her abusive father as an adolescent and as an adult, where he would introduce her in public as the "little lady," treat her with intimate warmth, and flirt with her as a lover. At one meal she overheard a man at another table say, "Look at John's new mistress." His comment pierced her deeply, because she had "sort of" known for years how her father treated her in public. She had not faced the facts, because she was systematically unwilling to trust her intuition in any situation.

The other element of the relational distortion is a proclivity to reach contemptuous deductions. Data may be observed ("Dad is flirting with me"), but the assessment is inaccurate ("I must have led him on"). The accurate, though painful, conclusion ("Dad is a wicked man") is too hard to accept, therefore it is not considered as a viable option. Often this unwillingness to trust one's intuition leads to extensive excuse making and patterns of deceiving others: "Dad was not being inappropriate, he just shows his affection in a different way." One woman described a family reunion at which, in front of ten relatives, her father crawled over to her, laid on top of her, and would not get off when asked. She could feel his stiffening erection and heard the uncomfortable laughter of her relatives; nevertheless, she excused his behavior as childish rather than abusive.

Patterns of distorting facts and conclusions in one's own mind lead eventually to the necessity of deceiving others. At times the lies are intended to elicit support or care by sharing details about fantasized past pain or exploits that do not require the real past to be acknowledged. Or the deception of others may be a subtle form of taking power over them. The deceiver always knows something that the hearer is unaware of. As subtle as the distortion may be, chronic distorters are often addicted to the power of deceiving and the thrill of the chase. More often than not, people who distort and lie are unaware of the extent of their own fabrication and of the sophisticated denial they've developed to keep their deception in place. The consequence of hypervigilance, suspiciousness, and personal and other-centered distortion is the fragmentation of relationship.

THE CONSEQUENCES OF BETRAYAL

The consequences of betrayal are similar to the damage done by powerlessness. The major difference is that the focus is less on personal competence and control and more on the prospect of *hope* in relationship. The damage of powerlessness is the onslaught of doubt, despair, and deadness that leads to a loss of a sense of self. *The damage of betrayal is the deepening conviction that relationship can neither be enjoyed, trusted, nor expected to last.* The consequences are the loss of a hope for intimacy, strength, and justice.

Loss of the Hope for Intimacy

Intimacy is either elusive or dangerous for those who have been sexually abused. Intimacy, or the experience of pleasurable connection with another, is viewed as the pot of gold at the end of the rainbow: a nice dream, but unreal. True intimacy that provides the opportunity for deeply giving and richly receiving is not possible; what is possible is not *oneness*, but *nearness*. Keeping others near us can keep at bay the overwhelming hunger for something more. Being isolated and lonely can be far more painful than being lonely in the midst of the noise, hubbub, and the daily requirements of meals, laundry, and business projects. All that is required for nearness is the occasional sacrifice. A distant husband will not require depth of intimacy. He wants sex, a hassle-free environment, and a happy wife. An uninvolved wife will not require depth of intimacy either. She wants a successful provider, help with the children, and a comfortable life. Distant, parallel lives are the replacement of true intimacy. Nearness satisfies some of the ache and does not threaten the wounded heart.

The loss of the hope for intimacy is an understandable

defense. Intimacy was used to open the door to abuse. *The defensive loss of hope is the heart's refusal to be tempted again to love or enjoy.* The person who has been betrayed fears her own longings for connection with others, because her longings tempt her to move out of isolation and want something from others, which will surely destroy her. The best solution is to kill her longings and avoid all the "predators" in the world. Self-contempt serves her well: "If I can't destroy those who might hurt me, the only way I can be sure we don't connect is to hate myself. If I can rail on myself enough when my longings begin to arise, I can keep others at bay and myself off limits."

If the heart has been crushed by betrayal, at least future pain can be minimized if one abandons the prospect of oneness. Yet all modes of giving up hope, however reasonable and understandable, lead to greater alienation and isolation.

Loss of a Hope for Strength and Justice

We exercise strength on behalf of others out of either duty or intimacy. A policeman risks his life to protect us against a criminal, because it is his job. His calling involves the responsibility of risk-taking on our behalf, regardless of whether he likes us or even knows us. On the other hand, protection is also a natural byproduct of care. If one of my children were threatened by an assailant, I would not wait until the legally recognized "protector" arrived in his squad car. I would act—probably without reflection or conscious decision—to do what I could to rescue someone I love. Love is the core ingredient of protective strength.

No wonder an abused man or woman gives up hope for strong protection. If in a core relationship, strength was exercised to use and destroy rather than to protect, why would the victim assume that in a less intimate relationship, sacrificial protection would be provided—especially when authority figures, like teachers, pastors, Scout leaders, and other adults chose to ignore the signs or outward pleas for help? A number of abused persons either hinted or directly told an adult about the abuse. Rarely does an adult in a position of authority do anything with information about abuse other than ignore it. Even worse, many children were told never to repeat such a terrible lie again.

It only takes one encounter with a malevolent authority figure to learn that trust is foolish and invites even greater harm. This is particularly true in the church. Who will be believed: a nine-year-old girl or a fifty-year-old, well-respected deacon? If the allegation is true, the loss for the deacon is enormous. He may lose his job, his family, and his reputation. Even if the allegation is true, all the little girl loses is being believed (or so it seems). "Let's just call the situation a lose-lose enterprise, cut our losses, caution the deacon, and forget the whole mess." Those words were recently uttered by a respected pastor. I understand the sentiment, but it is unacceptable if one has seen the damage done to those who have lost the hope for protection and justice.

What will be the response of a child, and later an adult, to this loss? In most cases, the response will be *an entrenched commitment never to want intimacy or need protection.* The mode of independence may be socially responsive or outright rude, subtle and endearing or brutally obvious and alienating. The intent will be the same: autonomy and safety. The brick wall blocks the development of intimacy and ensures that an intruder will never be permitted through the front door. The difficult to comprehend, almost unimaginable, fact is that while the front door is shut tight to intimacy, often the back door is left wide open to an obvious abuser. The next chapter will help explain this odd reality.

CORE IMAGES RELATED TO BETRAYAL

When a victim of sexual abuse feels powerless, she will see herself as weak and incompetent. When she feels betrayed, her core image will reflect these questions: "Why did the abuser treat me so badly? Why was I not loved and protected?" The answer may be because the victim failed or was incompetent, but in most cases that does not explain the severity of the abuse. Generally, the answer will be found in some *terrible flaw* in the soul or body.

One woman wept: "If I had been priceless china, my mother would never have allowed me to be used and discarded. Therefore, I must be no better than an old, used paper plate." The metaphor accurately describes the image of betrayal. One does not abuse a valued possession. Many men and women have wept angry tears over the fact that their parents spent more time washing the car, tending the garden, or perfecting a golf swing than facing and dealing with their wounded heart.

The experience of being used and discarded provokes images of being undesirable and ugly. Physical features are the most obvious and easy explanation of undesirability. Few escape evaluative scrutiny and shameful remarks about their physical features, especially in regard to their sexual anatomy or attractiveness. It should come as no surprise, then, that someone who has been sexually abused will develop strong contempt and obsessive self-consciousness about his or her body. The result may be an excessive attention to physique, health, and diet or an extreme disregard for the body. In either case, the supposed ugly flaw that is at the foundation of the abuse is under control.

For example, one woman I worked with ate sparingly, exercised daily for several hours, and weighed herself constantly. Her only hope for intimacy was through keeping her body attractive and sensual. She *was* her breasts, thighs, and buttocks. There was nothing more to her than her physical attractiveness to a man. Another woman weighed sixty pounds over her desirable weight, and though she regularly dieted at two meals, she would almost always binge at dinner or during a late-night snack. She hated her rolls of fat, but she also recognized that she was not at risk in dating as long as she was physically unattractive.

I have found that most abuse victims will concentrate on one, if not several, body parts as the focus of their self-contempt. The part will become a symbol for the whole person and will take the brunt of the past abuse, even if the association has never been made between the self-contempt and past events. Much of the energy behind fad diets, compulsive exercising, plastic surgery, and body consciousness is a demand for perfection and a freedom from shame that is, at least for some, related to an undealt-with past of sexual abuse.

Contempt can be leveled just as effectively at character qualities—qualities that have to do with one's relational desirability.

"If only I'd been more friendly, warm, funny, or sophisticated, I would not have been abused." Doubt about one's relational desirability can spark as many "fad" self-help regimens as can disgust with one's body. The person who is endlessly "working on herself" through another seminar, tape, or book is often the one who has the most contempt toward her own character.

The damage perpetrated in an abuse victim's heart through the experiences of powerlessness and betrayal is great. But the most serious blow is the experience of ambivalence. No other aspect of sexual abuse is more devastating to the victim's capacity to embrace life and love in adulthood.

SEVEN

Ambivalence

The final category of internal damage—ambivalence—is probably the most difficult to describe. It also has the potential to produce more shame and contempt than either powerlessness or betrayal, although both factors are intricately intertwined with ambivalence.

Ambivalence can be defined as *feeling two contradictory emotions at the same moment*. A good friend of mine, a single woman, recently returned from the wedding of one of her good friends. She described in glowing terms the joy she felt for her friend, but her eyes were noticeably moist and sad. I asked her how she felt at the moment, and she said, "Weird." The description of her inner state as weird mislabeled her enormous maturity as something deficient and odd. Her good heart rejoiced for her friend who was chosen and honored in ceremony, gift, and relationship. Her friend's joy, however, brought into even sharper focus her own loneliness. She has not been chosen to be a bride. She lives alone, makes decisions by herself, and struggles with questions about her desirability. Her pain was deep, but it did not erase her joy for her friend. Her experience of ambivalence, or contradictory feelings of joy and sorrow, was not a mark of "weirdness," but was a sign of her deeply attractive maturity.

Unfortunately, emotions that are labeled as weird, crazy, stupid, or even worse, ungodly, are just as often inner experiences that reflect great spiritual maturity. This is particularly true with respect to the experience of ambivalence generated by sexual abuse.

In order to minimize confusion and misunderstanding, I must discuss what I do not intend to say as well as what I am attempting to say. Ambivalence revolves around the experience of relational, sensual, and sexual pleasure that, in most cases and to some degree, was experienced during the first three stages of sexual abuse.

Sensitive men and women will shudder at the thought of how that may be heard by either naive or malevolent ears. One abusive father I worked with told me that kids like sex. He coyly remarked, "I didn't do anything that she didn't ask for first." I asked him what she did to provoke the fondling of her genitals. He said, "She climbed in my lap and told me to hold her, and so I did." He assumed, wickedly and inaccurately, that her desire for cuddling was a cue for sexual foreplay.

The fact is that sexual arousal is possible in an unsuspecting victim because a small child has arousal receptors in his penis or her clitoris that do respond to touch. But that fact does not justify the sexualization of relationship. Nor can it be argued that a child "wants" and actively seeks sexual stimulation, unless he or she has been repetitively conditioned to associate sexual pleasure with relational intimacy. The archaic and perverse notion that a woman wants to be raped or that a child seeks out sexual contact is a patently stupid and God-dishonoring presumption. Nevertheless, the experience of pleasure in the midst of powerlessness and betrayal sets off a profoundly convoluted spiral of damage.

Sexual abuse creates destructive crosscurrents and undertows in the human soul. How is it possible to experience pleasure in the midst of agonizing physical pain or crushing relational betrayal? One man recalled being laid across the top of a fence post, having his pants pulled down, and then being anally raped by his father. The pain was excruciating. There was no sexual pleasure in the experience. But occasionally his father would end the ordeal by masturbating him. For those few moments, he struggled between giving in and having an orgasm and an equally strong desire not to ejaculate, thus depriving his father of the perverse joy of seeing his pleasure. The battle always ended in mingled pleasure and intense self-loathing. His only relief came when he was unable to have an erection. His impotence was a source of enormous shame, but the rage he was able to express toward his father by remaining flaccid was a sufficient gain to withstand his father's whithering disgust. Sadly, he remained impotent through most of his eighteen-year marriage.

A young woman who was "teased" about her maturing body by her brothers, uncle, and father recalled feeling a sense of power, dominance, and attractiveness when they commented on her shapely form. She had never been valued for any of her academic or social success, but when she was fourteen she began to be the center of male discussion in her family. It dawned on her that she had something that men, including her male relatives, wanted and valued. Her hungry soul soaked up the attention, though she felt embarrassed and cheap. When she blushed and responded with girlish discomfort, which was misconstrued as a flirtatious come-on, the comments became more aggressive and sexually descriptive. Her pleasure turned to disgust, but the initial pleasure of being wanted lingered in her soul, and eventually was conjoined with contempt. Her anger toward her relatives and the confusion over her own internal response to their suggestive comments was hidden under a growing prim-and-proper aloofness that remained in her relationships with men and women thirty years after that period of abuse.

In both cases, the unacknowledged and undealt-with ambivalence established patterns of relating to others that carried the past abuse into current relationships. It is imperative to understand the roots of ambivalence. What is its cause, cost, and consequence? What core image of herself will a victim develop as a result of her ambivalence about the abuse to her body and soul?

THE CAUSE OF AMBIVALENCE

The cause of the distorted feelings related to abuse includes factors that involve the past, present, and future. The past is clear.

An experience of relational pleasure (being invited to go fishing or being complimented about sexual attractiveness) or sensual pleasure (being hugged) or sexual pleasure (being touched on primary or secondary sexual parts) will arouse deep parts of the soul. Sexual pleasure in particular is both frightening and stimulating to a young child. The experience of sexual arousal feels like a taste of life to an empty heart. When the same pleasure is connected with the experience of being powerless, betrayed, and used, then untold damage will occur. The devastation is just as great when sexual arousal proper has not occurred, yet the victim enjoys other aspects of arousal in the relationship. A young man or woman may feel conjoint relational, sensual, and sexual arousal in the midst of an adult's flirtatious interaction. The inevitable feelings of both enjoyment and shame produce the anguish of ambivalence. *Central to understanding ambivalence is the fact that the very thing that was despised also brought some degree of pleasure.* The pleasure was, in most cases, the only taste of "life" available to the famished child. Nevertheless, later most adults cannot forgive their body or soul for betraying them.

The ambivalence about pleasure helps explain the chronic sense of irrational responsibility for the past abuse. Most victims feel as if they were somewhat responsible for what occurred, especially if arousal is viewed as "cooperation." As mentioned before, it is of little help to tell an abuse victim that it was not her fault. Though it is not wrong to offer this encouragement, it will not last, nor facilitate the process of deep personal change. The irrational roots of false responsibility are sunk deep in the soil of contempt, bolstered by the unacknowledged or hated ambivalence.

One woman remarked that her brother would never have abused her unless he had been aware that she would respond. The proof of her willingness was the fact that she enjoyed his touch. She occasionally left her door open, hoping that he would walk by her room and come in to "cuddle." The fact that something within her wanted and responded to his advances proved to her that it was her fault and her shame alone. In this case, so called cooperation was the natural by-product of a hunger for relationship and the normal enjoyment of sexual arousal. She also despised the abuse, but rather than seeing it as normal, she interpreted it as further proof that she was crazy.

Another woman who was cruelly raped by a distant relative hated the abuse, hated the abuser, and reported no awareness of relational, sensual, or sexual pleasure. Her life was filled with the remnants of loneliness, rage, and bitterness. She had a long history of conquest in relationship with both married and single men. She was not a practicing lesbian, but she had been involved with a number of female partners. She was cynical, hard, and sophisticated, but her heart was sick of hating her abuser. Her ambivalence was not related to sensual or sexual pleasure, but to an aspect of relationship that has not been stressed so far.

She recalled during the rape the confusion she felt as she heard her abuser moan. She had absented herself from her body by focusing her entire attention on a small crack in her bedroom wall, but at a few points she remembered feeling strangely curious and proud that she was causing him such apparent agony. She felt some sense of power over him, and in the midst of feeling so helpless and violated, the experience of his moaning was a small scrap of sustenance to hang on to. Her later conquests had the same pleasure in power. She could seduce and entrap and then abandon. She had power, but she also experienced profound loneliness. Her experience of pleasure over something that was clearly abusive confused her and deepened her sense of being evil and unforgivable. Ambivalence over pleasure, power, or the mix of emotions related to abuse swirl into the present with destructive force.

There are factors in the present that also create a vortex of self-hatred. One factor is the frightening intrusion of unexpected memories, dreams, and fantasies. Many abused men and women feel as if a portion of their mind is not under their control. Dream elements return that deposit past horrors before their eyes without rhyme or reason. Pleasant daydreams are suddenly interrupted by the hideous and contorted face of the abuser. A hidden recess of their mind's closet gets dumped into open view at the most unexpected and undesired moment. The fact that memories of events lodged so deeply in the past can return at all provokes a sense of being out of control.

Several clients have admitted that part of the horror of the memory intrusion is the experience of pleasure. One woman regularly awakened at night masturbating as she recalled the past abuse. Another man recalled at moments of tension and stress at work the day that his older sister gently fondled him in the bathtub. The shameful memory, in both cases, became exponentially more shameful when it was reused to comfort or stimulate himself.

The conscious use of past abuse to stimulate is another source of deep ambivalence. Unfortunately, the topic of fantasy is so unacknowledged in some Christian groups that its mere mention may be viewed as unnecessary and wrong. The fact is that sexual practice was never to be divorced from sexual longing and, by implication, sexual fantasy. It is nearly impossible to develop a hunger for a juicy steak that does not evoke images of past dining, current sensual arousal of the taste buds, and the motivation to pursue the pleasure in the future.

Arousal is always mediated by images; the pictures drawn from our ancient and current past are the only images available to comprehend our present and plan for our future. Is it any wonder that many abuse victims use their past victimization as the basis of "picturing" their current relationships and, in particular, their sexual arousal? This is known as the "sexualization of intimate relationships." *Intimacy once fused with abuse surfaces, to some degree or another, whenever intimacy is experienced in other relationships.* Many abuse victims misinterpret their longing for intimacy as lustful passion when they begin to care for someone of the same or different gender. Depending on the mode of relating to others and the style of contempt, the sexualization of intimacy may provoke the dissolution of the relationship or may be handled similarly to the mode used to deal with their past abuse.

For example, one woman could achieve an orgasm only when she visualized herself being raped by a man who stalked her and eventually overpowered her in private. At times that fantasy did not provoke sufficient arousal to lead to orgasm, so she then imagined the scene with the rape occuring in public before countless spectators. The greater shame and the crowd's contempt enabled her to relax sufficently to achieve orgasm. Like any pattern of self-protection, the contemptuous fantasy worked only for a time before it needed to be intensified and strengthened. Therefore, her fantasies became even more humiliating and destructive, until she was unable to engage in any sexual activity. The sudden intrusion of or the conscious use of past memories often radically intensifies the victim's shame and contempt.

Another factor involved in the cause of ambivalence is that the future seems doomed to repeat the past. Behavior is often compulsive and repetitive. Historians claim that if we do not know the past, we are doomed to repeat it. Psychoanalysts claim that man is apt to identify with the aggressor and repeat or play out the past abuse in current relationships. The writer of Proverbs states even more succinctly, "As a dog returns to its vomit, so a fool repeats his folly" (Proverbs 26:11).

As noted earlier in our discussion of powerlessness, revictimization is a common denominator for incest victims. But revictimization, measured in terms of sexual assault, is not the entire story. Much revictimization is not so easily or dramatically measured as tragic rape or other serious sexual assault. Rather, it involves the repetition of other more mundane, but equally destructive, patterns of relating to others.

For example, the prim-and-proper woman mentioned earlier consistently had to rebuff the sexual interests of married men. In a slightly pouty manner (with equal parts of naive confusion and confident daring) she asked me, "Why do you think men find me so appealing?" The prim-and-proper, demurely dressed fundamentalist was just a hairsbreadth away from eliciting an affair. I felt trapped. What was she asking? She certainly could not be accused of being seductive, but on the other hand, her words and her tone were provocatively sensual and naive. The precise combination of elements both invited seduction and allowed for indignation when a man attempted to do so.

Is it a surprise that an element of her confusion and hopelessness was the sense that her future will be like her past? The push and pull of her style of relating to men existed in the twilight of her consciousness. She was not wholly unaware of her impact on men, but she had never connected the past abuse to her current way of relating. She expressed her ambivalence by simultaneously loathing herself for her tight-collared seductiveness and feeling rageful, self-vindication in being a temptress.

All elements of the past, present, and future combine to create a swirling ambivalence that does not find resolution through denial or repeated efforts to control one's thought life. The cost of the convoluted vortex does more damage to the human soul.

THE COST OF AMBIVALENCE

The internal cost of ambivalence is the infusion of massive shame and contempt. The topic of sexual abuse is shameful. The sense of being isolated and different from normal, healthy adults is magnified beyond comprehension once the core ambivalence is acknowledged. One woman said with an air of sad mockery, "My husband will barely allow me to go swimming in mixed company. What do you think he'll do if he finds out that I had an orgasm with my father and that I fantasize about every man that shows me any kindness?" Her ambivalence during the past abuse and the sexualization of intimacy in the present shamed her. She was equally terrified of her dangerous passion and of being found out. Her plaintive question still haunts me: "Who in the church understands that I feel torn into pieces? Who can I tell or pray with who is not aghast, overwhelmed, or trite?" Shame intensifies the horror of the past.

Shame is compounded by personal confusion. How could I feel arousal and hatred at the same moment? Why do vile images return at the most disconcerting moments? Why do I feel sexually aroused when someone is kind to me? Shame is further complicated when others react to the victim's ambivalence with shock, disgust, or condemnation.

The false cure for the personal confusion and relational rejection is either self- or other-centered contempt. It protects the soul from the possibility that lust will surface and destroy. Or it propels the person into promiscuous relationships that validate what she fears may have been true: the abuse really was her fault. The proof that it was her fault is the pleasure she experienced or is experiencing in current illicit activities.

The hellish cycle of shame and contempt deepens the wound, and the secrecy keeps the wound from being touched by the normal healing effects of relational affirmation and support. *Intimacy begets longing, and longing is interpreted as sexual. Passion destroys; therefore, it must either be avoided or conquered.* On that basis, rich relationship is not possible, and when it does occur, the result is even deeper shame and contempt.

THE CONSEQUENCES OF AMBIVALENCE

The consequences of increased shame and contempt are a fear of pleasure, a profound hatred of longing, greater likelihood of revictimization, and chronic patterns of compulsiveness. The consequences stressed under ambivalence, of course, are not entirely related only to this one factor. There are unique contributions, however, that need to be underscored. The central consequence of powerlessness is a hatred for being weak. Betrayal increases feelings of undesirability and deepens a hatred of intimacy. Ambivalence robs a person of the joy of being alive as a man or as a woman. For an abuse victim, femaleness or maleness is so intertwined with shameful sexuality and the experience of perversity that it seems impossible to untangle. Consequently, femininity or masculinity is on some level despised and ignored. Most women who have been abused do not richly enjoy being women. Most men who have been abused do not enjoy their masculinity.

Ambivalence makes pleasure—any experience of enjoyment—highly suspect and dangerous. It is like a chain-link fence connected link by link so that each section is inseparably joined to the others. To pull one link forward is to pull the entire fence. Pleasure, of all types, is inextricably linked together.

When pleasure at hitting a good forehand in tennis opens the door to the confident exercise of one's physical prowess, that might be too frightening. Physical pleasure is linked to internal, personal pleasure, and both are linked to interpersonal, social pleasure. God has made us to be unified in body and soul in our relationship with others, so pleasure in one arena is bound to elicit pleasure in others. Therefore, intense pleasure in any area of life may provoke too many memories or stir too much sorrow.

I am not suggesting that all abuse victims are morose and joyless. Many past victims are wonderful storytellers, great fun at parties, and enjoy a good meal and caring friends. For many abuse victims, however, there is a limit, a stiff, angry boundary that will not permit cross traffic. Once the boundary has been reached, the guard goes up, and pleasure must be subdued, not enjoyed. *Pleasure, like its parent (legitimate longing of the heart), must be quietly watched and controlled lest something get out of hand.*

A second consequence of ambivalence is the hatred directed toward longing and passion—in particular, the longing of the soul that arouses the experience of maleness or femaleness. To some degree most abuse victims are cynical, suspicious, and terrified of deep-souled passion. The hunger of the human heart for touch, nurturance, and intimacy is intertwined with a revulsion for sex, either conscious or submerged, and a hatred of their own arousal. The overdetermined reaction to the wound is to become immersed in sexual passion to blunt the original ambivalence or to remove any sexual passion by deadening the soul and/or withdrawing from the body. Total immersion or complete deadness function similarly to eradicate the struggle with ambivalence.

Sexual passion, like any form of pleasure, is intimately connected to the deeper hunger for love and respect. Therefore, it is not uncommon for even nonsexual longings to arouse what is felt to be the turmoil of the past abuse. A friend of mine, an abuse victim, is loathe to receive or enjoy a compliment. When I tell her that she did a good job on a project she is working on, she blushes, subtlely demeans her effort, and is distant for hours. Her initial response usually indicates some appreciation for noticing, but she would have preferred distance. Warmth and appreciation touches a part of her soul that craves the affection she was denied in her dysfunctional family. Whenever she hopes someone will notice her new dress or appreciate her hard work, she feels alternately lustful and dangerous, and then cheap and frightened. She has found it less shameful and painful to want nothing at all from anyone. It's almost as if every time one wanted to spend a dollar in a store, a full security check was required to make the purchase. It would be easier never to go shopping. My friend views her longings as either a nuisance, a weakness, or an envoy of guilt.

It should be clear that she cannot afford to enjoy herself as a woman. Kindness is dangerous, because it invites her to respond with warmth and joy. The invitation may bring more to the surface than she or the giver of the compliment can bear. Anything that increases a sense of feminine responsiveness, therefore, is avoided as the germ that might cause a plague.

Imagine what will happen when someone does manage to arouse the longing in a sexual-abuse victim? Needless to say, the picture is not always pretty. The sexually abused woman seems to often get involved with men who are equally uncomfortable with sexual desire, or sexual atheletes who are looking for new fields of conquest. The sexual addict finds a reluctant, but willing, partner in relationship with some abuse victims, because their definitions of intimacy and love are similarly sexualized. The abuse victim can either choose to continue redefining herself according to that terrible, but comfortable, framework, or reject her partner and flee from all intimacy on the same grounds. In either acceptance or rejection, the ambivalence has never been exposed or dealt with.

Charlie and Jan are typical church-going, committed Christians who truly love the Lord and have been used by God in the lives of others. Their problem is simple: Every now and then their rage and hatred for each other rips through the house like a Louisiana twister. The cleanup is amicable, both feel guilty, and peace is restored for several months before another storm cuts its way through their hearts. The struggle is always the same: sex. He wants to make love at least once, if not twice, a day. She gives in and only occasionally initiates sex on her own. Other than that, they experience few obvious conflicts.

Jan is an abuse victim, and Charlie is a sexaholic. Their relationship worked well to the degree that Charlie experienced the intimacy, arousal, and power of sexual conquest. Jan functioned well by absenting herself from her body during sex. But when

Jan began to face the consequences of the past abuse in her life, she started to see her deadness as self-protective sin and Charlie's demands as abuse. Their relationship, seen as a model by other Christians, worked only to the degree that Jan ignored her deadness and Charlie, his demandingness. It was a functional, pleasant, but destructive mess.

The abused woman often chooses a partner who will not require deep-souled involvement. Even more, the spouse or boyfriend will often be the kind of person who deepens the victim's self- and other-centered contempt, thus diminishing her conscious struggle with ambivalence.

Another major consequence of ambivalence is a proclivity to compulsive behavior. The abused man or woman often handles the confusion of the soul by drowning his or her wounds in addictive activities. *Addictive behavior is the use of any object or repetitive mode of functioning to handle stress, struggle, or sorrow that both impairs personal functioning and relationships and cannot be stopped without extensive outside intervention.* Addictive behavior might include alcoholism, substance abuse, workaholism, sexaholism, eating disorders, perfectionism, or religious fanaticism. The common element of each is the bondage that is exercised over the individual by the object of obsession and the deleterious influence it has on his or her ability to love others.

The abused person is often captured by the awesome demands of something external, such as work, a dependent friend, food, masturbation, or alcohol. The compulsion refocuses energy away from the inner struggle, explains away loneliness, and deepens the legitimacy of the unrecognized contempt.

One woman I worked with was a chronic masturbator. She was enslaved and hated herself, but all efforts to stop were only occasionally successful. At times she doubted her salvation, and at other times cared little about her spiritual status. She struggled with deep shame about the past abuse with her older brother. Her hatred of her femaleness was intensified by a number of promiscuous relationships through her teens and early twenties. When she became a Christian, she ended all her sexual contacts. But soon after her conversion, she began to struggle with overwhelming dreams in which she was exposed as a whore, a hypocrite, and a renegade who would not be granted access to heaven. After every dream, she would awaken and masturbate. Soon her masturbatory practice became a regular nightime and then daytime activity. She recalled feeling very cheap, but somehow relieved in a way that could not be explained as merely the satisfaction of sexual desire. *She felt "confirmed."* Her behavior *proved* that she was a cheap, undisciplined, oversexed whore who had to hide her passion, her longing, and certainly her past behind a veil of secrecy and shame. Under the constraint of her addiction she found relief, a reorientation of her fears, and proof that her soul was stained and undesirable. All addictions are illegitimate worship of an object and gain, for a time, a false sense of control to eradicate the ambivalence and numb the wound.

CORE IMAGES RELATED TO AMBIVALENCE

The contemptuous picture of oneself begins with doubts about intelligence and competency (powerlessness), moves to questions about desirability (betrayal), and finally ends with the conclusion that one is dirty, vile, and cheap. The internal picture explains why arousal and cooperation ocurred, memories return, and patterns are repeated in the present. *The image of being vile explains not only why the abuser betrayed the victim in the first place, but also gives reason for the absence of deep relationship today.* The picture of being cheap, loose, or more graphically, a whore, explains why arousal occurred and lessens the sense of damage when revictimization occurs. The abused woman can use the core image of the whore as a scarlet letter to hide behind or as a shield to fend off any man who might seek a legitimate relationship.

Joan was a diminutive, sweet woman who felt like a whore whenever she developed a crush on any unsuspecting male. Her dress and demeanor portrayed innocence and naivete, but her mind was a cascade of sexual thoughts and images. Her prim demeanor belied a terrible passion. The self-image of a whore was a death sentence that was temporarily postponed as long as she was faithful and chaste, but only as long as she was under strict control. No wonder few had any idea of her struggle with such a vile self-image.

Lisa was a bold, carefree Bohemian who wore clothes that were just beyond the border of propriety. Her dress was not provocative nor obviously seductive, but her mood was loose, free, and sensual. She liked to see herself as a woman who was too much for any one man. She was confident and take-charge in relationships, but remained stiff in the face of relational intensity. Her self-image was vile and self-destructive: she was a toy, a plaything for fun. The lightness and confidence of her lifestyle belied the internal image of herself as a toy for abuse. The image of the toy served as a proud badge of her freewheeling lifestyle, but it equally represented the sad loneliness of her shattered heart.

The image of a whore—shamefully hidden or proudly exhibited—is seldom conscious or intentionally chosen. Rather, it is lived so deeply that one may be surprised by its presence and intensity. *Core images are contemptuous explanations of internal damage and maps for living out self-protected patterns of relating to others.* For that reason, the images caused by the internal damage of sexual abuse are most frequently seen in the way the person lives out her interpersonal relationships.

The next section of the book will be an evaluation of the external damage due to abuse. The focus will be on the secondary symptoms most commonly related to abuse and the typical styles of relating that are associated with the core images of internal damage.

EIGHT

Secondary Symptoms

Sexual abuse doesn't devastate only a victim's internal world. Whatever damage is done internally will eventually affect the external, observable life. Many abuse victims might argue that past abuse has not damaged their lives. In many cases, the claim is partly true. If the category used to evaluate "no effect" is sufficiently broad, many abuse victims do not show clear, measurable consequences.

For example, a woman I know well, who was abused by several people, argued strenuously that her conversion and growth in Christ removed all the damage of the past abuse. Her argument was based on 2 Corinthians 5:17: "If anyone is in Christ, he is a new creation; the old has gone, the new has come!" Her life is symptom free; she is not depressed, sexually inactive or unfulfilled, undisciplined, or struggling with a poor self-image. She feels in control of her world. If she were to fill out a questionnaire on the effects of abuse, she would be an example of someone who survived the trauma of abuse without deleterious consequences.

However, if the categories of measurement were allowed to be more refined and based on an outsider's observation, then her evaluation would be somewhat inaccurate. Her marriage is marred by her overbearing and patronizing tone. She is opinionated and, at times, insensitive. Her manner is kind, though formal and uninviting. She sees herself as a submissive, spiritual woman, whose perspective is penetrating and accurate, rather than sharp and critical. It is my opinion that she has not escaped the consequences of her past abuse. I find that many who claim no ill effect from past damage are often the ones who are most strident, adamant, and arrogant. An argument from observation, however, does not address the serious theological question raised by her assertion of "no effect."

THE LONG ROAD TO GLORY

The issue raised is a crucial theoretical concern: What is the nature, extent, and basis of personal and physical healing through the work of the Holy Spirit in our day? The issue is too large to address in this chapter, but a few theological observations will establish the parameters of my perspective.

First, the work of the Holy Spirit does not lead to sinless perfectionism in this life. Perfectionism of body and soul awaits the work of glorification. The passage mentioned, 2 Corinthians 5:17, cannot be used to argue that one's past, the consequences of one's own or others' sin, are erased and no longer play a part in the life of the present. It is not a statement about possessing a new personality or new "creational substance" in Christ, but rather an acknowledgment that we have been victoriously included in a new creation or kingdom that is different from the "world"; therefore, we are granted the opportunity to serve as messengers of the victorious King who offers reconciliation through the gospel. This Scripture passage is a statement about our place in a new kingdom order and the privilege of ambassadorship. Therefore, to assume radical change on the basis of conversion is to neglect the essential relationship between justification and sanctification.

Second, the Holy Spirit's "normal" process of change involves both the dramatic and the mundane. The Spirit knocked Paul to the ground, blinded him, and sent him to be ministered to by frightened Christians who would have preferred to have avoided him (Acts 9:1-19). Then he was sent to "seminary" for several years, assumably to read, ponder, and form his understanding of the gospel (Galatians

1:15-22). The spectacular work of his first encounter was not invalidated by the need for more homework and change. God's work of sanctification is slow, progressive, tailor-fit, and unfinished at every point during our earthly life. Spectacular change in one area does not negate the need for increased change in the same area or in other related areas.

Third, the normal work of the Holy Spirit produces crippled warriors who are used because of their brokenness, weakness, and powerlessness (1 Corinthians 1:26-29), and not because their struggle-free existence draws good press and large crowds. The assumption of most "healing" approaches is that past damage can be, and should be, removed in order to glorify the goodness and power of God. Unfortunately, that assumption flies in the face of much biblical teaching.

God's path is paradoxical. We are drawn to Christ because we want life, and life more abundant. He gives us life that leads to abundance via brokenness, poverty, persecution, and death. The life He invites us to lead causes us to lose ourselves so that we can find ourselves, to lose our life so that we can have life. The servants He often uses are young, ill-equipped, and unwilling. The path He takes His servants on is unexpected, perilous, and often unchosen. The Scriptures promise ultimate health and wealth, but the path to such enjoyment is not what most of us envision or naturally choose. Paul was left with his "thorn in the flesh," his path included untold suffering, poverty, and trial, and his earthly life ended with his execution as a sacrifice poured out for our sake. The specifics of Paul's life may not be ours, but the path of weakness and foolishness is the same, if we want to live out the call of Christ.

For those reasons, I would argue that change is possible and substantial, but not perfected until heaven. "Substantial healing," a phrase used by Francis Schaeffer, underscores the possibility of deep and meaningful alteration, without blinding our eyes to the fact that permanent and final change awaits the transformation of the world through Christ's return. The wounds of living in a fallen world with fallen people (including ourselves) make being damaged (internally and externally) a certainty.

EVIDENCE OF INTERNAL DAMAGE

The external outworking of the damage done by sexual abuse is evident in two broad forms: (1) secondary symptoms (depression, sexual dysfunction, etc.) and (2) the "typical" way the abused person relates to others. The style of relating to others is often the primary arena where the damage of abuse is lived out in a daily, discernable form.

That is not to say that the nature, extent, and severity of the damage will be the same for everyone who has been abused. In many cases, the abuse victim will not reveal secondary symptoms for lengthy periods of time, though the possibility for symptom generation or symptom return exists during periods of loss, stress, or repetition of past abusive dynamics. Symptom-free abuse victims, however, rarely escape the effect of abuse in their style of relating. The effects of their relational style are often destructive and result in another series of problems that provoke secondary symptoms.

In either case, it is not unusual for the abuse victim to overlook the connection between her secondary symptoms and relational style and her history of sexual abuse. I went through my case files for one year to evaluate the relationship between the reason people came to see me for counseling and the issue of sexual abuse. What I found staggered me. I worked with thirty women and fifteen men during that year. Twenty-six out of thirty women and eight out of fifteen men had been sexually abused. Not one man or woman came to see me because of the issue of sexual abuse, nor did anyone acknowledge or even wonder if their past abuse had any effect on their current problems. In a number of cases, abuse was recalled, but viewed as an unpleasant memory of childhood—similar to breaking a bone—that had no relevance to the current struggle.

In many cases, the inability to see the connection is not a lack of information, but an absence of memory. At the beginning of my work, only twelve out of twenty-six women and five out of eight men recalled the past abuse. The remainder became aware of the memories of abuse during the process of counseling. My figures are different now that I am known as someone who works with abuse victims, but a counselor, pastor, or close friend can usually assume that abuse may be a factor behind the internal and external struggles in a person's life, even if it is not initially reported, nor remembered.

In order to see the potential signs of abuse in the symptoms presented, it is imperative to know what to look for. Significant signs include the symptoms of depression, sexual dysfunction or addiction, compulsive disorders, physical complaints, low self-esteem, and particular styles of relating.

Each symptom must be understood as "potentially" related to sexual abuse, because it is quite possible to struggle with one or various combinations of symptoms without having experienced sexual abuse. A balanced perspective on these symptoms allows for an open, non-dogmatic tension between seeing abuse behind every personal and relational problem and being naive about the high level of incidence and the damaging consequences of past abuse.

My attitude is not to assume more than I am allowed, given the data, while being aware that abuse is most often ignored or forgotten. Therefore, when symptomatic patterns of abuse are consistently presented through symptom complaints and relational style, I follow my tentative hunch that past abuse likely occurred. Then I work toward dealing with those issues at the speed most appropriate to the person's own pace and desire.

DEPRESSION

Our discussion of the internal damage of sexual abuse has set the stage for an understanding of depression. Depression is often described as "learned helplessness." The symptoms of depression include a despondent view of oneself, the world, and the future. The depressed person has little hope for understanding, help, or change. It is not uncommon for a depressed person to feel that the weight of the world is on his shoulders, and no one is either able or willing to assist him in his struggle.

Those who are unfamiliar with depression are often surprised by the depressed person's swing between feeling helpless, alone, and unworthy to feeling cheated, abandoned, and angry. The swing corresponds to the difference between self-centered and other-centered contempt. In fact, depression can be understood as absorbed, self-annihilating hatred toward the soul for feeling alive and then being disappointed.

The person who struggles with chronic hopelessness often lived in an abusive environment that made the expression of longing, disappointment, and anger dangerous, if not impossible. The swing between hope ("Maybe Dad will be happy with my report card") and disappointment ("He didn't even notice my three As") opens the door to frustration, anger, and rage. Those emotions, most often associated with a sense of injustice, are dangerous, because the expression of anger might elicit even more profound abandonment or abuse. What is denied in depression is the accuracy of one's intuition that injustice has occurred, the legitimacy of one's longing for justice, and the knowledge of what would right the wrong. The rage is turned inward, but not without subtly attacking those who have perpetrated the damage. Depression is "selfless selfishness," or perhaps better said, "selfless revenge." The self is annihilated (a sense of injustice and longing for what is right is forsaken), while those around are made impotent to stop the downward cycle of despair and hopelessness (revenge).

Sexual abuse is often the foundation of the shame associated with longing and the contempt related to failure. It is quite common for depression — which is a deeply morbid and overpowering affect — to mask recalled memories and inhibit the return of new recall. Depression is often a cycle that many abuse victims pass through before major memories return. One woman spoke of the depression as "payment" for remembering the past. In most cases, the depression is a mask covering the real struggles of the soul; therefore, to orient the entire treatment to overcoming depression misses the dynamic function of the symptom.

SEXUAL DYSFUNCTION AND ADDICTION

Sexual struggle is almost an "expected" symptom of sexual abuse. Not every abuse victim will struggle with severe sexual problems; no doubt some will have successfully reclaimed the privilege of pleasure and reintegrated their body and soul into one whole being. On the other hand, many will experience little struggle because their soul is radically absent during physical acts of sexual intimacy. The absent soul does not experience direct, overwhelming affect; therefore, the body is left like a zombie to perform, at times with high arousal, sexual feats. It is only when a sense of self returns that sexual problems begin to be recognized. Couples who have had satisfying sexual relations for years often begin to develop "new" problems when one partner begins to explore his or her past sexual abuse. The "new" struggle is the result of built-up residue that comes to the surface in a safe and hopeful environment (often a counselor's office). Nevertheless, the examination of the old wound is often viewed as the process that ruined a so-called "good" sexual relationship.

The key phrase associated with many sexual problems is *lack of interest* or *disgust*. A man or woman may have little or no desire for sexual pleasure, even though there is an ability to experience arousal during sexual contact that leads to orgasm. I've heard both men and women remark: "My spouse is a good lover, but I get bored. Sex is not what it's cracked up to be." Lack of interest is often the soul's quiet rebellion to avoid the hidden memories and vague feelings that are stirred during sexual contact and arousal.

Disgust, on the other hand, is a more pronounced and active defense. Disgust is usually directed toward the sexual act or a sexual partner (person or gender). Disgust might be toward one's own body for feeling aroused, toward one's partner for being too masculine or feminine, or not masculine or feminine enough, or toward men or women in general. The last category implies a homosexual orientation, which is not uncommon for those who have been abused. Not every man or woman who is attracted to or involved sexually with the same sex, however, has had an abusive past.

Sexual perversion, normally labeled the paraphilias (exhibitionism, voyeurism, pedophilia, homosexuality, transvestism, and fetishism), is often highly correlated to abuse. Whenever a man struggles with a sexual perversion, I usually suspect a history of sexual abuse. This is even more true with a woman, because sexual perversions are a male symptom at a rate of over ten to one. Therefore, a woman who struggles with a perversion may well have a history of some sexual trauma in her past.

Sexual addiction is another probable sign of past abuse. Sexual addiction has some elements in common with other types of compulsive behavior. All compulsions, no matter how bizzare or destructive, provide a context to find relief and work out revenge. Relief is the easier of the two to comprehend. A chronic masturbator or a driven sexaholic obviously experiences great satisfaction during the sexual act. The pleasure of an orgasm, however, does not explain why a voyeur or exhibitionist risks family, reputation, and career for an orgasm that could be found in countless safer contexts. Nor does it explain the sexaholic's penchant to see all of life from a sexual standpoint. Something else is going on besides the desire for mere relief. Sexual addictions, promiscuity, and perversion can also be ways of expressing revenge.

Revenge is the working out of deep-soul hatred toward others (other-centered contempt) or toward oneself (self-contempt). Revenge exacts payment against both the perpetrator of the past harm and the victim for her supposed cooperation and ambivalent pleasure. At times, the symptom pattern is more obviously connected to self-contempt (masochism, being the object of battering or anal sex) and at other times toward other-centered contempt (sadism, predatory sexual promiscuity, seductive Don Juanism). More often, however, both sides of revenge (contempt) are played out in the same behavior.

The chronic masturbator often struggles to remain pure until some event either increases frustration or arousal. For example, one woman I worked with felt compelled to masturbate whenever she felt rebuffed by a man she wanted to get to know. A combination of arousal and frustration led to an overwhelming desire. She would masturbate and during the process fantasize about winning her reluctant suitor. The "winning over" phase was a power fantasy in which he was unable to resist her beauty, sophistication, and charm. In her fantasy she owned him and controlled his every desire. After the pleasure of masturbation subsided, she scorned herself for the act, her adolescent fantasies, and her lack of self-control. Other-centered revenge (power over his passion) quickly melted into self-hatred. Usually self-hatred – or as some might call it, guilt – motivates the person to rectify the wrong through some form of penance, the process of paying for one's own sin through sacrifice and guilt offering. Guilt often propels the person toward change and moral behavior until the rocks of disappointed longing snag the soul on the same desperate reef, and the same process is played out again. The compulsive cycle looks something like this: longing, disappointment, power (other-centered revenge), shame (self-contempt), self-hatred, penance.

Sexual dysfunction or compulsiveness is often a sign of undealt-with rage. The rage that is worked out through self- and other-centered contempt must be exposed and connected to the past abuse if it is to lose its compulsive edge. The dilemma is that shame masks not only the symptom but also the role of revenge. It will require a great deal of time to help a person face the confusing interrelationship of relief and revenge, and to separate the elements of both factors that are legitimate and God-honoring from those that are destructive, illegitimate, and God-dishonoring.

For example, a woman who has little interest in sex needs to admit that she is depriving her husband of legitimate intimacy and pleasure. But that fact will not increase her desire nor improve the sexual relationship, even if she forces herself to have sex. She must be willing to face that her lack of interest is a form of both relief (avoidance of unpleasant internal realities) and revenge (withholding intimacy and pleasure). This acknowledgment will open the door to the question: Why do I find relief through avoidance, and revenge through withholding? Now she can view her problem as an internal (intrapsychic) and moral (interpersonal) issue rather than as a mystery or an irreversible fact.

Desire can never be commanded, but desire should always be assumed. It is not that a homosexual lacks heterosexual desire. The fact is that the legitimate, God-built passion is not absent, but blocked. The task is not to inculcate or teach passion, but to remove the obstacles that hinder its legitimate expression. Therefore, once relief and revenge, as internal and moral categories, are faced and their function understood, the block can begin to be dissolved.

COMPULSIVE DISORDERS

The same dynamic of relief and revenge fuels other familiar compulsions as well: alcohol and substance abuse, eating disorders (anorexia, bulimia, bulimarexia), perfectionism, and workaholism. For the sake of brevity, I'll choose to look at only one example. I've observed that bulimia is the "symptom of choice" of many abused women. Again, not all abused women will struggle with bulimia, but I believe that many bulimic women have a history of sexual abuse.

Bulimia fits the relief and revenge model of compulsive behavior. The relief is found both in maintaining a certain body weight consistent with the woman's vision of beauty and in the experience of instant gratification through binging. The experience of feeling physically satiated through binging is the physical counterpart to feeling soulishly filled through intimacy. When the soul is aroused and then disappointed, the stomach can be filled to compensate for the loss. As one woman said, "Why should I take the time to have an affair or masturbate, with all the work and guilt required, when all I need to do is eat a pint of ice cream and in a few minutes have the same relief?"

A strange combination of relief and revenge is found in the process of purging. Even the term purge implies removing something that is noxious and undesirable. Many bulimics have told me that hidden away in their fantasies is the hope that something vile and shameful will be discarded (other than the food) when they vomit. More often than not, the "it" is unknown. The relief, however, is present the moment "it" has been removed.

The relief and revenge toward others is found in the singular focus of the bulimic: All of life, including relationships, is supplanted by food. Imagine the powerlessness of being married to a woman whose every thought is of food. Though many anorexics and bulimics may be gourmet cooks, man does not live on bread alone. The bulimic woman's propensity to make others second to a dish of pasta is a form of other-centered revenge.

The relief/revenge toward self is not subtle at all. Vomiting is a self-destructive act that punishes the soul for some unknown offense. Most bulimics hate themselves for being powerless to stop the compulsion. The hatred is intricately wed to the relief, and that in turn leads to a convulsion of shame: "How could I hate and enjoy the same vile act?" Ambivalence over bulimia often mirrors, and yet obscures, the confusion of cooperation and arousal that occurred during the past abuse. Again, the compulsive drive of bulimia will not be diffused unless the symptom is understood in light of the past abuse.

PHYSICAL COMPLAINTS

It has long been known that the division between the body and the psyche is an artifical distinction. There are differences between the two, but there is a clear, though imperceptible, bridge between our inner health and our physical well-being. The relationship between body and soul is too complex to throughly explore here, but the fact is that physical symptoms are often a sign of deep inner struggle.

It is as if the body is warring against the soul by blocking memories or dreams that would unleash a torrent of anguish. The physical armor that protects against those memories produces a rigid, exhausted frame. The body was never meant to be at war with the psyche, and when it is, physical symptoms occur. So-called stress-related disorders include ulcers, intestinal problems, lower backaches, stiff neck, tight jaw, and chronic headaches. Again, physical symptoms are not always related to a history of sexual abuse. I had severe lower back problems for years that were finally diagnosed as a congenital defect. I would have hated being told my problem was in my head, a "psychological" defect that could be resolved if I were "normal." But physical complaints, regardless of their cause, are at least intensified by internal, moral issues. Chronic physical complaints, unabated by competent and multistaffed medical care, should be considered and treated from the perspective of probable past abusive trauma.

SELF-ESTEEM

Struggle with a poor self-image or its counterpart, narcissistic grandiosity, is another common feature of an abusive past. The picture of oneself as a weak, stupid, naive, worthless, stained, cheap whore does not produce a God-honoring, accurate self-appraisal (Romans 12:3). The symptoms of a poor self-image are most often unseen and can only be inferred by observing a person as she relates to others. A common element, however, will be the presence of strong self-contempt. The person who undercuts, devalues, and sabatoges her life and deeds is often a person who harbors a past that pollutes every pleasure and discolors every gift given to her. The person who feels unworthy and guilty for every kindness and who has the unnerving quality of being able to snap defeat from the jaws of victory, more than likely struggles with an undealt-with abusive past.

STYLE OF RELATING

All the symptoms described have some common dynamic and behavioral components. However, the differences between people who display similar symptoms can be profound to the point that drawing conclusions based on an analysis of all bulimics, for instance, distorts the idiosyncratic nature of the symptom. Yet we can draw some helpful conclusions if we see each symptom from a larger perspective, *one's style of relating*. A style of relating is *the characteristic manner of both offering and protecting oneself in social interactions*.

One's style of relating may well be called one's *personality*, if that term denotes a flexible array of behaviors that are used habitually in dealing with both internal pain and external circumstances and relationships. (This definition of personality is in opposition to some modes of personality "typing" that assume a person's style and behavior are static and genetically determined.) Consequently, we can know our style of relating or personality only to the degree that we reflect on our manner of dealing with others. To do this productively we must be willing to move beyond the simplistic assumption that we are the way we are because that's the way we are. I am quite aware that environmental and biological factors play an important role in personality formation. I am concerned, however, with the simplistic and fatalistic notion that people are who they are and others must simply understand and accept that they are rigidly choleric or whatever type system is used to justify behavior. My understanding of personality assumes that style of relating can be substantially altered through repentance—a concept I will explain more fully in chapter 11.

Why is style of relating important? Simply put, it is the primary x-ray that tells us the condition of our heart. What we believe is expressed best in the way we live. The best way to know our attitude toward God is to look at how we deal with Him and others (Mark 12:28-34). Do we love selflessly, passionately, boldly? Or are we committed to self-protection, to the autonomous oath that we will not be hurt again? The next chapter describes typical defensive styles of relating that people develop when they have been sexually abused.

NINE

Style of Relating

Although obvious secondary symptoms of sexual abuse are not always present, past damage will inevitably show itself in one's style of relating to others. For clarity's sake, several important foundational concepts need to be covered before we explore the particular elements of relational style: (1) What is a relational style? (2) Why is it important? (3) How is it formed?

WHAT IS A RELATIONAL STYLE?

A relational style is the "typical" way of protecting oneself in contact with other people. Self-protection is, in essence, the commitment to never be hurt again, to never be powerless, betrayed, or ambivalent in the way we once were. Isaiah 50:10-11 provides an excellent picture of the idea of self-protection:

> "Who among you fears the LORD and obeys the word of his servant? Let him who walks in the dark, who has no light, trust in the name of the LORD and rely on his God. But now, all you who light fires and provide yourselves with flaming torches, go, walk in the light of your fires and of the torches you have set ablaze. This is what you shall receive from my hand: You will lie down in torment."

The context of these verses indicates that the Suffering Serv-ant is in the midst of physical harm, mockery, and contempt. Though his experience can be described as dark (full of confusion and struggle), his heart is resting on the vindication of God. The opposite of trusting God in the midst of darkness is the word-picture of lighting one's own fire. Consider how reasonable it is to turn the light on at night in a strange hotel room. The placement of furniture is unlike your own room, so when you arise in the dark, the natural response, in order to avoid harm, is to switch on the light.

The so-called reasonable desire to avoid pain, discomfort, or shame compels us to light our own fire. Fire lighters are those who take charge of the dark (particularly, struggle or confusion in relationships) by their own means, for their own purposes. It seems that the natural desire to avoid pain directs us toward a path of independence, when, in fact, the desire for relief and satisfaction, if the hunger is deeply felt, will lead to a path of chosen dependence on a Person greater than ourselves.

How can this be the case when past trust has led to abuse? Protecting oneself and relying on one's own resources for self-preservation has seemed like the only reasonable way to live in a fallen world. There is an inherent and radical battle in the soul of the abused person toward any change that may open the door to revictimization. So how does facing one's style of relating lead to a deeper experience of life as it is meant to be lived?

The Scriptures indicate that fire lighting (a self-protec-tive strategy) leads inevitably to torment. The honest man or woman will eventually acknowledge that self-preservation has not worked and, even when it seems to, leads to a diminishment of the soul. The person who takes the initiative to keep her soul intact will violate the nature of her being to accomplish the impossible task. Any effort expended to remain intact is doomed to failure, because it is the attempt to *find* one's life—an attempt that results in *losing* one's life. The self-absorbed interest in keeping intact ultimately leads to a violation of love, which in turn diminishes the essence of who we were designed to be (representatives of God's love in a doomed world). To the degree that we labor to keep ourselves intact, we become less human, less loving, and more like those who cavalierly abuse and dehumanize for their own survival. The honest person will admit that even though her fire-lighting strategies have won her a certain sense of safety, she is not living as she was created to live, and in the hollow chambers of her heart she is lonely as hell.

Reasonable but nonreflective living inevitably leads to subtle autonomy and overt rebellion. The expression of our sinful independence will be most evident in the quiet, deep, fire-lighting patterns we practice in our relationships with others.

WHY IS STYLE OF RELATING IMPORTANT?

If you ask Christians where they struggle with sin, the answer, in many cases, revolves around an act or a behavior, such as a lack of discipline (I don't spend enough time studying God's Word, or I don't obey the speed limit) or a failure to perform (I'm not as sensitive as I should be, or I don't witness enough). True enough, those issues constitute a failure to love God and neighbor. But if sin is defined as merely behavioral, the more subtle and wicked sins are often ignored.

Honoring God ultimately means boldly and sacrificially loving Him and others; yet it is in relationships that we are most committed to avoiding pain. The call to love and the determination to dodge hurt set up a radical contradiction in the soul. One will give way to the other, and the outcome will determine the quality of our walk with God. If we ignore or trivialize our self-protective manner of dealing with people, we will inevitably overlook the deepest sin of the heart: our fallen commitment to take charge of our life so we will never be hurt or shamed as we were in the past. And if we fail to recognize and repent of the sins of the heart, we will not deeply change. We will not deeply love.

HOW IS A STYLE OF RELATING FORMED?

Past abuse, capital-A (physical, emotional, or sexual abuse), or past abuse, small-a (the byproduct of so-called "normal" sin), sets the scene and tone for the development of our self-protective styles of relating to others. The raw material used to form a style of relating is often found in our God-given attributes and talents. The fact that one person chooses to keep others at a distance by detached, academic brilliance may not be an option for a person with a lower IQ. Culture also plays a role in relational style. The haughty disdain of the landed aristocracy is in form quite different from the swagger of the inner-city adolescent, but the cause and function are the same.

The cause is found in the heart's hatred of being alone and unloved, used and out of control. A person made in the image of God was never meant to be alone and unloved, but the fall of man into sin brought about both loneliness and a passionately deep commitment to control an uncertain world.

I spoke to a man whose wife was turned off by his Christian piety and pressure. She was in a sexual-abuse therapy group where she found intimacy and meaning for the first time in her life. He wanted her to stop and "come back to the Lord." She wanted nothing to do with his passionless, pressured, performance-oriented religion, even though she was a Christian. He saw her as the sinner who needed to repent, and all his comments of concern were spoken with quiet disdain and distance. The door opened for change in the relationship when he realized that his style of relating was cold, formal, emotionless, and critical. It reflected his deep commitment to control his wife (and thus his own life) rather than love her.

SPECIFIC STYLES OF RELATING

There are as many styles of relating as there are people. Nevertheless, there are some general patterns that can become common styles of relating for those who have been sexually abused: the *Good Girl*, the *Tough Girl*, and the *Party Girl*.[1]

The Good Girl
The Good Girl is the classic helper, a kind-hearted, gentle woman who lives to keep the peace and sustain those with whom she is

in relationship no matter what the cost may be to her.

The Good Girl is pleasant, but rarely alive. The woman who described herself as a "house with the lights on, but never at home" was a Good Girl. She responded with pleasant warmth and social ease, but she never viewed herself as alive within herself. The idea that Christ makes His home in us always struck her as a strange thought, since *she* didn't even live inside herself.

Internal Dynamics

The internal world of the Good Girl is full of self-contempt, which is usually private and hidden. For example, Good Girls will likely struggle with fantasies and the sexualization of close relationships, but will pay a terrible price for their sin. The penalty will be heavy-handed self-hatred and contempt, often intensified by lengthy periods of penance and guilt-racked restitution. After time, the burden that comes from feeling sexually alive requires too great a price, therefore sexual realities are either forbidden or permitted only if the soul is disengaged.

The pattern of limiting and controlling emotion is true in other areas as well. The Good Girl allows herself only a small portion of pleasure or pain. Her soul is disengaged from most feelings except guilt. If a Good Girl is hurt by someone, she is likely to feel pain only up to the point where she feels either too intense or too angry, then the hurt will dissipate into guilt: "I know I shouldn't feel so hurt," or "I am so terrible for not forgiving her, but I feel so helpless." The guilt often intensifies her sense of alienation and discord in relationships.

A number of Good Girls have acknowledged that they feel as if they don't have a "voice." One woman recalled watching her two-year-old son play with an older boy who hit her son in the head with a toy. The other boy's mother was in the room, so my client turned her back on the assault and for a time ignored her son's tears. Later, she felt overwhelming hatred and contempt for her passivity, but at the moment of the assault, she felt speechless and powerless to do anything to protect her son. The internal world of the Good Girl is controlled, lonely, passive, and full of self-contempt.

External Dynamics

The external world of the Good Girl is usually organized (but never sufficiently in control), pleasant (but rarely alive), and sacrificial (but seldom inviting). The Good Girl is often an energetic worker, organizer, and performer, but a woman who lacks the courage and godly humility to impose on others. Consequently, as long as her effort is sufficient to resolve a matter, it usually goes well; but when it requires delegating or direct solicitation of help, then either the task or the Good Girl unravels.

The Good Girl would rather allow her health to deteriorate than ask for help. One Good Girl, who had hernia surgery three weeks after giving birth by C-section, was told to stay in bed for at least a week. Food was to be provided, and her home was to be cleaned by friends and church acquaintances. Before each person arrived to "help," however, she cleaned the house and washed the dishes so that no one would be inconvenienced.

A Good Girl faces the world alone and usually manages well, until the inevitable limits of her physical and mental health are stretched beyond the breaking point. She is organized and competent in her lonely war, but she is aware that her unseen, fragile core may come unglued if deep realities are faced.

One Good Girl described her style of relating as "plastic fruit." The appearance was good and tasty, but something real, alive, and nourishing was missing. One husband of a Good Girl said, "I've never worried about my wife's fidelity, but most of the time it doesn't really matter since she won't give herself to me anyway." Her husband felt both respect and contempt for his martyr-wife. She was faithful, responsible, clean, orderly, reverent, and always prepared, but she lacked the passion of soul to yell when he was a jerk and the freedom of soul to laugh when he told an uproariously funny story. The Good Girl lives without passion for anything or anyone other than the drive to keep things smooth and conflict-free.

A Good Girl, a martyr, sacrificially gives without ever inviting the recipient to taste or enjoy her soul. A Good Girl is far more comfortable in giving her husband or friends her hands than her heart. If a friend points out the contradiction between receiving her help instead of her love, guilt, self-contempt, and depression can easily occur. For that reason, many men married to Good Girls learn that it doesn't pay to bring up problems because the confrontation will be met by self-deprecation or hurt withdrawal.

A Good Girl is also likely to be a person who works, that is overworks, at relationships. She will not rest until she thinks that others are pleased with her. I've known Good Girls who would babysit sick children, risking infection of their own kids, simply because Good Girls cannot stand to say no. For the Good Girl, peace and harmony must be assured, no matter what the cost, nor how little the gain. The thought that someone may be upset by her actions might cause a Good Girl a loss of appetite or a sleepless night. One can imagine how apt she is to ask for forgiveness. She will likely be a professional apologizer. Asking for forgiveness, or saying I'm sorry, looks so Christian, but in fact is often a demand on others that they be pleased with her. In that sense, her apologizing is self-centered and a burden to others who must continually reassure the "sinner" that she is still welcome and wanted.

The effect of a Good Girl's style of relating is to gain superficial involvement from others without earning their deep respect. A Good Girl's hard work is often designed to get others to marvel over her commitment, zeal, or love. In truth, her sacrifice is often seen as subtly manipulative and empty. The person involved with a Good Girl often feels invited to use or take her for granted. Who wouldn't like someone who lives to tend to the nuisance details of life for your sake? There may be no desire to use the Good Girl, but it is almost impossible not to step on her as she labors underfoot to keep the path clean and trouble-free.

It is not hard to see that the Good Girl is a woman who has disengaged herself from the wounds of her soul. In many cases, she will recall some elements of her past abuse, but will either mislabel them or believe they were her fault. Often she was an ally of the abuser, or at least the ready helper to whom others turned for comfort and support. She was the good listener who was valued for her care and used because she was quiet. She often looks comfortable in her attractive clothes or pretty in her Sunday dress, but at heart, she is critical, and even hateful, toward herself as a woman. She has handled the damage of abuse by faithfully enduring the repeated mistreatment by others with quiet, resilient, pleasant detachment.

The Tough Girl

The Tough Girl is the classic take-charge, task-oriented, no-nonsense ramrod, whose heart may be as good as gold, but is usually just as hard. The hardness is often the result of being controlled by other-centered contempt. If the Good Girl could be called a woman who does not live inside herself, then the Tough Girl is a woman who lives behind thick, impenetrable walls.

Internal Dynamics

Internally, the Tough Girl is above her own feelings, suspicious of others' motives, and arrogant and angry in her evaluations of others. She views human need as childish and unnecessary. It would be unusual for a Tough Girl to gently hold a crying child for any length of time. A more standard response would be to permit tears for a moment and then get the child busy in another activity. Or another standard option would be to shame the weak child to toughen up his or her exterior: "You are just a crybaby, so if you continue crying, I'll just have to get a diaper for you."

A Tough Girl views her longings as sentimental, sloppy, and weak; they are a defect that must be eradicated. It is not that human hunger is entirely denigrated, because a Tough Girl is often able to justify her response toward others as a demonstration of realistic concern. She sees herself as an able mother, desires her children's respect, wants her husband to be more involved, and is sensitive when she is snubbed. At her core, however, her hunger for involvement is severely undermined by her refusal to be dependent on anyone. She views her longings as a sign of weakness whenever she cannot resolve her heartaches on her own. Whoever manages to provoke her intense hunger for rich relationship is to be scorned or avoided. Emotions are to be conquered and controlled so that no one can cause her pain again.

All of this makes the Tough Girl suspicious and critical. She perceives others' movement toward her as their attempt to dominate; therefore, she spurns kindness and human warmth as not only unnecessary, but dangerous. She views compliments as a "buttering up before the kill," or a prelude to being used.

With such an internal disposition, the Tough Girl is often accurate about motivational issues. Her refined sense of perception often can spot a phony miles away. Suspicious perception, however, though often accurate, is also a self-fulfilling prophecy. Family members and friends will sense her defensive and hostile attitude and over time their fear of judgment or attack will make them standoffish and critical in return. Their defensive and hostile behavior is then interpreted by the Tough Girl as proof of her suspicions.

The Tough Girl's suspicious mood is further expressed in opinionated arrogance, which is really a cover for her pervasive anger. Tough Girls know how to run their families, invest their money, run the youth group, rectify the wrongs in city government, plan the Fourth of July parade, cure hives, and take an average chicken and turn it into a gourmet meal. Tough Girls don't usually ask questions unless the question is a pretext to deliver their own opinion. One Tough Girl recently asked me what I thought about the increased interest in the topic of sexual abuse. Before I had the chance to open my mouth, she heralded her thoughts and was off on another topic. She was offended when I brought the discussion back to the original question.

Arrogance shows itself beyond know-it-all-ism and a lack of interest in the thoughts and experiences of others. It is also manifested in a desire to control, or have a preeminent say in the activities of other people. The assumption seems to be: "I know best." A Tough Girl who visited our new home and saw some of our recently acquired furnishings said, "It's a nice home, but . . ." and proceeded to offer her suggestions regarding color scheme, decor, and needed furniture. My wife and I felt demoralized and furious. If we had wanted an interior designer, we would have paid for one, but we didn't comment, because a Tough Girl has the potential either to erupt in anger or nurture a grudge for a long time.

The Tough Girl's internal hardness, suspiciousness, superiority, and criticalness may not be as obvious as one might assume. Of course, some Tough Girls advertise their disdain for emotion, their suspiciousness of those unlike them, and their preeminent superiority in all affairs. Others, however, are more subtle, softening their contempt behind a more socially acceptable and restrained demeanor.

External Dynamics

Some external realities will almost always be part of the Tough Girl's style of relating. First, there will be an edge or wall that keeps people from drawing close. The edge may be nothing more than a haughty glare. I know one pastor's wife who has perfected the disdainful look. Her eyes look straight through you with a mild sneer. Needless to say, few in the congregation willingly oppose any of her plans. The edge might also take the form of a biting, sarcastic wit, or a busy, "please don't disturb me" air. In any case, the edge functions to assure both intimidation and distance.

Second, the Tough Girl is and will be in charge. She is a good researcher and organizer. She knows where the best deals are, who is a reputable gynecologist, and who in the neighborhood is likely to have an affair. There is nothing wrong or unusual in being competent and confident in one's area of expertise, or for that matter in a number of fields. The clincher is what happens when a Tough Girl loses control, makes a mistake, or is challenged on one of her pet opinions. A battle usually ensues. While the Good Girl is committed to not ruffling the feathers, the Tough Girl would rather eat the bird than be found wrong. A Tough Girl may not "enjoy" fights, but she is willing to go toe to toe in heated combat for the sake of her black-and-white (I'm-right-and-you're-wrong) values.

Finally, the Tough Girl is emotionally impenetrable. A Good Girl will handle a compliment by depreciating her ability or motive or by insisting that the Lord, not her, deserves the full honor. A Tough Girl will often appear to receive a compliment or a thank you, but she will not be touched by the giver's kindness. Like a tennis ball hit against a wall, the kindness always returns, close to the same level of force, but without the intention of further interaction. Both giver and receiver are left feeling cold and lonely. The Tough Girl's relational wall withstands the force of the ball and sends it back, but she indicates no desire to give in return.

The people in a Tough Girl's domain react to her hostile edge, control, and impenetrability by keeping their distance. Often they respect the accomplishments or boldness of her will, but they do not enjoy her presence or essence. The Tough Girl makes a great surgeon, trial lawyer, or prime minister, but not a desirable friend, spouse, or parent. The Tough Girl is appreciated for her perseverance, ingenuity, and hard work, but feared because of her critical eye and contemptuous power. The honest Tough Girl is a lonely woman.

The Party Girl

The Party Girl is the classic easygoing, good-time lady, sometimes intense and other times mellow. She is predictably inconsistent, hard to read, and impossible to pin down in close relationships. One factor behind her capricious style is her ability to use competently both self-centered and other-centered contempt. It's as if she has mastered the ability to hate herself *and* you at the same time. She has the skill to easily draw a person into relationship and then, in an instant, turn her back on him. Her manner is affable, warm, and inviting, but in a flash she can become irascible, demanding, and whiny. The Party Girl can be as bombastic as any Tough Girl, sacrificial as any Good Girl, but then easily hurt, frightened, and fragile.

Internal Dynamics

The Party Girl is complicated. She is usually fragile and funny, sincere and phony, blunt and dishonest—a series of paradoxes.

When she allows herself to agonize over loss or hurt for a brief time, she views her anguish as neither selfish (Good Girl) nor weak (Tough Girl), but as pointless. There is an acknowledgment of longing and anguish, but "so what?" Feelings are felt, but not deeply faced.

Internally, the Party Girl is inconsistent and ambivalent. She is like a constantly changing, unstable storm front—bright one minute, dark the next. Her emotions will swerve and undulate without a recognizable cause. The reason, in part, is the presence of both self- and other-centered contempt. Her demeanor will often depend on whom she hates most at the moment: herself or you. The chaotic mood and behavior fluctuations drive most people crazy. One just does not know what to expect from a Party Girl.

While the Good Girl wallows in guilt and the Tough Girl brims with rage, the Party Girl struggles with fear and ambivalence. She handles her simultaneous or fluctuating hunger for and hatred of relationship through superfical analysis ("Life will work out"), minimization ("The abuser was just insecure, not sinful"), and cynical withdrawal ("That's just the way life is"). It's as if the Party Girl won't allow herself to be too troubled, because she knows it will lead to a point that requires honesty, commitment, and strength. It is far easier to laugh or cry over her pain and then walk away from it, than it is to actually enter the unknown.

External Dynamics
The external aspects of the Party Girl include fickleness and seduction in relationships and chronic dissatisfaction. Loyalty—that is, the commitment to persevere in relationship for the sake of the other—endures only as long as pleasure is found. Once the enjoyment of a new relationship begins to fade or requires hard work, the Party Girl finds some way to terminate or sabotage the union. Often a Party Girl will go from relationship to relationship, replaying a pattern that involves start up, enjoyment, use, and then sabotage.

One woman described her style of relating as "discarding

old soda cans once the good stuff is gone." This is similar to the behavior of a tick. A tick does not have the ability to produce its own blood, therefore it is dependent on a host animal. The tick remains connected until the host runs dry and then moves on to another host. The Party Girl, similarly, draws out life from a host until commitment is required or the parasitic manipulation is discovered. Then she moves on to find satisfaction somewhere else. The Party Girl is committed to pleasure and relief more than to honor, values, or relationship. Loyalty, consistency, perseverance, and longsuffering are not her hallmarks.

Seductiveness is another characteristic of the Party Girl's style of relating. Her seduction can include a sexual element, but it must be understood in the larger context of enmeshing the "host" in relationship and keeping him or her responsive. Seduction might then be as obvious as the provocative wink and coy comment of the flirt or as subtle as the deep depression of the "fragile" mother whose son does not respond to her complaints. For example, the woman who "loves" her son to the point that she would do anything for him, suffer any deprivation, endure any insult is often the first to turn on him or exhibit whiny hurt and fragile disappointment when he moves away from their enmeshed and dependent bond. The commitment is not one of loyalty but of demand; her love is parasitic and life-dissolving, not liberating and life-giving. In either case, a flirtatious or a fragile Party Girl is luring the object of her desire into a web of relationship through lust or guilt. The result will be the same: enmeshment, control, and the power to destroy.

Often the first evidence of the Party Girl's seductive control is her "host's" feeling of being deeply needed and valued, to the point that the Party Girl cannot enjoy life without the host's special help. The intoxicating thrill of being special and needed often blinds the eyes so that many a pastor and counselor have had affairs with sincere, struggling Party Girls who deeply appreciated the kind and gentle counsel of a choice helper.

Another clue to a Party Girl's seduction is the guilt a person feels when he "lets her down." He will feel like a catastrophic failure in light of the needy girl's disappointment. The Party Girl is a master of "I'll live with it" dissatisfaction. She is never entirely happy, even if she has what she wants. Her dissatisfaction not only seduces the host into guilt-bonded relationship, but it also justifies the termination of the relationship. Why should she stay in such an "unhealthy" relationship? The other person is demanding too much involvement, commitment, time, energy, and money, to justify the relationship's continuation.

A Party Girl is a two-fisted excuse maker who may be hard and angry one moment and confused and needy the next. She seems to have an insatiable hunger that can never be filled. One man, whose wife and mother are Party Girls, lamented: "I can never do enough to make them happy. It's as if there is an emotional tapeworm that dissolves all the food I give, so that they are never nourished by my care."

The insatiability of the Party Girl keeps every interaction superficial and dissolves all potentially good relationships. The dissolution of good relationships resolves the uncertainty and anxiety generated by ambivalence and opens the door to destructive, abusive unions. In turn, the mutual manipulation, destructive consequences, and deep loneliness of the abusive bond serves to quiet the Party Girl's hunger for pure and satisfying care.

It is easy to stereotype (somewhat accurately) the Good Girl as the typical downtrodden housewife or perfect pastor's wife; the Tough Girl as the typical liberated woman, driven executive, or ministry staff director; and the Party Girl as the barhopping, promiscuous gadfly. Those stereotypes, however, belie the complexity of the matter. Many Party Girls are committed, moral Christians who laugh off problems or use prayer and Bible study (in the way that some unbelieving Party Girls use alchohol and drugs) to superficially muddle their way through the struggles of life. On the other hand, many Good Girls, deadened by their own guilt, engage in repeated illicit affairs. Promiscuity is not the sole province of the Party Girl, nor is drivenness the exclusive domain of the Tough Girl.

Tendencies in style of relating are open to countless variations and apparent contradictions. Why would this be the case?
In part, the answer is simple. Each style of relating emphasizes
one kind of contempt over another, but not to the point of
excluding the other. Every Good Girl has a deep streak of other-
centered contempt, often unmined and untapped, but waiting to
show itself at the right moment. Similarly every Tough Girl hides
a sizable stock of self-contempt, though she is more comfortable
with hating others. And every Party Girl has an uncanny capacity
to glide between self- and other-centered contempt with equal
facility.

Nevertheless, at the risk of stereotyping, the three styles of
relating can be briefly summarized: the Good Girl is committed
to pleasure and relief through faithful attendance to relationship;
the Tough Girl, to the exercise of power through control and
intimidation; the Party Girl, to enmeshment and control through
seductive lust and/or guilt.

The Good Girl will draw support and pleasantness from
others, but in the long run will be lonely and more deeply
abused. The Tough Girl will draw respect and distant admira-
tion, but will be lonely and feared. Her intimidation will keep
abuse at a minimum, but in the long run her arrogance and
abusive interactions with others will provoke retaliation and
vengeance. The Party Girl will elicit laughter and anger, good
will and hatred; at core, she will confuse and frustrate others. She
will invite involvement, but intimacy often will degenerate into
rage or fear, leading her to abuse others or be abused by them.
In the end, she will have deeply harmed others and be equally
devastated by their frustration and withdrawal.

The Good, Tough, and Party Girls are both victims and
agents. Their styles of relating are not only byproducts of their
past abuse, but also of their futile attempts to find life apart from
a dependent, vulnerable relationship with God.

The disentangling of the true person from a defensive style
of relating is the thrilling work of Christian growth. Nothing can
be done to take away the heartache or failed relationships of the
past, but our hope is that in Christ the past need not stain the

present nor shape the future. A perspective on the damage of the past abuse, both internal and external, sets the stage for an understanding of how relationship with God is central in the change process.

PART THREE
PREREQUISITES FOR GROWTH

TEN

The Unlikely Route to Joy

The guiding assumption in the previous chapters is simple: A problem cannot be substantially resolved until it is honestly faced. The most common error in some Christian groups is to ignore the problem or offer true solutions in a trite way. But people struggling to face their problems honestly make an equally destructive error if they spurn spiritual solutions because they appear simple and irrelevant to the complexity of the problem at hand.

Unfortunately, those who cling to spiritual answers often view with suspicion those who reject shallow truisms. And those who grapple with understanding the effects of living in a fallen world often disdain those who find comfort in simple truths. In either case, the contempt, though understandable, addresses neither the horror of the damage nor the wonder of the good news. Those who desire to honor God and the redemptive work of Christ must embrace both the simplicity and complexity that exists in the problem and the solution.

The remainder of this book is devoted to sketching a picture of what is required for change. Change is possible. Change, in fact, is assured for any who desire to grow. Growth, however, is surprising. In all respects it is both natural and utterly supernatural. We were made to grow, to learn, to change as human beings.

However, sin not only inhibits growth but makes it the exception, not the rule. When we move toward loving God and others, we can be sure that something radical and supernatural has intruded to alter the process of self-centered stagnation and decay.

Change is always a process. This truth cannot be overemphasized. Many abuse victims feel their progress of change is taking too long. The assumption is that if God is involved, then the process will be brief and not too messy. If that were true, then why did God take forty years to teach Moses humility and leadership skills in the sheep fields of Midian? Deep healing, supernatural change, may take years of struggle, trial and error learning, and growing in strength to make the next significant move of faith. No one ought to judge another's growth timetable.

What surprises can an abused person expect if he or she chooses to cooperate with God's supernatural work? The process involves the surprising route of weakness, brokenness, poverty, and death. These words are apt to alienate, disgust, or frighten the honest person. The man or woman who has been abused already feels weak and broken (powerless), poor (powerless and betrayed), and dead (powerless, betrayed, and ambivalent). The thought that the cure is worse than the disease, or at least as bad, makes the prospect of a spiritual route seem totally undesirable.

For that reason, many secular and Christian approaches to the problem dilute the biblical process to make it more palatable. Fallen human nature wants control and guarantees, and any system or model of change that offers relief through the faithful execution of clear steps touches a basic desire of the fallen soul.

The biblical path allows for choice and responsible action, but it involves walking through the valley without lighting a flaming torch in the darkness. It involves losing our life in order to find it, trading death for life (John 12:24-25). *Trusting in God involves the loss of our agenda, our flaming torch, so that we die to our inclination to live a lie.* It requires forfeiting our rigid, self-protective, God-dishonoring ways of relating in order to embrace life as it is meant to be lived: in humble dependence on God and passionate involvement with others.

A CRUCIAL QUESTION

Before reflecting any more on the prospect of change and the route to joy, we must step back and ask ourselves a crucial question—a question whose answer will determine whether we will embrace the biblical path or pour contempt on it. The question is this: "Do I believe that God is a loving Father who is committed to my deepest well-being, that He has the right to use everything that is me for whatever purposes He deems best, and that surrendering my will and my life entirely to Him will bring me the deepest joy and fulfillment I can know this side of heaven?"

If the answer is yes, then the biblical path, though rocky at times, will be smoothed by a faith that acknowledges the infinite love, unsearchable wisdom, and severe mercy of God. The process of turning from our self-sufficient, self-protective modes of existence will be humbling and painful, but successful. We will recognize the sinfulness of our commitment to construct a "life" according to our own definition, and we will move faithfully in the direction of repentance. Trusting God will be reasonable, if not easy, and will lead to the right hand of God where there are pleasures forevermore.

If, on the other hand, the answer to the question is no, the biblical path will seem more than absurd; it will be impossible to embrace. How can we willingly forfeit our own strategies and agenda if, deep inside, we feel like this: "The last thing God seems to be is a loving Father. He's the One who allowed me to be abused in the first place, so how can I trust Him to have my best interests at heart in the present? As far as I'm concerned, God is selfish and demanding, and I'm tired of being 'used' by Him and everyone else. Surrendering my will and my life to God can't result in anything that's really good for *me*. In fact, I'm sure it would be the end of me, once and for all. It's a miracle I've survived this long, no thanks to Him."

What if we're closer to the second position than the first? What if trusting God and surrendering our all to Him seems like the mockery to end all mockeries?

First, we need to consider again what is and is not biblical trust. Most assume that trust is quiet, serene, selfless dependence on God. Though there is an element of truth to that view of trust, more often than not such serene faith is a byproduct of wanting very little from God. It is frighteningly easy to appear trusting when in fact one is simply dead (in denial of the wounds, hunger, or struggle of the heart).

Genuine trust involves allowing another to matter and have an impact in our lives. For that reason, many who hate and do battle with God trust Him more deeply than those whose complacent faith permits an abstract and motionless stance before Him. Those who trust God most are those whose faith permits them to risk wrestling with Him over the deepest questions of life. Good hearts are captured in a divine wrestling match; fearful, doubting hearts stay clear of the mat.

The commitment to wrestle will be honored by a God who will not only break but bless. Jacob's commitment to wrestle with God resulted in the wounding of his thigh. He would never again walk without a limp. But the freedom in his heart was worth the price of his shattered limb. The price of soul freedom is the loss of what has been deemed most secure (the tight grip over one's soul, the commitment to be one's sole provider and protector) but is intuitively known as no security at all.

The wonder of the gospel that ultimately captures the wounded heart is that in spite of our hatred and rebellion toward God, Christ died for us, and His Spirit pursues us to the ends of the earth. His faithful pursuit is not stymied by our hatred or ambivalence, our lack of faith, or our refusal to trust. In fact, His steps doggedly pursue even when we assume we are most incapable of receiving or even desiring grace. At times His penchant to pursue in the present invokes even greater hatred than did His silence or inactivity in the midst of the past abuse: "Why won't He just leave me alone?"

But He won't leave us alone—for our sake. The only thing that will ultimately produce change and joy in our lives is recognizing our sin and receiving God's grace. For the person who has not yet begun to deeply trust God (or even deem Him worthy of trust) the rest of this book may be quite difficult to read, embrace, and apply. But a new day can come for even the most fearful. God will faithfully work in a willing heart and bring it to repentance and surrender. As humble, dependent children of a merciful and powerful Father, we will find the courage to enter the darkness and peril of the valley, and we will emerge blazing with His redemptive light.

THE STEP APPROACH TO CHANGE

How is this unusual route to life, through the valley of the shadow of death, different from the do-able step approach that many choose to pursue? The latter path usually has at least three steps that mark its predictable process and results. The first step helps an abuse victim feel and own her emotions (self-discovery). The next helps her find the freedom to express her inner world (self-expression). The ultimate goal is to train her to establish boundaries in relationship to others so that she is never used or abused again (self-protection).

These objectives are so close to the biblical ideal that it is difficult to articulate the difference through the written or spoken word. I would suggest, however, that the difference is profound.

Self-discovery, or owning one's feelings, though necessary and legitimate, often becomes focused on the goal of learning more about oneself in order to require others to take into account one's pain. When self-discovery takes place in a truly biblical way (with the focus on how one can better love others), it annihilates any hope of self-justification and intensifies the need for grace. Biblical self-discovery exposes the abused person's wound and rage, loneliness and self-protective isolation. It doesn't stop at reclaiming repressed feelings, but faces the self-serving comfort found in living with a dead soul. The primary purpose in facing victimization is not simply to know how one feels about it, but to expose more clearly the victim's subtle patterns of seeking life and comfort apart from dependence on God.

What about self-expression, the second step of the common route to change? Freedom to express what one thinks and feels often becomes an opportunity to vent defensive accusations. The phrase, "I was just being honest," is often used as a means to seek revenge under the guise of openness and authenticity. In relationships the question should never be merely, "Have I been honest?" as much as, "Have I been committed to the other person's good?" Honesty of expression should always serve to honor the other person.

Finally, the setting of boundaries to prevent possible use and abuse often leads to self-centered, arrogant, autonomous self-protection. One woman said with a barely hidden sneer: "I don't care what you think. I've learned to say yes to myself. I'm no longer going to be a pawn of anyone's demands. I'm going to do what I want for a change." Her relationship with her husband and all others could be called codependent in that she functioned in life without a soul, a will, or a heart, and she was controlled by the whims of everyone around her. She faced her victimization and the need for reclaiming her inner world, but she was so enraged by facing the past harm that she never looked at her part in her codependent victimization. She was never humbled and broken by her sin, because the path of boundary building never exposed her codependence as damaging, sinful self-protection designed to keep her from having to live boldly, authentically, and humbly in relationships. In facing her victimization, she longed for a courtroom in which to vent her indignation and demand justice. She never faced her own sin; therefore, she never asked for grace.

The concept of boundaries is legitimate. I accept, to some degree, my own limits as a human, finite, and sinful person. Consequently, I establish boundaries to better serve those with whom I am in relationship. A boundary like the number of hours I sleep at night is seldom violated, because I am able to function better when I get seven hours of rest. I seldom interrupt my time with my children to talk over the phone, because I am not owned by the phone. I am not required nor indebted to talk to everyone who might want to talk with me. Boundaries are an acknowledgment of my finiteness and a gift of mercy to my soul.

I am not insensitive to the fact that abuse victims have often lost the ability to set and maintain legitimate boundaries, nor am I opposed to helping them identify boundary violations and strengthen their ability to set limits. The objective behind boundary building, however, will determine whether it is consistent with loving God and others or if it is merely self-centered humanism.

The objective must be to bless the other person rather than to make sure we are not abused again. We are to draw a boundary in order to better love the one to whom we are relating. We cannot wholeheartedly give if we live in fear of another. Most boundaries are allowed to be violated because we are afraid to offend or lose the paltry relationship that currently exists. *To love is to be more committed to the other than we are to the relationship, to be more concerned about his walk with God than the comfort or benefits of his walk with us.*

I talked to a woman who has been immersed for years in a secular approach to boundary building. Her mother is an evil, hard, critical woman who would rather destroy her daughter than admit that her husband abused the girl. For years, the daughter set appropriate boundaries and "took care of herself." She had more peace and ease, but little joy or gentleness of soul. She was supposedly learning to love herself, but in so doing she'd lost the legitimate, God-honoring thrill of giving herself fully to another. In order to keep her boundaries high, she had to continuously reaffirm the necessity of protecting herself and harden her heart to the sadness of her mother's life. She was transformed from a weak-kneed wimp to an angry, tough wench. And that was called growth.

Is it possible that love implies and requires its own boundaries? In order to love, we must both honor the dignity and expose the depravity of the person with whom we are in relationship. We cannot love if we distance ourselves or overlook the damage of another's sin; neither can we love if we fail to move into another's world to offer a taste of life. In both cases, the lover often is a martyr for the sake of the gospel, sacrificing personal comfort for the sake of helping the other experience his own longings and need for grace.

Love has boundaries, but often boundary setting is a means of fleeing the requirements of love. A good heart will always feel unsettled by any path that does not offer the opportunity of sacrifice for the sake of the gospel. The common route of self-discovery, self-expression, and self-protection seems reasonable, but the byproducts are often not true strength, tenderness, or faithfulness.

THE BIBLICAL ROUTE TO CHANGE

Real life requires death. Death involves the experience of suffering. Suffering is required for growth.

Even the Son of God was required to suffer in order to enter the fulfillment of His maturity and mission:

> In bringing many sons to glory, it was fitting that God, for whom and through whom everything exists, should make the author of their salvation perfect through suffering. . . .
>
> Although he was a son, Jesus learned obedience from what he suffered and, once made perfect, he became the source of eternal salvation for all who obey him. (Hebrews 2:10, 5:8-9)

Suffering is equally necessary for us because it strips away the pretense that life is reasonable and good, a pretense that keeps us looking in all the wrong places for the satisfaction of our souls.

Annie Dillard, in a passage of savage clarity, uses a description of a burn victim to expose the pain that lurks near the well-manicured, verdant green ease of the good life:

> Once I read that people who survive bad burns tend to go crazy; they have a very high suicide rate. Medicine cannot ease their pain; drugs just leak away, soaking the sheets, because there is not skin to hold them in. The people just lie there and weep. Later they kill themselves. They had not known, before they were burned, that the world

included such suffering, that life could permit them personally such pain.[1]

For the Christian, how can fully embracing personal suffering (rather than self-protectively deflecting it) lead to hope instead of despair? It has to do with the way deep suffering can lead us to place our trust where it ultimately belongs.

Suffering of any sort points to the fact that something terrible, unnatural, and wrong has occurred, and that something better, more fitting to beauty, righteousness, and justice must await. Otherwise, why would our desire for more be so strong, if in fact this is our home, our only home?

It would not be right to indicate that all suffering is necessary or profitable. Many suffer under the weight of their sinful contempt. Others languish with the demand that someone take away their pain. I would not call such suffering good, but it nevertheless reveals that our soul knows it was meant for more.

Christ's suffering was in bearing the disgrace and shame of the Cross; our suffering is in losing ourselves and taking up His Cross so that we can find who we are really made to be.

The path of the valley or the Cross, requires biblical expressions of honesty, repentance, and bold love. *Honesty* removes the pleasant, antiseptic blandness of denial. *Repentance* strips away self-contempt and other-centered hatred and replaces it with humility, grief, and tenderness. *Bold love* increases power and freedom through the exhilaration of loving as we were made to love. The Good Girl, Tough Girl, and Party Girl become stronger, more passionate, more free, inviting, and faithful.

THE REWARDS OF THE BIBLICAL PATH

The joy that lies ahead on the unlikely path involves three internal realities: (1) enjoyment in being soft (tender), (2) deepened capacity to respond to others from the soul, and (3) freedom to make difficult and unpopular choices.

The enjoyment of being soft—or a word more suited to a man, tender-is the experience of being inviting. One woman said she longed to be the kind of person with whom others could relax. She wanted to be like a large, lovely tree that invited creatures to come and nest, whose leafy arms held the promise of comfort and rest. Clearly, this is the antithesis of the Tough Girl.

The capacity to give to others out of the depths of one's soul is a rich delight. Being a good neighbor who is willing to lend a hand to someone in need is pleasant enough. How much more delight is there (or at least there should be) in offering one's soul — one's core possession that will last for eternity — to another for his supreme good? The joy is beyond words. Clearly, this kind of giving and involvement doesn't compare to what the Party Girl is capable of offering in relationships.

Finally, the freedom to make difficult and unpopular choices is exhilarating. Such freedom enables the heart to live a bold, value-controlled versus frightened, people-dependent life. The capacity to act on conviction instead of fear enlivens the soul and allows it to soar above the petty attacks and jealousies of a fallen world. Clearly, no Good Girl has even begun to sprout such wings.

The best summary of what is available for the person who has been sexually abused is found in Proverbs 31:25: "She is clothed with strength and dignity; she can laugh at the days to come." The woman who is clothed in strength and dignity is not a Good Girl; she has too much power and might of soul to be voiceless and dead. She is not a Tough Girl; she has too much passion and life to be hard and aloof. She is not a Party Girl; she has too deep a commitment to tomorrow to live hedonistically only for today. She is the truly loving, existential woman who lives passionately in today and faithfully for tomorrow.

What are the prerequisites for becoming such a woman or man? Honesty. Repentance. Bold love. The courageous and humble person will pursue all of these and reap the fruit of joy.

ELEVEN

Honesty

Honesty is the commitment to see reality as it is, without conscious distortion, minimization, or spiritualization. Honesty begins by admitting we are deceived, and that we would rather construct a false world than face the bright, searing light of truth. An honest person acknowledges his fondness for vague, half-truths that neither require change nor rip away the presumption of self-sufficiency.

Why must we admit what is true? Because dishonesty, or living in denial, is actually an attempt to dethrone God. It is an attempt to become as God with the power to construct the world and reality according to our desire. A person committed to denying hard truths must construct an alternate world and, then, like Atlas, keep it spinning on her own power. The creation of a false world is really an attempt to shut God out of our world. It's much like the child who says, "Unless you play by my rules, I'll take my ball and bat and go home." God does not play by our rules nor resolve our wound and ache as we desire; therefore, we leave God's world and create one that is more palatable to our taste, even if it robs us of life and love.

Honesty takes away the need for living a life of lies. At first, scrutiny of the lies provokes shame or rage—emotions that threaten the hope of intimacy and leave the lie maker alone and afraid. But eventually truth frees the soul, because it lifts the burden of bearing the weight of a false world. The work of keeping the gnawing dogs of truth at bay actually takes far more energy than admitting the awful reality. At first truth may be hated, but it is a taste of relief to a tired, burdened, and lonely heart. When one is committed to honesty, she knocks on the door of truth, open-handed, hungry and persistent, until the door opens and the Bread of life is deposited in her hands. If a person devotes herself to change through honesty, she must fully acknowledge the internal and external damage caused by sexual abuse.

THE INTERNAL DAMAGE

An honest victim of sexual abuse must be willing to acknowledge the eight truths that have been highlighted in the previous chapters:

1. I have been abused.
2. I am a victim of a crime against my body and soul.
3. As a victim, I am not in any way responsible for the crime, no matter what I might have experienced or gained as a result of the abuse.
4. Abuse has damaged my soul.
5. The damage is due to the interweaving dynamics of powerlessness, betrayal, and ambivalence.
6. My damage is different from others' in extent, intensity, and consequences, but it is worthy to be addressed and worked through no matter what occurred.
7. It will take time to deal with the internal wounds; the process must not be hurried.
8. I must not keep a veil of secrecy and shame over my past, but I am not required to share my past with anyone I feel is untrustworthy or insensitive.

An honest heart that embraces the internal damage will at some point be face to face with the memories of past abuse. The experience will be similar to holding onto the ends of a live electrical wire that burns and sears the soul, shaking it and transforming it into an altered, alien state. The new state is so unfamiliar and terrifying that many victims opt to not recall memories at all. Others recall only parts of the past, or even recall all the details but stay detached from them as if what happened didn't actually happen to *their* body or *their* soul. These three positions (no memory, partial memory, emotionally detached memory) provoke three questions: What is the point in recalling the past, because it cannot be changed? How much needs to be recalled for change to occur? If one cannot recall, or can recall only certain memories, how hard should she push to reclaim the memories that remain submerged?

What Is the Purpose in Recalling Past Memories?

A woman approached me at a seminar trembling with intense energy. She asked what I thought about the use of sodium pentothal for recovering past, blocked memories. She could recall only momentary snapshots of the past. All memories before age nine were absent. She felt as if she were losing her mind. She cried often and had fainted several days before our talk. She was desperate and wanted assurance that a "truth serum" would help her reclaim the past and free her from the awful pain of the present.

I asked her if she really wanted to know about the past. My response unnerved her. Her incredulous look belied her confusion and irritation. She responded, "Of course not, but I will if it will bring relief to the conflict." She admitted she did not want to face what might be behind her amnesiac block, but wanted to be symptom free. She saw drugs as a way of reclaiming the past without having to make a soul-engaged decision to enter what she did not want to face. I told her that any data she gained without choice would, most likely, be denied or distanced even if it was recalled.

Certainly not every victim who is open and devoted to reclaiming memories will be "rewarded" with graphic recollections of past events. Sometimes the abuse is so submerged in the subconscious, or the events happened at such an early age, that recall is impossible, even if the victim is willing. But more often than not, choosing to open oneself to memories will, over time, draw them to the surface, where they can begin to be dealt with constructively.

The purpose of regaining memories is threefold: removal of the denial, reclamation of the self, and movement toward real change. The denial is an affront to God. It assumes that a false reality is better than truth. It assumes that God is neither good nor strong enough to help during the recall process. Ultimately, the choice to face past memories is the choice not to live a lie.

Second, we are as much our past as we are our present and our hopes for the future. To cut off the past is to erase part of our story, our journey, our self. The reclamation of the past involves the courage to be all that we are so that we can be all that we will be in our relationships to others.

Finally, facing the past enables us to see the present more clearly. The past clings to the present like an intractable barnacle, an unseen drag that slows the progress of the vessel. Facing the past memories gives the victim a sense of legitimate control. Nothing has been hidden that might spring out at some unexpected moment. Nothing lurks to expose her as the ugly duckling, the soiled woman she fears she might be.

How Much Needs to Be Faced for Change to Occur?

The question is similar to a question I recall asking as a young believer: What is the minimum level of obedience that is required to be a Christian? Can I still get drunk? Do I have to go to church? Witness? Give? The question has no answer, because it begins with an inaccurate premise.

Similarly, the question of how much needs to be recalled is built on the premise that change is the result of doing the right thing, or at least just enough of the right thing. The deepest change, however, is a byproduct of repentance—in this case, turning from the dark, hazy fog of disbelief that it could have happened to me, or incredulity that my father or brother or uncle or neighbor could have been so bad as to have abused me.

But a legitimate concern remains: When is enough really enough? There are two answers. First, the process of reclaiming the past is a lifetime endeavor. God does not require perfect growth overnight. The average American eats twelve to fourteen tons of food in a lifetime. Imagine the horror of being told to eat several tons, let alone the whole thing, at one sitting. In the same way, growth is apportioned for a season, for a choice time. Our part is to be prepared; God's part is to orchestrate the process according to our personality, our need, and His good purpose. Consequently, God will graciously return memories in His own time, according to His sovereign purposes.

Second, memories often will return slowly, progressively, toward a major event or experience that unconsciously serves as the foundation for the deepest shame. The progression is often toward what I've called the "ace in the hole." The ace-in-the-hole memory is often the experience that involved soul-shattering violence, or arousal or gain, that serves to prove that the abuse was warranted, desired, or enjoyed.

One woman vaguely recalled countless experiences of abuse. She was quite aware that many memories were fuzzy and sensed that more occurred than she could recall. Her dreams were traumatic whenever she recalled a door to a room in the basement of an old farm house. She could not recall what occurred behind that door, but she knew it was profoundly unnerving.

Our work helped her recall a number of terrible experiences, but each gain was nullified by a sense of dis-ease that more needed to be faced. Eventually, the scene behind the door became an overwhelming reality. It was a ghastly experience of barbaric abuse involving rape, beastiality, and torture. The memory returned, I believe, after her soul had experienced sufficient change to warrant the unconscious confidence that she would not be destroyed by the memory.

How much is enough? The answer is ultimately whatever God desires for us to see. Our part is to face whatever will help us better love those whom we have been called to serve.

How Hard Should I Work
to Reclaim Vague or Submerged Memories?

The answer is simple: be *open*—but not demanding; be *curious*—but not frantic; be *vigilant*—but not obsessed. The principle is much like trying to recall the name of a high-school friend. The harder you work, the deeper the loss of memory. It's at the point that you are concentrating on an utterly unrelated task that the name returns.

A choice attitude toward openness is best expressed by the psalmist:

> Search me, O God, and know my heart;
> Try me and know my anxious thoughts;
> And see if there be any hurtful way in me,
> And lead me in the everlasting way.
> (Psalm 139:23-24, NASB)

Openness is similar to a beggar whose hands are lifted, humble, hungry, and expectant. Openness is not merely a state of passive receptivity, expressed with the attitude of, "Well, I'm open. If God wants me to see something, then He can sure drop it in my lap." Neither is openness a demanding attitude. *Openness is the hunger to know coupled with the humbleness to wait.* It is a precondition for the return of memories, even when the memories are said to be unwanted.

I've worked with countless men and women who feel as if the memories have a life of their own; the memories intrude at their whim and control the world. The fact is, however, that the memory would never have returned unless, at some level, it was desired. In spite of the victim's inevitable ambivalence about recalling painful events, the return of any memory is a byproduct of a desire to address the past. The openness that prompts the memory's return, however, cannot be regulated by a mere, conscious act of the will. Memories do not normally return the moment we've prayed for God to search our heart. His ways are far more autonomous and mysterious than a light switch.

Curiosity is similar to childlike exploration. A child senses his way through life, smelling, tasting, and touching his world to learn about his place in the universe. A curious person inquires and ponders, without frantically trying to put everything into a well-grooved cubbyhole. The person who has been abused must be willing to listen, reflect, and ponder the data of her life. The process is not like an intense scramble through her purse looking for her keys; rather, it is the progressive sensing and touching of her inner and outer world as she learns her place in the universe.

Vigilance is similar to the prepared alertness of a mother who walks with her young child across a busy street. The mother is not so oriented to her child that she loses sight of the traffic, nor so aware of the cars that she forgets her child. Vigilance is a mind-set of preparation ("I am equipped to grapple with whatever occurs") and anticipation ("I am looking for something to occur"). Obsessiveness distorts perception and shuts down the return of past memories. Openness unlocks the door, curiosity opens the door, and vigilance awaits what will enter.

Facing with honesty the internal damage can be summarized as facing the horror of being a victim. Victimization, when properly faced, directs the focus toward the external damage.

THE EXTERNAL DAMAGE

The external damage of sexual abuse reveals both the victim's assaulted dignity (victimization) and the perpetrator's self-protective depravity (agency). Many Christian professionals argue that the "coping" or "survival" behaviors a person uses in adulthood to deal with the past abuse are to be "honored" and not exposed as sinful or illegitimate. No option was available to the young victim other than survival, so she need not examine her current coping behaviors too closely. The important thing is to face the ineffectiveness of past survival behaviors and, in her own time and space, begin to experiment with new, more positive trusting behaviors.

The argument makes sense and seems reasonable. But there is one flaw: Sin is sin. A child finds ways to protect or numb herself from the ravages of victimization, and her "coping" behaviors are not to be judged. But when, as an adult, she allows these behaviors to continue in a way that keeps her from deeply entering into relationship with those she is called to love, she is no longer simply "coping" in a legitimate way. She is violating God's highest commandments. Sin that is ignored or denied lingers like an untreated infection. It drains the soul of joy and robs the sinner of relief. In turn, the soul requires more energy to sustain its activities, while ignoring the brooding infection.

The plea for understanding, if satisfied, is never as sweet as the grace given in response to the cry for forgiveness. It would be a grave error to imply, however, that a desire for "understanding" is illegitimate. The abuse victim who is committed to growing will be unable to quickly alter her current self-protective patterns at will once she has begun to face the internal damage. She will occasionally stumble and fall on the long climb to maturity. She does not need a "friend" who constantly harps on her style of relating or incessantly points out her self-protective distance. One abuse survivor told me about her husband who came to my sexual-abuse seminar. She sadly reported: "Now that he has a little knowledge under his belt, he thinks he must be my conscience by pointing out all my faults." Nothing could make me sadder than to think my teaching might be adding salt to the already wounded heart. Repentance and forgiveness are the pinnacles of the journey, but a weary traveler cannot continue without a cup of cold water—rich understanding given from the kind hearts of those she cares about.

As she climbs toward the goal with the support of caring friends, honesty requires that the victim recognize her external damage and face the form, function, and failure of her current self-protective style of relating as a result of the past abuse.

The *form* of self-protection is seen in a specific style of relating—such as the Good Girl, Tough Girl, or Party Girl. As mentioned before, no one fits one type all the time, every time. It is far more important to ask, "When and with whom am I a

Good Girl, Tough Girl, or Party Girl? When or at what points of my life have I lost my voice, turned a cold shoulder, or seduced an unwitting victim?"

Honesty about the form of self-protection also helps the victim see the small choices of life from a larger vantage point. For example, is a single woman's choice never to buy sensual lingerie a judicious use of finances, or a refusal to be alive as a woman? Is the choice never to say to one's husband, "You get the phone!" a choice to serve him, or a fear-based withdrawal of involvement? Those questions are nearly impossible to answer well without having a larger perspective on one's style of relating. Once that perspective is present, however, the victim can face the specifics of her pattern with growing sensitivity and wisdom.

The function of self-protection must be seen in light of both dignity and depravity. The victim, at age nine, who learned to tune out the abuse by staring at a spot on the wall, must not be told with an insensitive snarl that her choice was self-protective and wrong. I affirm her choice to survive. I am proud that she found a way to minimize the damage and survive to the next day.

Honesty, however, acknowledges that her adult adaptation of the child pattern is an outworking of her depravity, not her dignity. When, as an adult, she protects herself in relationship by tuning out, stiffening, detaching, or fleeing from a connection between herself and another that deepens the potential for intense enjoyment (and thus vulnerability), she does more than assure her own survival. She sins against another and dismisses God's right to use her as His instrument of love and grace in the world.

When a redeemed heart faces its bold commitment to autonomy and rebellion, subtle as it may be, change begins to occur. For example, it is not possible to glide as easily through an encounter as a Good Girl once that pattern of relating is exposed as self-serving.

Opening the door to the function of self-protective behavior naturally exposes its failure. Honesty requires entering the decaying and musty parlor of death. No one likes to frolic in a funeral parlor, nor idly tarry in a morgue. Then why is it better to be in the house of mourning than a house of rejoicing? The answer is that a house of death strips away pretense and clarifies the real purpose in living life. To face the failure of self-protection is to enter into the regret, sorrow, and shame of lighting our own fire. It is acknowledging the result of a self-protective lifestyle "to lie down in torment" and grieving the loss of what might have been as well as the damage of what was. Honesty will force a victim to face the fact that she never had a childhood, nor a safe, warm world. At the same time, it will expose the self-protective means she has used in adulthood to minimize her past pain as well as give her insights into her hungry, enraged heart.

I spoke to one woman who could not bear the fact that she was hated by her three children. She had been a ferocious Tough Girl who had both indebted and alienated her kids by her acts of brittle, self-centered, sacrificial service. She could see that she was arrogant, angry, and alone, but she would not face the agonizing fact that she could not recover the lost years or reengage her children by more acts of kindness. She hated herself and hated the abuser who caused the toughness and coldness of her soul. She hated her failure to redeem her relationships, and she wouldn't admit her helplessness in the face of the damage she had perpetrated. It is quite possible to hate oneself for a failure (self-contempt) without ever facing the consequences, shame, and sorrow of the sin (conviction).

THE PROCESS OF HONESTY

If a person chooses to face humbly and courageously the internal and external results of an abusive past, what is involved in the process? The answer comes close to what most readers have been waiting for since the first page of the introduction: a guide to what to do. Unfortunately, even this guide to honesty lacks a step-by-step formula. However, I do believe it is possible to outline a path that needs to be followed, even if the specific steps are unclear. The process involves openness, priming the pump, listening to the data, and drawing logical connections from the data.

Openness

Openness is involved whenever a victim's memories return and she acknowledges past sexual abuse. For most people the eruption of the past does not feel like the choice of an open and willing heart. It seems to just happen. Actually, however, the choice to face the past abuse is a response to the quiet promptings of the Spirit. The victim feels drawn and nudged, if not shoved, into facing the abuse. The memories require a response. The response must, at some point, involve a conscious choice to acknowledge the truth of the memories or the intuition of past abuse.

A second choice must be made to deal with the abuse. Ambivalence is to be expected, but to the degree it dominates the process, change will be hit and miss. A major turning point is reached when a man or woman says, "I feel shaky about moving into the areas of my life that feel both dead and painful, but I know I cannot settle for life as it has been. I want to deal with the abuse." Openness as an articulated desire must not be required or rushed. It will occur as the person lingers between denial and hope. One can only postpone birth so long, and it is unwise to push before the right time.

Priming the Pump

Old pumps had to be primed to draw water from the well. The process of priming the pump is active and purposeful. Water does not pour forth unless effort is exerted. In a similar way, honesty does not bring forth its benefits unless it is active and purposeful.

"Priming the pump" involves the spiritual disciplines of prayer, fasting, and reading the Bible. Prayer expresses the deep hunger for intimate relationship with God; fasting exposes the soul to its emptiness and the temporal shallowness of all earthly satisfaction; the Word of God feeds the soul and satisfies the hunger like no other bread can do.

The pursuit of honesty without active openness will set the heart on a path that may evoke honest reflection, but will not carry it toward the deepest issues of the self. It is not my intent to describe how to execute each discipline, as much as to identify the benefits of active honesty in regard to sexual abuse.

Prayer

In a word, prayer is conversation—a human-divine interaction that is our opportunity to face God as a son or daughter whose presence is welcome and desired. Prayer begins with the assumption that the infinite, all-knowing God knows every thought and intent of the heart before it is conceived or spoken. Prayer does not inform God; rather, it draws us into His presence and invites Him into our life. Prayer is involvement through the spoken word. In that sense, prayer of any kind and about any subject delights God's heart. The Lord desires for us to want Him, adore Him, thank Him, need Him, love Him. To ask God to reveal, confirm, instruct, guide, heal, bless, convict, or comfort, invites Him to enter our situation and accomplish what He desires. Prayer opens the door to the unacknowledged anger, sorrow, and hunger of our soul.

I always recommend that an abuse victim begin praying aloud, on walks, in quiet places where the conversation cannot be overheard or interrupted. Prayer should be an honest expression of what she feels, thinks, and wants in relationship with God and others. It is an invitation to the Holy Spirit to bring to mind whatever He desires to make known, in whatever way He chooses to reveal. It is an invitation to reestablish a relationship that has often been ignored or spurned—albeit, subtly—for years. It is the acknowledgment of hunger and desire for a closer relationship with God.

Fasting

Fasting is the choice to put aside legitimate satisfaction, for a time, to concentrate on a more pressing spiritual pursuit. It is not merely an abstaining from pleasure, though the absence sets into play an awareness of our gnawing dependence on temporal satisfaction. It is not simply an exercise in self-control, though it does solidify our resolve to pursue a calling higher than comfort.

Fasting is an expression of single-minded intention to pursue experiential knowledge of God.

I often encourage the abuse victim to set aside times during the month when a fast can be joined with a significant period of silence in a retreat to a favorite quiet spot to read, write, or simply sit and meditate. A fast opens the soul to the hunger that so often is satiated by the whims of the world. A fast begins the process of removing false satisfaction.

Reading the Bible
While prayer invites exposure and fasting intensifies hunger, study of the Word exposes, awakens, and ultimately satisfies the heart by taking it into the mind of God. The Scriptures orient the heart to ask the questions that are of greatest concern to God. He asked Adam after the Fall: "Where are you, Adam?" He asked Cain: "Why has your countenance fallen?" In both cases, God pursued the central issue that broke His child's relationship with others and Himself. With Adam it was shame; with Cain, rage. The Word of God searches us and probes the thoughts and intentions of our heart (Hebrews 4:12-13).

Listening to the Data and Drawing Logical Connections
Listening to the data that is gained through prayer, fasting, and study of the Bible involves quiet attention and meditation. Learning is a process—a slow, at times torturous, inch-by-inch grasping of what is to be known. One woman I worked with told me about three memories: her father standing before her naked, herself sitting uncomfortably on his lap, and rough play with him and her sisters. The memories were slow in coming. As the weeks passed, she finally sensed a connection between the three distinct memories, though she could not recall a specific event. She sensed that she was forced to sit on his lap when he was naked and play rough. She did not recall actual contact, but the utterly inappropriate, highly suggestive behavior on his part must be considered a sexually abusive interaction. Pondering, journal writing, and talking with a counselor and trusted friends opened the door to the data that was central to her process of change.

Pondering

Pondering is similar to the process of a cow chewing her cud. The slow, grinding absorption of facts turns the grass into the raw material that eventually produces milk. Pondering an event—by recalling what you wore, what you were doing, what you said, how you dealt with the interaction, what occurred after the event ended—opens the mind to details that are often central to understanding the internal and external damage of abuse.

One woman brought me a photo album of pictures taken when she was a child. Her face was sweet and gentle in one picture and then tight and vacant in another. What had transpired between the two pictures was rape perpetrated by a preschool teacher. She took the pictures and pondered the two expressions, the two very different little girls. Memories poured back that were powerful and illuminating. They helped her see the patterns of the past and exposed the path of the present. She was a vacant Good Girl, pleasant but distant. The more she pondered the picture, the more connections she made to her self-protective patterns with her friends, counselor, and husband. Pondering looks at a memory, picture, or fact from countless perspectives in order to grasp its meaning.

Journal Writing

Research and experience has demonstrated that writing—placing the facts and feelings of an event into written words—solidifies the experience and allows it to be more real. I recall sitting at my computer after facing the fact that I had been abused and writing over and over again this sentence: "I have been abused and I feel sick." I felt both numb and strangely alive. The words were a witness that I could erase, but they faced me as evidence that I could not deny.

Much has been written about how to journal and about what questions and issues to address. My only suggestion is to begin. It is better to ramble incoherently on paper than to spin the wheels of one's brain in endless cycles of confusion. I have found that the self-discipline of writing eventually forces me to put on paper the essence of my struggle, whereas when I sit and obsess in mental isolation I endlessly pass the same point until I quit in frustration or boredom, resolving nothing and learning little.

Talking to Others

Conversation with fellow travelers is one of the best means to evaluate which route to take and what to look for on the way. Talking to others can easily be a substitute for quiet reflection, prayer, and Spirit-guided insights, but even with the benefits of the Spirit and the means of spiritual discipline, we are not meant to deal with our pain alone. If we are to learn, we must talk to other human beings.

Conversation requires honesty and risk-taking as we expose the past, our shame, and our sin. I believe that the issues of abuse were never meant to be addressed in isolation. It is advantageous to find at least one other person to talk to about the past, the memories, the internal wound, and the self-protective patterns of the present. In most cases, I further recommend involvement with a group of fellow travelers who are progressing toward the same objective: maturity. In a group, reality testing, defenses, and wounds can be dealt with in an environment of safety and with people of like mind and experience. Conversation has a unique way of raising the past, exposing the present, and opening the door to the possibility of change.

I recommend that you search high and low, pray and ponder, until you find a person who is neither judgmental and expecting rapid change, nor condescendingly sympathetic and concerned only with your victimization. Trust is neither something to expect nor to give too quickly; therefore, listen to your intution, your hunch as to a person's capacity and willingness to hear.

Honesty opens the door to the heart. Openness is essential if the past is to be recovered. A willingness to pursue God is essential if the data is to be used in a way that produces fruit. If honesty opens the door, repentance invites God to bring about dramatic change.

TWELVE

Repentance

The process of change begins with honesty, which is a form of repentance. Repentance is an about-face movement from denial and rebellion to truth and surrender — from death to life.

In the beginning, honestly facing the characteristic lies and denial associated with sexual abuse usually intensifies the experience of victimization. For the first time, memories return that rip apart the pretense of a happy childhood or a loving family. Not only is the perpetrator faced as wicked, but other family members are seen as aiding the abuser by their complicitly, denial, or minimization of the harm. Often the abuse victim realizes that the same patterns that allowed the abuse to occur and go unaddressed are equally operative in her life today. Victimization is usually not only an event in the past; in most cases, it is an ongoing, day-by-day experience.

The return of horrific memories, the exposure of past and current betrayal, the acknowledgment of internal damage, the recognition of current self-protective, destructive patterns — all are nearly overwhelming. Thankfully, the process of absorbing the data is slow and progressive, rather than sudden and final. Nevertheless, the process is disruptive and tumultuous. It is impossible to say what the internal process will be like for the honest abuse victim, but a general path that many experience may serve as a guide.

First, the process of honesty opens the door to stunned acknowledgment. The initial shock is somewhat analogous to physical shock. Reality is seen, but in slow motion. The observer sees the awful truth, frame by frame, as a known but distant memory. Often the unreal, distant memories arrive through current disappointment in a relationship. A birthday forgotten or the inability to receive a compliment shakes the foundation of current coping strategies. The pretense that the past is the past and the present is satisfying begins to crumble in the face of deepened hunger and discontent.

Disappointment often turns into rage. Rage at the hypocrisy of the family. Rage at the idiotic illusion of the good life. Rage at the failures of those who claim to love, but seem to adore only the image of being loving. *Rage is the thrashing of the soul when it fully awakens from the nightmare lie.*

Rage may be directed first and foremost toward the self. The self-contempt infused through the past abuse may come to the surface with a vengeance, though the victim will often direct some of the rage toward the abuser, family, friends, or spouse. Because the rage is in fact there, the process of sanctification will include facing its ferocious intensity. Growth never allows pretending. Recovering the anger, however—and this must be said strongly—is not the cure. It may feel good, freeing, and energetic to face one's rage, but simply owning anger is not maturity. No matter how alive the soul feels in the midst of recovered anger, rage does not heal the wound or satisfy the soul. In most cases, the rage will lead only to deepened despair.

Despair, or a fatalistic, who-cares emptiness, is the pendulum swing from honesty to a second round of deceit. The question that surfaces—now far deeper than during the first round—is, "What use is there in dealing with reality, or God, or my pain, or those who harm me, or my sin?" Once her emptiness overtakes the initial experience of disappointment and rage, the victim must face a major crossroad. The path taken is either toward more radical denial and plastic functioning or toward deep change through repentance. If honesty is the first phase of the healing process that is experienced with shock, pain, and anger, then repentance is the second phase that is entered through sadness, grief, and sorrow.

Sorrow alters the damage of the past and present. The process of honest grief over the damage of the abuse and one's autonomous response to it integrates the past into the present without carrying over the burden of hardness and vengeance. Sorrow begins to melt the victim's calloused hatred toward herself and others.

Not all weeping is either restorative or repentant. Grief may permit deeper acknowledgment of past pain and restore a greater sense of wholeness, but it may equally strengthen the resolve never to be hurt again.

Grief may lead to two separate routes: the path of *sorrow unto life* and the path of *sorrow unto death*. One route involves a re-owning of lost parts of the soul for the purpose of humbly crying out to God with all that we are for grace and strength to live the God-glorifying, other-centered life. The second is a reclaiming of lost parts of the soul for the purpose of developing a case against the abuser, a wicked world, and ultimately against a God who did not intervene—a case that supports our right to exist independently of a disappointing, cruel world and the God whose eternal Kingdom will replace it. The difference in the paths of sorrow is found in a contrast between repentance and penance.

WHAT IS REPENTANCE?

Before defining repentance, let me state two important points. First, the abuse victim is never called by God to repent about the past abuse. Many victims have anguished before God, crying out for forgiveness for what occurred or for what they experienced—things that are in no way their fault. Second, repentance is a surprising, wholly unexpected experience that is rarely, if ever, a simple choice of the will to do right and not do wrong. Repentance is poorly understood and rarely enjoyed.

It is not necessarily transforming for those who labor to simply do right. For that reason, we must clearly define what is and is not repentance.

Repentance is *an internal shift in our perceived source of life.* It is recognizing that our self-protective means to avoiding hurt have not ushered us into real living (the reckless abandon to God that ultimately leads to a deep sense of wholeness and joy) or to purposeful, powerful relating. Repentance is the process of deeply acknowledging the supreme call to love, which is violated at every moment, in every relationship — a law that applies even to those who have been heinously victimized. The law of love removes excuses. The pain of past abuse does not justify unloving self-protection in the present. The damage the victim does to others by her failure to love God and neighbor with all her being deserves judgment — that is, the just penalty of death and separation from God.

The weight of the holy requirement of perfect, unbroken love is more than any person, except Jesus Christ, can bear. Love silences explanation, penetrates excuses, and humbles the heart, preparing that heart to be captured by the gospel of grace. Ultimately, repentance is a hungry, broken return to God.

One of the greatest pictures of repentance is found in the story of the prodigal son (Luke 15:11-32), which makes several points about the coming-home process. First, repentance begins in the belly. A return to God the Father begins with the recognition that sin is degrading. As the rebellious son sat slumped in a pigpen, he had to face that eating the food fed to pigs was beneath a Hebrew, who would not even eat pork, let alone pig slop. Living the way he was, independent of his father, was unbecoming and distasteful. In one sense, repentance begins with the recognition (which may at first sound selfish), "I am hungry, and there's something right about wanting better. I was built for the food fed to the son or daughter of a King, yet I am eating refuse."

Repentance often begins with dissatisfaction. The prodigal son admitted that even the least in his father's household ate well, and he was a fool not to return. It takes profound humility to come to one's senses and admit what is true: "I am eating garbage. Others are happy; I am not happy. I am not staying here. I'd rather risk untold shame, facing rejection from my father and taking the lowliest position in my father's house, than stay in this muck." It takes brokenness of soul to move back toward the Father, admitting what is true. Humility sometimes begins with seeing that our efforts to make life work have taken us to the pigpen. And worse, nothing we've done is excusable. Seizing our inheritance prematurely was not only stupid, it reflects our sinful commitment to preserve our own life.

Notice the response of the prodigal's father to his son's return. He weeps, restores, and celebrates. The father is a fool, at least a fool in the eyes of his older son, and undoubtedly in the eyes of his community. The father likely had experienced ridicule and shame for allowing his son to leave with a large portion of the family wealth. He must have felt pressure either to turn his back on his child, or at least to require a period of penance before allowing his boy to return to the family table. Instead, the father threw a party, a public spectacle that restored full rights and privileges to the errant son. The father did not even listen to the penitent litany the son rehearsed before he came into the father's presence. Repentance is met with full restoration and celebration.

The contrast of such a response of life is the reaction of death, exhibited by the older son. He viewed the father as a stringent taskmaster who could be pleased only by discipline, obedience, and a martyr's denial. He blamed the father for never giving him a party. The father's response indicated that a party was all his for the asking, but the older son never humbled himself to ask. The tragedy is that the older son actually despised the father more than the young prodigal. The prodigal, at least, trusted the father's goodness enough to ask for the money in the first place and to return in hunger once it was gone. The older brother asked for nothing and, in arrogant self-justification, chose to avoid the party to prove he was more righteous than the father. Jesus told the story to shatter the presumptive facade of the righteous Pharisees; in so doing He tears away our false assumptions about what pleases God.

What is repentance? Although difficult to define, *repentance involves the response of humble hunger, bold movement, and wild celebration when faced with the reality of our fallen state and the grace of God.* The Father wants us to be hungry and dissatisfied with our pigpen cuisine. He wants us to return in absolute dependence and dine on the fatted calf.

Repentance flows from the energy of being stunned, silent, and without excuse for the harm we've done to ourselves and others and for breaking the heart of God. It includes a hunger-based refusal to wallow in anything that makes us less human, strips anyone of his dignity, or damages our relationship with the Lord.

A caution is in order for the person who is ready to come alive. It is right to refuse the defensive method of numbing one's soul to cope with pain. It is right to come alive with all that we are, to proclaim the fullness of our existence as a man or woman who longs for the relationship and impact we were designed to enjoy. It is right to abandon self-protective maneuvering in a way that requires others to take us into account. But, as we move in this good direction, we approach a line which if crossed takes us into a subtle humanism where proclaiming our existence becomes the point of our existence.

Biblical repentance always leads us toward coming alive for the explicit purpose of having more to give to others for their well-being and to God for His glory. Without a radical commitment to seeing our entire existence as wrapped up in furthering God's purpose in other people's lives, recovering our souls can strengthen our tendency to think more about all that happens within and to require that others treat us with tenderness and respect. Longing for love from others is a beautiful part of our dignity as image bearers, but it is self-centered to recognize our existence in a way that makes our longing for involvement the most important reality of life. *The point of living is giving, not getting.* By God's grace, we've already received what we long for but do not deserve. Now we are privileged to enter into the very nature of ultimate reality: other-centered relating. Repentance moves us in that direction.

REPENTANCE VERSUS PENANCE

What is the difference between true repentance and what might be called "penance"? *True repentance admits helplessness; penance presumes the ability to make amends on one's own.* Repentance is a humble declaration of longing; penance is a self-abasing declaration of arrogance. The arrogance (and rage) of penance, similar to the pride of the prodigal's older brother, assumes that sin is not that awful; therefore, it can be resolved by right behavior. The father is a slave driver with no heart, who cares only about himself; therefore he can be placated by returning to him with interest what was originally his due. *Penance is a payback; repentance is a plea for mercy.*

The effects of repentance and penance are entirely different. Repentance softens; penance hardens. Repentance creates a willingness to be humbled. The person who knows the joy of being lifted up by God is willing to transform laughter into mourning and joy into gloom in order to humble herself before the Lord (James 4:8-10). If she knows that forfeiting her self-centered agenda opens the door to life, then she can view trials of various kinds as friends and not enemies (Romans 5:3-5, James 1:2-4). Repentance takes away her terror of shame because her soul has already admitted it is naked, wanting, and undeserving. In being accepted as a sinner, she has nothing to hide or fear; therefore, she is free to love others without fear of their response or rejection (Luke 7:47). Being restored to the Father plants her hope firmly in His goodness and the coming day of perfect justice and union with Him for eternity. She realizes that not even death can destroy her; she need not fear obliteration. Therefore, she is free to live passionately and boldly because she knows that whatever injustice is served her on the path to loving others will one day be vindicated.

Penance, in contrast, deepens the victim's hardness. Once she's paid for her sin, the sin must be canceled; therefore, no one has a right to require more from her. Many perpetrators of abuse, who admit their sin, feel as if the past should be dropped and life lived only in the present. I've heard abusers say, "I've repented, but she won't let the thing drop. The burden to change is on her, not me." The proof of penance is a hardness (though it may come with violent tears of self-pity) that refuses to be humbled by dealing with the damage of the past.

A second characteristic of repentance is a sorrow that glows with passion, energy, and other-centeredness. The apostle Paul confronted the sin of the Corinthians and wounded their arrogance (2 Corinthians 7:11-13). He was sorrowful to have caused them pain, but thrilled about their repentant response. Their godly sorrow over their sin produced an increase in earnestness, eagerness, indignation, and longing for justice. They pursued change out of conviction of wrong, not out of self-contempt. Contempt (self- or other-centered) is the energy behind penance. It produces a sense of being downtrodden and worthless and leads eventually to rage and murderous hatred. The result is an unredemptive sorrow that is full of self-pity and despair.

Genuine conviction of sin, on the other hand, leads to a softening of the heart that dispels other-centered contempt in the wake of the recognition that we are no better, at core, than those who have abused us. *Self-contempt is Satan's counterfeit for true conviction.* Contempt attacks the perceived source of the problem to gain control and then attempts to regain relationship with others and God through penitent deeds. Conviction humbly recognizes the need for grace and embraces a sorrow that leads to life and sacrificial love.

A sorrow unto life is a merger of the bitterness that arises from breaking God's heart and the sweet joy of being restored to His embrace. The bitter heartache of wounding the heart of God and the pleasure of dining in His presence, welcome and wanted, is unlike any other emotion. Repentance decreases shame, increases passion, and welcomes restoration. Penance increases contempt, decreases life, and resists involvement.

REPENTANCE AND THE SEXUAL-ABUSE VICTIM

What will repentance look like for the abused man or woman? It will involve a turning from death and a movement toward life in the internal and external arenas of life. In reality, it is impossible to truly separate the internal and external. All true internal change will bring about the clarity, desire, and energy to make external changes in behavior. And all truly repentant external changes will be undergirded by substantial shifts in the heart. Nevertheless, for the sake of description, we will look separately at each aspect.

The internal shift will involve at least three elements: (1) a refusal to be dead, (2) a refusal to mistrust, and (3) a refusal to despise passion. Each refusal must finally be energized by a realization that offering all that we are in the service of others is the essence of life.

The external shift will look different for each individual, but it will be characterized by an active humility before God and a deepened commitment to vulnerable involvement with others.

THE INTERNAL SHIFTS OF REPENTANCE

A Refusal to Be Dead

To live with a dead soul makes deep sense to an abuse victim. It seems natural and reasonable. It numbs the ravages of the past abuse, it quiets the demons of contempt, and it simplifies current relationships by destroying the desire for more.

Deadness, however, is the choice to rob others of our God-given humanness. It dehumanizes relationships, making the response to others robotic and mechanical. Most of all, it is an assault against the Creator God, who is the Author of life. To live as a dead being before the living God is to say that death is preferable to life with Him. In essence, the choice to be dead is the choice to turn one's back on the Author of life, to deny Him the opportunity to touch our lives deeply and to use us fully according to His good purposes.

The refusal to be dead is the choice to admit and embrace our existence: "I am not a shadow, a quiet ghost, a substanceless vapor. I am a person who can enjoy and be enjoyed by God and who can relate to others in a way that draws them to an enjoyable relationship with God." It is the recognition that nerve endings exist in the soul as well as in the body and that they are good. A victim refuses to be dead when she gives herself permission to acknowledge and feel the reality of both past and present.

This aspect of repentance—the choice to be alive for the sake of others—does not feel, in most instances, like a pious, religious event. In most cases, it does not begin with a ritualistic statement of, "Dear Lord, I confess my sin of deadening my soul." It begins as a simple acknowledgment of fact ("I am dead") and is furthered when conscious choice is made to reject death ("I will not deaden myself with this bowl of ice cream"). It is brought forth kicking and screaming as a newborn baby when a dramatic moment (as big as the choice to have an affair or as apparently small as the choice to buy a new dress) is used by God to present the option of life or death.

A refusal to be dead will evoke sadness initially. Sadness, in most cases, is the experience of disappointment with oneself or others. A woman who refuses to be dead will feel and desire—and inevitably experience hurt. When she is disappointed, however, she will not resort to heart-numbing strategies. She will not rationalize or excuse a hurtful phone call. She will not blame herself when an exchange of pleasantries replaces the more substantial interaction she allowed herself to desire. The acknowledgment that it is unbecoming and unworthy to be dead will free her soul to face sadness, grief, and sorrow—and ultimately, joy.

These three words—sadness, grief, and sorrow—often are viewed as synonyms. To a large extent, the three overlap in meaning, but there are a few subtle differences that help explain the process of repentance.

Briefly, *sadness* is an experience of disappointment. Usually, it is focused on current loss with regard to unmet hopes and expectations. If a friend forgets our birthday, we may experience sad feelings. The feelings are often temporary, because the loss was usually not that severe and is often easily filled.

Grief, on the other hand, is an intensified experience of sadness involving the loss of something deeply important that cannot be regained or replaced. The death of a child or the loss of a spouse through divorce cannot be made up for by a change of friends or activities.

Sorrow accepts sadness and grief but adds a new dimension: recognition of damage done to others. Sorrow over the harmful impact of one's life on others is a sorrow unto life. It is the core of repentance. Biblical sorrow acknowledges and moves beyond the loss of oneself and enters the wounds in others, perpetrated by one's own capacity to abuse through defensive or hostile behaviors.

Sadness opens the heart to what was meant to be and is not. *Grief* opens the heart to what was not meant to be and is. *Sorrow* breaks the heart as it exposes the damage we've done to others as a result of our unwillingness to rely solely on the grace and truth of God.

For example, many abuse victims begin the process of repentance, without even realizing it, when they acknowledge hurt and sadness in current relationships. The choice to groan inwardly—that is, face the effects of living in a fallen world—opens the heart to a desire for a better life. The choice to feel sad is neither selfish nor sinful. It embraces what is true, but it is not sufficient to produce redemptive change. Grief is a necessary next step.

Many abuse victims lost their childhood and adolescence. They never learned to enjoy a sense of being special, uniquely loved, and purely enjoyed. Their sense of themselves was significantly twisted by the experience of powerlessness and despair. No matter what they do to replace the inaccurate images of the past with more biblical images, the loss of a childhood, the loss of innocent, unself-conscious enjoyment of themselves and others cannot be replaced, or recovered through surrogate parents or therapy.

Grief does not regain what is lost, but it breaks the tendency to resort to self-hatred to resolve the anguish of the loss. Grief exposes the hardness of the contemptuous heart and replaces it with supple tenderness and vulnerability.

I asked an abused friend who hates herself for being uncomfortable in the presence of people (especially men) what she would do if my nine-year-old daughter withdrew from her:

Would she warmly pursue her, or ignore her in disgust? If she saw my little girl cry, would she angrily accuse her of wanting attention, or would she gently hold her while she wept? Of course, she said, she would pursue my child without disgust or anger; but she would never allow herself to want someone to pursue her without feeling disgust for herself. Her alive heart felt grief over her capacity to be tender toward others but not toward herself. The difference between how she would deal with my daughter and herself allowed her to weep over her sin of contempt for the first time.

Repentance involves admitting we were victims who were unrighteously deprived of life. From this juncture, however, we have two distinctly different paths from which to choose. The path of sorrow unto death faces grief and in turn vows: "Never again. I have a right to life, and I will never be deprived again." This approach to grief actually exchanges self-contempt for even deeper other-centered contempt. The second route, sorrow unto life, moves from grief over our own victimization to an acknowledgment of the damage we have done to others as a result of our choice to live dead and dormant. A biblical path to handling life always steers us away from self-centeredness and reflects the foundational Christian ethic of loving others for their sake.

A Refusal to Mistrust

A refusal to be dead sets the stage to deal with a refusal to mistrust. Repentance in the area of trust is difficult to explain. The opposite of mistrust would naturally seem to be trust. Therefore, it might seem that an abuse victim ought to trust those whom she currently doubts or suspects of harm. Nothing could be further from the truth. The problem with mistrust is that many persons are not worthy of trust, or at least deep trust; therefore, to encourage an abuse victim to trust is tantamount to asking her to more deeply doubt her intuition and to open herself to more abuse.

The opposite of mistrust is not trust, but *care*. When we view a person with mistrust, it is as if their life no longer matters. We "write them off." Mistrust prejudges their every word and deed so that they cannot ever reach our heart. A protective shield descends whenever we're around them, and relationship is severed.

To review comments made earlier, boundary building often encourages us to harden our heart so that care, or a receptivity to relationship, is lost. Repentance, or a refusal to mistrust, reengages the God-given desire to care, to be kind, to comfort, and to be concerned about the temporal and eternal destiny of those who have harmed us.

A refusal to mistrust, however, is neither gullible nor stupid. It looks at evidence, evaluates the past, and makes decisions about trust based on conclusions reached through deductive reasoning. The Lord Jesus commands us to be "wise as serpents and innocent as doves" (Matthew 10:16). Evidence may force a woman to see that her spouse is an enemy, one who is bent on doing harm. A Good Girl may begin to face evidence that compels her to doubt the word of a good friend. Is that repentance—a refusal to mistrust? I would say absolutely yes. Her insipid, naive trust is not a commitment to care; it is denial designed to alleviate the need to be fully engaged in relationship. An acknowledgment of data that implicates others as untrustworthy can be a renewed commitment to be involved, to care about truth, one's own soul, and the lack of integrity in another. Trust is conditional; however, care is not. To care is to use all that we are for the good of others while not walling off the deep parts of our soul. By not writing off others, we tenderly and strongly offer relationship.

Offering relationship must be viewed from the vantage point of the heart, not merely from the standpoint of behavior. There are certain behaviors that may look highly relational yet are not, as well as those that appear nonrelational yet are ultimately caring. For example, a Good Girl who bakes a cake for her abuser may be hiding behind her culinary gifts, covering over his sin and her feelings of her "kindness." If she were to thrust the cake in his face, few would argue that she has loved him well. In the majority of cases, cake throwing is likely unloving. But observing her behavior alone will not reveal her heart's intent. In other words, tender and strong gifts of the heart will be those that uniquely touch the lives of others, for their ultimate good.

The process toward rich caring begins with sadness. Sadness acknowledges the countless times trust has been betrayed and misused. Every relationship, even the best, involves betrayal and misuse. One abused woman would not admit how devastating it was to her that her husband was insensitive and angry. Her defense was that he was pressured and overworked. A refusal to mistrust involved opening her heart to how deeply she cared about his betrayal. It was devastating, because she profoundly wanted him to be tender and strong.

Grief intensifies the sadness by facing the irretrievable loss. The abuse victim will never be able to relax fully in another's care without at least a hint of discomfort and anxiety. Suspiciousness and strains of paranoia will exist as long as her sin nature exists. Grief admits there are scars that can be removed only in heaven. The woman mentioned above had to accept the fact that she would always feel a certain ache whenever she made love to her husband. Although the ache may eventually lose some of its intensity, her loss of a dream for perfect love in a man could not be recovered until heaven.

Sadness and grief will soften the ravages of self-contempt and give way to a deeper sorrow: the sorrow of knowing that by not deeply caring for those she has mistrusted, the victim has committed the same sin of betrayal that, in essence, was committed against her. There is sorrow in facing the fact that we have given another a taste of harm that once was such a bitter meal for us.

The deepest harm of mistrust is perpetrated against God. God is seen as a games player, a cosmic sadist who twists the screws of pleasure to entice and pain to frustrate His victims. God is someone to placate and ignore or disdainfully despise. The one who does not care is indifferent. She is the kind of person Jesus described as neither hot or cold:

"I know your deeds, that you are neither cold nor hot. I wish you were either one or the other! So, because you are lukewarm—neither hot nor cold—I am about to spit you out of my mouth." (Revelation 3:15-16)

Lukewarm indifference ("I just don't care") is more destructive to relationship than hatred.

Sorrow develops as the believer begins to see that her demand for God to prove He cares is a mockery of the Cross. The death of Jesus Christ is sufficient proof of the trustworthiness of the heart of God. Such indifference breaks the heart of the Father, who eagerly awaits the return of the prodigal son and the brokenness of the elder son. When the humble child of faith sees the Father weep rather than retaliate and eagerly wait rather than turn His back, the wellspring of sorrow and passion begins to churn with life.

A Refusal to Despise Passion

Passion, for most abuse victims, is dangerous. Passion is a door that, if opened, may allow rage and lust, violence and promiscuity to pour out like the opening of a Pandora's box. Passion can be defined as *the deep response of the soul to life: the freedom to rejoice and to weep*. One of the most difficult commands to fulfill is to "weep with those who weep and rejoice with those who rejoice" (Romans 12:15). It requires open-hearted, other-centered, reckless involvement. Passion is tasting pleasure with delight, brokenness with tears, and evil with hatred.

A gifted counselor asked me to supervise her work. In one of our interactions I commented on how she uniquely intertwined gentle acceptance and relentless pursuit in her dealings with clients, two qualities not often found together. She first politely thanked me and then over a few minutes turned formal and cool. Something significant had changed in her demeanor and style of interaction. We eventually talked about what had occurred. She acknowledged that she felt initial delight and then terror when I commented on her character. It turned out that she had a significantly unaddressed history of sexual abuse. She literally became nauseous when she received a compliment or felt pleasure.

A refusal to despise passion embraces pain and pleasure—particularly pleasurable arousal of the senses—as God-given, wonderful and desirable. It also embraces the sadness of ambivalence. A fear of passion makes it nearly impossible to receive deep involvement from others. To some extent the abuse victim has lived in a flat, two-dimensional world distant from human touch, tenderness, and ardor. I worked with a woman who admitted with terrible shame that she was more devastated when the family dog died than when her father passed away. She hated herself for feeling pleasure when she thought of romping in the fields with her canine friend. She experienced untold self-contempt in wanting to hold her cat more than her husband. Repentance—a refusal to despise passion—required her to examine this self-contempt when she thought of her dog. Her animals were gifts of God to keep her heart believing in the potential of contact, warmth, and involvement with people. She felt sadness when she considered how many times she had deprived herself of legitimate, God-given passion.

Sadness opens the door to grief—a grief over the loss of unself-conscious spontaneity and unashamed responsiveness to the human touch on soul and body. The loss is permanent on this side of heaven. A child's freedom to cuddle in her daddy's lap with complete confidence and sensual comfort will not be imaginable for the abused person who never experienced it.

Grief, in turn, will yield to the experience of sorrow over defrauding others of passion. The woman who felt more alive with her animals than her husband admitted that all enjoyment, all pleasure, eventually triggered revulsive thoughts about sex. She deprived herself and her husband of the thrill of intimate, physical oneness. In facing how she deprived her husband of intimacy, she was sorely tempted to grind her soul under the millstone of contempt. She felt pressure. In turn, she felt renewed hopelessness, streaks of anger, and disgust. What did it mean for her to repent?

Repentance for her meant to cry out to God for grace so she could admit what was true: she hated sex, her husband, her abuser, her counselor, and God. Crying out in hunger meant not fleeing back into the numb, insipid pressure of dead works. It was a deeply moving point of repentance—a refusal to be dead—for her to admit that God preferred hot or cold passion to the lukewarm pablum of her dutiful obedience. She was alive, but she was a mess.

A refusal to mistrust meant that she could not ignore her husband's irritating demands for sex and his boorish withdrawal when she hinted at her answer. It meant caring enough to say no and then explaining why. As a Good Girl, her explanations in the past had been apologetic and profuse, capped with a hidden rebuke. A repentant explanation, for her, was short, kind, and bold. Repentance required her to put a hold on sex until the relational issues in the marriage were acknowledged, prayed over, and dealt with. She was caring, but still not free to laugh and cry.

A refusal not to despise passion allowed her to admit that she felt arousal in the presence of certain strong men. She hated herself for feeling any arousal. She came to acknowledge, however, that her arousal was both awful and wonderful. Her arousal in the presence of a strong, caring man other than her husband was less than God intended; it was sin. On the other hand, the experience of arousal itself was good and to be enjoyed.

Godly sorrow makes room for bittersweet joy—bitter because we have damaged ourselves and others, and sweet because of the wonder of God's grace and the judgment He spares us.

THE EXTERNAL SHIFTS OF REPENTANCE

The core of all change is internal, but its fruit will be visible, tasteable, and nourishing. What will it involve and what will it look like? Repentance will involve a purposeful, active choice to return to God. In each individual life the external changes will be unique, but a few examples will hint at the basic shifts.

The Good Girl will reclaim her voice with her spouse or friends for the sake of her spouse and friends. Instead of deferring choice to others she will begin to take hold of her desires and preferences by strongly (though not with a shift to Tough-Girl hardness) saying she would prefer not to eat at a certain restaurant.

The Tough Girl will pursue feedback rather than intimidate

those around her into never expressing their anger and hurt. When she gets the feedback, she will acknowledge how hard it is to hear, how easy it is to want to retaliate, and how deeply she wishes she could receive the thoughts with greater warmth and tenderness. She will make the choice not to lash out, even though the desire will be strong.

The Party Girl will choose to return to relationships she has defrauded and acknowledge her tendency to bail out when the storm winds blow or the calm waters swell. She will admit her proclivity to sabotage and take steps to ensure her fidelity. She will deepen her commitment to talk over her dread of relationship and how it shows itself in manipulation.

Repentant behavior will be markedly different between and within each style of relating, so it is impossible to make conclusions about what are the "right" things to do or not do on the road toward change. All that can be said is that change for any style of relating will never involve the choice to pursue sin. A Good Girl can never say that it is growth for her to have an affair. A Tough Girl can't justify lying in order to keep her anger from coming to the surface. A Party Girl can't persevere in a behavior that is enabling another to continue in destructive sin.

The goal is to move away from self-protective patterns, often in what appear to be the most simple and reasonable ways but which are, for many, the most difficult. An act of repentance for a Good Girl may be as "simple" as going shopping for a new dress, taking a long hot bath, or getting a baby-sitter so she can have a day away from the pressures of the family. For a Tough Girl, repentance may involve getting a soothing message, taking unexplained and unneeded days off, or frolicking with a pointless and inane romantic novel. A Party Girl's repentance may involve being quiet at a party without pouting, faithfully returning answering-machine phone calls, and writing to a friend within days of receiving a letter.

Repentance will always have one central quality: *the purposeful movement of a humble, hungry heart toward a God who will receive and lift up.* James states the picture in the most profound and simple words:

REPENTANCE

Wash your hands, you sinners and purify your hearts, you double-minded. Grieve, mourn and wail. Change your laughter to mourning and your joy to gloom. Humble yourselves before the Lord, and he will lift you up. (James 4:8-10)

Repentance is facing what is true: "I am a sinner and double-minded, and I deserve to be separated from God." *It is a shift in perspective as to where life is found.* It is a deep recognition that life comes only to the broken, desperate, dependent heart that longs for God. It is a melting into the warm arms of God, acknowledging the wonder of being received when it would be so understandable to be spurned. It is taking our place at the great feast, eating to our fill, and delighting in the undeserved party being held in honor of our return.

Repentance is a process that is never accomplished once and for all. It is a cyclical, deepening movement that, like a snowball, picks up weight and speed as it rolls. Repentance opens the heart to the bitter taste of sin and the sweet joy of restoration. It clears the senses in a way that exposes depravity and affirms dignity. It awakens our hunger for our Father's embrace and deepens our awareness of His kind involvement. And when we are deeply, truly touched by His love, we will move boldly into the bittersweet privilege of loving others.

THIRTEEN

Bold Love

The process of change involves honesty—an open heart that acknowledges the damage of victimization and reactive self-protection; repentance—a humble heart that enters the damage we have done to ourselves, others, and the Lord; and bold love—a grateful heart that pursues passionate relationship with others.

The sequence from honesty to repentance makes clear that an abused person does not need forgiveness for having experienced powerlessness, betrayal, or ambivalence; she needs forgiveness for turning her soul against life with little thought of serving the deepest well-being of others. Honesty opens the heart to the battle, and repentance softens the ravages of the past abuse. But more is required if life is to be deeply restored. Honesty and repentance are preconditions for life, but love sets the soul free to soar through the damage of the past and the unrequited passion of the present. The sweet fragrance of forgiveness is the energy that propels the damaged man or woman toward the freedom of love.

But what is love? What does it mean for an abused man or woman to love those who do harm—especially the past abuser and the other countless abusers who make up our world? Is it even possible?

WHAT MAKES LOVE POSSIBLE?

The answer to what makes love possible is surprisingly simple: the love of God and the fear of God. The love of God is seen in the cross of Christ. Peter puts the cross at the core of the return to the Father:

> He himself bore our sins in his body on the tree, so that we might die to sins and live for righteousness; by his wounds you have been healed. For you were like sheep going astray, but now you have returned to the Shepherd and Overseer of your souls. (1 Peter 2:24-25)

Christ's willingness to become a curse for our sake so that we would never bear the curse of God is our freedom and joy (Galatians 3:10-14). It is incomprehensible that the God of blessing would curse His own Son for the sake of offering us His gift of restored relationship. The gospel is an astonishment, an unexpected and unnerving intrusion into a fallen world.

But what comfort is the Cross to an abused man or woman? The questions still linger: Where was God when I was abused? Why doesn't He take away the pain, struggle, memories? Why didn't He intervene before I made destructive decisions? The Cross neither resolves nor negates pain. John Stott, in his wonderful book *The Cross of Christ*, states:

> I could never myself believe in God, if it were not for the cross. The only God I believe in is the One Nietzsche ridiculed as "God on the cross." In the real world of pain, how could one worship a God who was immune to it? . . . There is still a question mark against human suffering, but over it we boldly stamp another mark, the cross which symbolizes divine suffering. "The cross of Christ . . . is God's only self-justification in such a world" as ours.[1]

The Cross confuses us when we are certain that cruelty rules the world. It unnerves us when we see no proof of a caring God who is in control of this universe. The Cross does not directly deal with the question of "Why me?" but it sets the stage for a response to an entirely different question: *"Am I loved?"*

The Cross is the proof of the everlasting, sacrificial love of God, but it is more; it is also the evidence of the wrath of God against sin. God is enraged over sin. He is deadly serious about not letting His own creation succumb to its ravages. He is so serious as to place the wages of sin on the perfect Adam, the second Man, as a perfect atonement for human rebellion. The Lamb of God took the righteous judgment we deserved. The Father poured out His wrath on His own Son, who endured the shame of the Cross for the joy that was set before Him (Hebrews 12:2).

How do we, as human beings, find the energy to love? The answer involves the daily intertwining of holy fear of and love for the One who purchased our redemption. The fear of God begins with the conviction that a man reaps what he sows. Paul said, "The one who sows to please his sinful nature, from that nature will reap destruction; the one who sows to please the Spirit, from the Spirit will reap eternal life" (Galatians 6:8). Because of love we come to the Father; because of fear we refrain from sin. When we are gripped by the good news that a just God has spared us death and condemnation and restored us to eternal relationship, we will discover the motivation to love. Our gratitude for the perfect love of a merciful God will propel us toward pouring ourselves out for the sake of others.

WHAT DOES IT MEAN TO LOVE?

Love can be surprising. It can look quite different from what we may expect. Love is not weak, fear-based compliance. Jesus was silent and, some might say, passive on the cross. May it never be said! Peter tells us that "when they hurled their insults at him, he did not retaliate; when he suffered, he made no threats. Instead, he entrusted himself to him who judges justly" (1 Peter 2:23). His quietness reflected His trust in God's righteous judgment, which would, at the right moment, destroy those who opposed His rule. The Father was neither passive nor silent; He was simply waiting for the right moment to pour out His wrath.

Love is not an absence of anger. Unfortunately, Christians have often neutered love by putting it at odds with anger. Love is not inconsistent with a holy hatred; in fact, an absence of right-eous anger makes love anemic and devoid of passion (Romans 12:9). Listen to what it means to be motivated by the fear of God: "To fear the LORD is to hate evil; I hate pride and arrogance, evil behavior and perverse speech" (Proverbs 8:13).

Love also does not minimize or forget past harm. Christians are regularly (and wrongly, I believe) taught to "forgive and forget," to literally forget and no longer feel the pain of the past. God is said to have forgotten our sins (Jeremiah 31:34); therefore, we are told forgiveness equals forgetfulness. The Bible also tells us that God has removed our transgressions from us as far as the East is from the West (Psalm 103:12). Both pictures of forgiveness — forgetfulness and distance — are metaphors that are not to be literally mimicked in our life. Imagine trying to find the spot where the East and West are farthest apart to deposit anoth-er's transgression against us. Literally forgetting the harm done to us would be as difficult as finding that geographical point. The only way to do so would be through unbiblical denial. Obvi-ously, holding on to a memory for the purpose of demanding redress or justifying hateful distance is not biblical either. Biblical forgiveness, however, is not minimization or forgetfulness.

Finally, love is not pious other-centeredness that is devoid of pleasure for the giver. Many Christians feel that if self is involved in a gift of love, then the gift is tainted. We are said to ruin love if we enjoy giving and notice the pleasure in doing so, or if we are disappointed when a gift is not received. Nothing could be further from the truth. Paul ran the race for the prize. He was willing to be poured out in death like a drink offering for the crown of righteousness, which will be his and ours if we have longed for Christ's appearing (2 Timothy 4:6-8). In one sense, all we do is conditioned by the hope for reward. In the same chapter in which Paul waxed eloquent about his future hope, he also lamented the absence of friends, a warm coat, and writing paper (2 Timothy 4:9-13). He was profoundly alive in Christ and still affected by loneliness, persecution, and lack of creature comforts. Love that is so spiritualized that it reflects an absence of humanness is neither spiritual nor human.

WHAT THEN IS LOVE?

Love is essentially a movement of grace to embrace those who have sinned against us (Matthew 5:43-48). It is the offer of restoration to those who have done harm, for the purpose of destroying evil and enhancing life. Love can be defined as *the free gift that voluntarily cancels the debt in order to free the debtor to become what he might be if he experiences the joy of restoration.*

The role of forgiveness in the healing process may seem profoundly difficult, but clear and necessary. The necessity for forgiveness is not always recognized in secular literature. A major work in the field, in many ways a remarkable and helpful book, intones with invective against anyone who would dare make forgiveness a part of the healing process.

> Never say or imply that the client should forgive the abuser. Forgiveness is not essential for healing. This fact is disturbing to many counselors, ministers, and the public at large. But it is absolutely true. If you hold the belief survivors must forgive the abuser in order to heal, you should not be working with survivors.[2]

Considering how forgiveness is understood by many Christians and most unbelievers (forget the harm, pretend everything is fine, be nice and allow more misuse), it is little wonder that secular therapists are loathe to affirm such an unbiblical notion.

Forgiveness can be defined in terms of three components: (1) a hunger for restoration, (2) bold love, and (3) revoked revenge.

Hunger for Restoration
For many abuse victims restoration is the most difficult element in forgiveness. One abused woman told me, "I am willing to love

him, but don't ever ask me to want to be with him. I can't imagine ever seeing him in this life, and the thought that I might have to spend eternity with him sounds more like hell than heaven."

A victim will not hunger for restoration until the obstacles of deadness, mistrust, and the hatred of passion are removed. Once the disastrous effects of powerlessness, betrayal, and ambivalence are entered through honesty and transformed by repentance, the potential for living courageously with others will feel like a desire rather than an onerous burden. Meanwhile, shouts of evangelical fervor about loving the abuser fall on deaf ears.

Forgiveness is not something to be pushed on the abuse victim. It is an aspect of the healing process, but not a bitter pill to swallow. It must be assumed not commanded. A heart that knows something of the joy of returning to God will be drawn to offer restoration like God.

Maturity will come through the process discussed in earlier chapters. The return of life, care, and passion will set the stage for addressing the issue of forgiveness. The process may take years; there is no timetable for maturity that is a uniform standard for everyone. Each journey is different, sometimes profoundly so. The common factor in the process is that it will lead to a *freedom to love*.

For an abuse victim to forsake the call to love, even to love the abuser, is tantamont to saying her heart is no better than the one who abused her. One woman, in convulsive hatred, shouted, "I'd rather be dead than restored to him!" I asked her what she would do if God gave her two options—one: press the left button and God would totally destroy the abuser, so that not one molecule of his being existed next to another; or two: press the right button and God would totally restore him to be the man, father, and husband that God designed him to be. She wept with longing for a father, but not her father. I said, "Your father is wicked, perverse, vile, and worthy of condemnation. I did not ask if you wanted to be restored to who he is today, but to a man who is broken and contrite—a father who could weep over the harm done to you and to the Lord. Which button would you choose?" It was a moment of writhing pain and anguish, but her soul had tasted the joy of her own restoration, and she did not want to withold the possibility of joy for him. To have done so would be to deny her own salvation and to call her own good heart evil. She was unwilling to do so, and in that moment, she began to be able to imagine restoration. The ability to imagine what the abuser could be if he repented and was redeemed opens the way to hunger for a pure and righteous restoration of relationship.

There are many obstacles to deepening a desire for restoration that revolve around confusion over what it means to love and how to deal with the desire for revenge. What is the goal of love, and what will happen if we forgive?

Bold Love

Bold love is a commitment to do whatever it takes (apart from sin) to bring health (salvation) to the abuser. A metaphor may help explain what that means. A surgeon who sees a cancerous mass in a patient's neck knows it will kill him. His commitment is to destroy sickness for the sake of returning the body to health. He may stick a knife in the man's neck, or bombard the mass with chemicals or radiation, producing nausea and weakness, in order to eradicate the alien presence. Or he may strengthen the man's diet, provide rest and ease until more heroic measures can be implemented. The basic commitment, irrespective of the "intervention," will be to restore the man to life.

Bold love is reflected in Paul's command: "Love must be sincere. Hate what is evil; cling to what is good" (Romans 12:9).

Love is to be without hypocrisy; it is to be unfeigned. The Proverbs also state, "Better is open rebuke than hidden love. The kisses of an enemy may be profuse, but faithful are the wounds of a friend" (Proverbs 27:5-6).

In both passages, love is viewed as alien to feigned support and deceitful kisses of kindness. *Love is a powerful force and energy to reclaim the potential good in another, even at the risk of great sacrifice and loss.*

For example, if another's arrogance destroys the possibility of relationship with us and with God, we must hate his arrogance and see it as a cancer to be destroyed. In one way, the cancerous mass can be said to be part of the man, but in another sense it is a foreign, alien thing that is not part of God's original design. If we are to hate what is evil and cling to what is good, we are constrained to detest all that is consonant with evil and bind ourselves to whatever is good. Therefore, love is not anemic unconditional acceptance that ignores evil in others or ourselves (Matthew 7:3-6). It is not contradictory to love someone, desire their good, and equally work toward destroying their cancer through bringing them to repentance and faith.

The mind-set of the one who loves boldly is summarized by C. S. Lewis in his sermon "The Weight of Glory":

> The load, or weight, or burden of my neighbor's glory should be laid on my back, a load so heavy that only humility can carry it, and the backs of the proud will be broken. It is a serious thing to live in a society of possible gods and goddesses, to remember that the dullest and most uninteresting person you talk to may one day be a creature which, if you saw it now, you would be strongly tempted to worship or else a horror and a corruption such as you now meet, if at all, only in a nightmare. All day long we are, in some degree, helping each other to one or other of these destinations.[3]

Love means courageously using our life for the purpose of reclaiming in another the ground lost to the weeds, thorns, and thistles of satanic intrusion. It might be through direct, frontal confrontation (Luke 17:3) or patient, slow kindness (Ephesians 4:32). The goal, in either case, is restoration.

Two questions are often asked: "What does it mean to boldly love an abuser who is not a Christian?" "What does it mean to boldly love an abuser who will not deal with the past abuse?" Both questions require more words than are possible in this chapter; however, at core, both have the same answer: There are no certain steps or techniques to loving boldly. The heart of the lover must be free (through walking the path of honesty and repentance) to imaginatively ponder what it means to give grace to the abuser. There are no short cuts, no clear and smooth paths to follow.

Revoking Revenge

The courageous work of hating evil and clinging to good is further clarified by Paul as not repaying evil for evil (Romans 12:17) and forsaking revenge to leave room for the wrath of God (Romans 12:19). Bold love seeks to restore good and destroy evil, but such a view comes perilously close to justifying destructive expressions of rage toward the perpetrator under the guise of concern for his well-being. There is a profound difference between righteous anger and wicked revenge.

The desire to do harm to another is not always the same as wanting him to pay for his sin. Many times I have prayed for harm to come to a blind, arrogant, harmful man or woman in order to bring them to their senses. Paul encourages us to pour burning coals on an evildoer's head rather than strike back in revenge. John Stott argues that "pouring burning coals" is a New Testament metaphor for shaming or causing embarrassment. Coals turn the face red, the same color produced by shame. He suggests that our feeding and offering drink to an evildoer humbles and shames him and opens his heart to the possibility of redemption.[4] The purpose for doing good is to destroy evil. Many abuse victims who want to do harm to the abuser have not recognized the redemptive desire behind their fantasy of revenge.

A desire for the just repayment of sin, in general or toward a particular person, is not incompatible with godliness. The imprecatory psalms look forward to the same sentiment Paul expresses in the close of his letter to the Romans: "The God of peace will soon crush Satan under your feet" (Romans 16:20). The day will come when the unrepentant evildoer will be dashed to the ground and drowned in manure (Isaiah 25:10-12). The desire to see the abuser pay is honorable and consistent with the longing for the day of judgment. Again, what makes this attitude different from seeking revenge?

There are three important components that separate a

hunger for justice from fantasies or actions of revenge. First, revenge leaves no room for restoration. The judgment is final. The dilemma is that we will be measured and judged according to the same categories we use to judge others (Matthew 7:1-2). If I condemn you for being insensitive, I will be held accountable to the same exacting standard I use to reject you. Jesus puts the issue in hard words: "But if you do not forgive men their sins, your Father will not forgive your sins" (Matthew 6:15). The desire to see justice done and sin punished must always begin in the beholder (Matthew 7:3) before it moves to the sinner; but be clear, the removal of the log in our eye does impel us to deal with the speck in the other's.

Second, revenge gets in the way of God. Our acts of revenge are puny; His are perfect. Paul does not condemn the Romans for *wanting* revenge, only for *seeking* it. Most Christians are uncomfortable with the righteous rage of God. A passage that has given comfort to many is the picture of the feast of the Bridegroom when we will be dressed in white linen, spotless and pure for our betrothed (Revelation 19:6-9). The great supper of God, however, includes the apocalyptic picture of judgment, when the flesh of kings, generals, and mighty men will be devoured by animals and birds of prey (Revelation 19:11-21). Quite a scene for an after-dinner floor show! God is angry; we are too. But we've been invited to wait for the day, which is soon to come, when we can crush the neck of Satan with our feet. The desire for revenge is honoring to God; getting in the way of His patient call to repentance and His righteous judgment is foolish.

Finally, God gives an opportunity for conquering and overcoming evil today: Do good. Notice the kind of good He suggests: providing sustenance for the legitimate hunger and thirst of the body (Romans 12:20-21). What does evil expect? The answer is more of the same. Evil avoids the light; it expects the abuse victim to fear shame. Evil feeds on subtlety; it expects the abuse victim to live behind masks. Evil rejoices in death; it expects the abuse victim to withhold life. Evil despises legitimate satisfaction of the soul; it expects the abuse victim to hate nourishing passion.

Paul strikes a death blow against evil when he tells us to give evil life. It is like pouring life-giving water on the Wicked Witch of the West—she melts. Life and death do not mix. And when life, light, and love—in all its humble beauty, broken strength, frail boldness, and passionate other-centeredness—encounters evil, evil must flee or be transformed.

WHAT WILL IT LOOK LIKE TO LOVE AN ABUSER?

It should be clear by now that we live in a world of abusers, both capital-A abusers (those who wreak sexual, physical, and emotional harm) and small-a abusers (those who harm through "typical" human sin). In that sense, every person has abused and been abused. Many have never capital-A abused another or been capital-A abused, but the core of sin and the damage is the same for us all. Therefore, it is not sufficient to focus solely on the one who sexually abused the victim. We must expand the focus to include what it looks like to love all those who harm us.

There are three categories of abusers: the average abuser, the abuser-surrogate, and the capital-A abuser. To illustrate the theory, mood, and specifics involved in loving each kind of abuser would require a number of lengthy stories. Every abuse victim's situation is unique and requires face-to-face discussion of the specifics with other thoughtful, growing believers. Even after such individualized attention, however, the victim is left alone to wrestle with the difficult implications of what it means to love, from her redeemed heart, a person who has violated her body or soul. Bold loving for one victim might look entirely different from another victim's movement toward those who have harmed her. But there are some basics to the process of giving grace. These foundational principles can be applied to relationship with any type of abuser.

Average Abusers
An average abuser is the store clerk who snaps at us when we return an item, the next door neighbor who lets his dog fertilize our lawn, or our child who won't pick up his room. Average abuse

inevitably occurs in a fallen world where few care or provide in the way God intended.

What does it look like to love the average abuser? The answer is simple: set boundaries, deepen relationship where appropriate, grin and bear it, and keep moving toward the qualities of the soul that are not lost in the midst of pain and conflict.

For example, when my flight was canceled moments before another air carrier left for the same city, I was rude and obnoxious. No one knew me, my profession, or my commitment (or lack of) to Christ. But the rest of the day I thought about how I could easily have set off a chain of abuse. I added evil to an already wicked world. The airline probably cheated me. The ticket agent was curt. I had reason to be angry, but there was no call to abuse. If I had taken the data down, the agent's name, the time of cancellation, the flight number, and the time the other flight left, it would have been appropriate to write and complain. I had no opportunity to develop a relationship with the agent, so I'm left to grin and bear it and choose to use the event to help me develop the fruit of the Spirit.

The grin-and-bear-it stage is an important aspect to dealing with an abusive world. It does not imply denial or a *laissez-faire* attitude. To grin is to smile at a fallen world. There are times that the crazy mixture of incompetence and sin is befuddling and mind-boggling. A good friend made twenty phone calls to get a paper delivered to his home. He was told that his home was in a nondeliverable area, yet every evening for weeks a salesman for the paper called to get him to subscribe. He was kind at first, but day by day he became more and more perturbed. Finally, he spoke to one of the vice-presidents of the corporation and found out that the head of delivery lived two streets away. The executive promised that a paper would be delivered the next morning, or else! At six a.m. my friend went to his front door to find a copy of the rival morning paper; the other paper was nowhere to be seen. After yet another week of phone calls, he finally received his chosen paper.

A grin-and-bear-it response is most appropriate to this kind of abuse (perhaps not at the moment of intense frustration) because we can anticipate a brighter, kinder day. An alien and a pilgrim ought not expect (in any final sense) a sinless, hassle-free journey. To bear up under the weight of a fallen world is to faithfully endure hardship, learning to suffer well, for the sake of a higher call. More is required in practice, however, than a good attitude. There must be an offer of both grace and respect. Both can be accomplished by clarifying boundaries and offering kindness.

The kind of boundaries to be set will depend on one's typical style of relating. In response to the neighbor's dog making deposits on her lawn, the Good Girl might hand the neighbor a shovel; the Party Girl may do it herself, without a joke or a subtle punishment; and the Tough Girl might warmly laugh and ignore it or ask her husband to remove it for her. The issue is not, "What is the right thing to do?" but, "What will give us a greater opportunity to love?" The Scriptures say, "If your brother sins, rebuke him" (Luke 17:3), and "Love covers over a multitude of sins" (1 Peter 4:8). So which do we do: rebuke or cover over? It depends on the unique interplay of persons, situation, and timing, but the goal is to build-up and give life (Ephesians 4:29). Therefore, boundaries always serve to enhance relationships: What will give us greater opportunity to speak truth in love? For that reason, no detailed picture will ever capture what it means to love another average abuser. It must rest in the heart of the lover, whose soul is warmed by the gospel, whose imagination is set free by repentance, whose hands are free to serve and mouth free to rebuke.

Abuser Surrogate

There are similarities but significant additions in dealing with the abuser-surrogate. The abuser-surrogate is usually the person who offers the abuse victim the most intimate relationship in principle or actuality. It will be the relationship where all the past damage and self-protection is intensely played out. It seems that a spouse is most often the abuser-surrogate. In the marriage relationship, intimacy, trust, and sexuality are set against the issues of powerlessness, betrayal, and ambivalence. As stated before, the abuse victim usually will have chosen a relationship with a man who is dead to intimacy, untrustworthy (or too dull to be untrustworthy), divorced from passion or a user of passion. The marriage of an abuse victim is usually dull and stable or painful and chaotic. It is not unusual for a marriage to swing between the two ends like a ride on a roller coaster. It is not possible, at this point, to discuss all that needs to be addressed to revoke revenge and pursue bold love in a marriage relationship. Some women are married to hard, angry, cold, but somewhat open men. Others are enmeshed with extremely closed and self-centered men, or worse, with men who are evil, cold-hearted, and potentially violent. To address all that needs to be said is beyond the scope of this section; however, in most cases, perspective can be gained only in the context of some sort of marriage counseling. If a husband will not pursue counseling with his wife, the woman can still benefit from a counselor who will help her explore what it means to love a man who will not involve himself in the process of change.

What are the basics of loving the abuser-surrogate? The process includes building consistent boundaries, deepening intimacy, learning to sorrow and rejoice, and persevering in faith toward God's redemption of one's spouse as a person clothed in dignity and strength.

It is imperative to build relationship-enhancing boundaries. For example, many abuser-surrogates do not know about the fact of past abuse. One reason may be that the surrogate cannot be trusted to properly hear and respond to the history. Therefore, the couple must acknowledge and work toward resolving the issues that block trust before such heartbreaking information is shared. This hard work is not the sole responsibility of the abuser-surrogate. The victim herself must be willing to address the couple's difficulties no matter how risky it may feel to her to be exposed as both vulnerable (wounded) and self-protective (sinful).

For example, an abused woman refused to share with her husband the fact of her past abuse. He was unresponsive and uninvolved whenever she shared other significant (but minor in comparison) wounds of her past. She determined that, if he was so unfeeling, he would never have access to her deepest hurt. She hinted at her displeasure and occasionally attacked his cold front, but she never boldly pursued him with tenacious, honest, and passionate energy. In a more subtle way, she was just as guilty of self-protective, sinful relating as he was. Her part in building trust in their relationship involved opening herself even wider to his potential passivity and rejection, allowing him to see her pain over his response, and letting him know how deeply she longed for a richer relationship between them that would allow her to give herself to him completely.

Though there are exceptions, normally the victim of abuse should discuss her past with her spouse at some point in order to expose the destructive fire that started years before the marriage began. In turn, that will help clarify where the spouse has added fuel that keeps the fire burning years after the past abuse.

Other relationship-deepening boundaries need to be formed. For example, many—but not all—abuse victims will need to put a hold on their sexual relationship. Often, arousal is either not present, or available only through soul-damaging fantasies. To continue perpetuating the same abusive process in the midst of what should be an intimate sharing of the soul is like a dog returning to its own vomit. Often, putting sex on hold will dissolve an already weak and nonexistent marriage. The tragedy is that the dissolution would not have come about if the victim had remained dead. Even more grievous is the fact that the surrogate may use the hiatus to do even more harm, rather than following Paul's injunction: "Do not deprive each other except by mutual consent and for a time, so that you may devote yourselves to prayer" (1 Corinthians 7:6). Ideally, the sexual hiatus will allow the bonds of intimacy to be reestablished and sexual issues to be discussed before physical intimacy is resumed.

If the relationship deepens through honesty, travail, and repentance, it is unlikely the spouse will be used as a surrogate. However, when new boundaries and pursuit of depth in relationship result in irreconciled division, the victim will find it even more of a battle to boldly love her spouse who, in turning against her, has become a capital-A abuser.

Regardless of whether the marital relationship improves or disintegrates, the victim's passion for life will increase. Her tears will be deeper and her laughter will be richer. Ultimately, living out honesty, repentance, and bold love will draw her good heart toward the Author of life and His character qualities will become hers.

Capital-A Abuser (Past and Present)

What does it look like to love the actual abuser? Obviously, this question assumes that the perpetrator is still alive and the victim knows his whereabouts. If the abuser is unavailable or deceased, then I do not encourage memory healing, Gestalt conversations with an empty chair that represents the perpetrator, or any other means that works toward a cathartic explosion of rage and an imaginary forgiveness process. I'd rather focus attention on dealing with the abuser-surrogate, because in the absense of the actual abuser, the unresolved dynamics in the current relationship are often even more intense than if he were present.

Loving the capital-A offender sometimes involves confronting him. The victim should carefully consider her motives, however, before calling confrontation love. If her desire to confront is to more deeply heal herself, then her motive is basically self-centered. The goal of healing is secondary to the primary call of living out the gospel with strength and dignity, and care.

What, then, is a valid motive for the choice to confront? There are two: concern for the abuser and concern for those he may still be abusing. It is a known fact that abusers are likely to abuse again. Unaddressed abuse often allows the perpetrator to harm others in the future. The abuser himself must live with some level of anguish in his soul. He must have a secret spot in his soul that has neither forgotten or justified his past abuse. His anguish may not be observable to others (or even to himself) because it may be so well-hidden behind shame-based rage and arrogance. The arrogance, however, is in fact proof of the great distress in the soul—the soul of an image bearer who was created to love but has instead destroyed. The anguish neither exonerates nor excuses the past abuse, nor the current failure to repent. Nevertheless, the anguish still exists and should be of concern to the victim who is considering confrontation.

It is, of course, up to the abuse victim, if and when a confrontation will occur. However, she should not move toward confrontation until she has moved from honesty to repentance in her own heart. There should also be some experience of bold love in less threatening relationships (with friends, counselor, children, or spouse) before she attempts to deal with the perpetrator and the nonoffending parent(s). The victim should never go out to battle without first strengthening her soul and skill through basic training.

If the time becomes right for confrontation, what will it look like? For one thing, it is usually not effectively accomplished in a single meeting; it is a process of building a new kind of relationship. The process includes several elements: building consistent boundaries, rebuking and inviting the abuser to repent, offering relationship, deepening intimacy, learning to sorrow and rejoice, and persevering in faith toward God's redemption of the abuser as a person clothed in dignity and strength.

Before the victim attempts to directly rebuke her abuser and invite him to repent, she should have made substantial shifts in the style of relating she has habitually used to distance herself and seek revenge against him and others. There should be a sense that the relationship has been put on notice: "Life is different and good, and I would like for you to know the joy of restoration with God." The notice will rarely involve direct preaching or teaching. The perpetrator will perceive it because the victim will be strong where she was once afraid, kind where she was once distant, and passionate where she was once dead. The basic change will be in the internal realm, resulting in corresponding external shifts in sometimes minor, but highly significant areas of interaction, whether that interaction is daily or infrequent.

For example, a Party Girl who was normally light and bubbly sat at a Thanksgiving feast with her family (including her abuser) and said very little. The change in her behavior may seem minor, but her family was distraught and incensed. She was neither moody nor withholding in her interactions, but she chose to speak only when her soul was stirred rather than on cue when the family silences beckoned her to act the clown in order to quell their discomfort. Her change was a step toward eventual confrontation with the abuser and the nonoffending parents.

Actual confrontation must involve *rebuke*.

Jesus said, "If your brother sins against you, rebuke him and if he repents, forgive him. If he sins against you seven times in a day, and seven times comes back to you and says, 'I repent,' forgive him" (Luke 17:3-4).

Rebuke often opens the door to repentance. Rebuke ought to clarify the offense, its consequences, and the means for restoration.

It is usually best for an abuse victim to invite the abuser to a confrontation, not hiding the purpose for their meeting. The meeting ought to occur in a safe, public place (usually a high-class restaurant). It is good to have a friend or two at another table or out in the parking lot praying and supporting the interaction. A confrontation should never be attempted without prayer.

The rebuke must follow a logical sequence, and if a step is not passed, the rebuke cannot continue. The issues that block a step may be discussed between victim and abuser, but resolution cannot occur until the issues are dealt with. In order for a rebuke to be effective, the abuser must take the following steps:

1. When the victim reviews the details of the abuse, the perpetrator must agree that the abuse occurred.
2. The abuser must accept complete responsibility for the abuse—without excuse or blameshifting.
3. When the victim describes the past and current damage from the abuse, the perpetrator must evidence some grief and acknowledgment of harm.
4. When the victim exposes the abuser's current relational failures that inhibit the potential of reconciliation, he must be open to consider the data and deal with the barriers.
5. When the victim describes the process for moving into

a new kind of relationship, the abuser must express a
willingness to pursue the path and seek additional help
(through church discipline, counseling, seminars, or
reading).

If the perpetrator, and later the nonoffending parent, is
willing to move through all five steps, the victim can offer relationship and take steps to deepen intimacy. If repentance does
not occur, the victim can still forgive by offering bold love, *but
relationship cannot be restored.*

If, after the initial confrontation, the abuser totally denies
the past abuse and its damaging consequences, the victim ought
to offer to pursue the subject again after a short period of time
(several weeks). She should make it clear that she will not drop
the subject in order to make the abuser comfortable or relieve
the relational tension. If the abuser continues to rebuff her invitation to a restored relationship through repentance, then at some
point the victim must sever the relationship. She should explain
that the estrangement is entirely reversible if the abuser should
decide at some point to begin the restoration process. This form
of excommunication is actually a gift, a respectful choice to honor
the abuser with the consequences of his own destructive choice,
in hope that loneliness and shame will draw his cold heart back
to the fire of relationship (2 Thessalonians 3:14-15).

One man, who was raped repeatedly as a child by his father,
was told by him that the abuse never occurred. He also asked
his son, at the same time, for a loan to get medical treatment.
The son's choice, though it did not seem like honoring or loving his father, was to deny the loan. In fact the father had
ample money, but he did not want to cash in his stock when
the market was low. The son's refusal alienated his father; his
father proceeded to defame his son throughout the family. When
the son received phone calls from his brothers accusing him of
turning against his father, he asked if they would like to know
the whole story. Several brothers did, and others did not. He
shared enough detail to indicate the strong need for repentance
on his father's part. One brother turned against him and told

him the past is the past and he should forget it like a good Christian. Another brother wept—first for him and then for himself as he acknowledged their father had done the same to him.

A refusal to normalize a wicked relationship is a gift of excommunication that waits for the sinner's return, but does not offer deep relationship until he acknowledges and deals with his sin. The offer of restored relationship (based on repentance), in honest, open-hearted kindness, is living out the gospel, even if the offer is spurned and condemned.

In the case just mentioned, the son chose to close the door to relationship with his father at great cost, given the hatred of other members of the family. He honored his father by giving him the opportunity to repent and taste the restoration of relationship with the righteous Father. The door to relationship was closed, but not locked. Several months after the event, his father asked him to perform a relatively easy task for a brother. He kindly told his father that if the brother wanted the job done, he was free to call. He spoke warmly and directly, but reminded his father of his desire to see the relationship properly healed. His father hung up on him. Months later, his father called again, asking for restoration, but without dragging either of their memories through the mud. The son, in tears, declined. The father, in a fit of rage, slammed the phone down. I would love to report a happy ending to this sad story, but only time, and the clarity of heaven, will provide the desired finish. Nevertheless, in his sorrow, loneliness, and occasional bouts of confusion, this son has found a deep, if intermittent joy in being used to call his wicked father to repentance.

What is to be done with the abuser who admits the past but either deals with the damage in a cavalier, cheap-grace fashion ("I'm sorry for the past, but I am forgiven and your attitude is unChristian and unloving") or cries for forgiveness with self-serving self-reproach? In other words, what is to be done if the abuser blocks real change with other-centered or self-centered contempt? A key to the answer is preparation. The victim ought to have reckoned with such a possibility, especially knowing the heart of the abuser from other contexts. Her battle plan should include a means of stripping the abuser of his "normal ploy" to escape rebuke. One woman stated to her father: "Dad, I know how you've handled every minor confrontation with Mom. You've simply told her how sorry you are, which relieves you of the need to look more deeply into her pain. Is that what you plan on doing with me as I begin to share the damage you brought into my life?" She surprised her father with her insight into his usual defensive tactics. Exposing his contemptuous maneuvers paved the way toward an open discussion of the past abuse.

The process of redeeming a relationship is not after the initial confrontation, even if it goes well. It will require a continual returning to each step, forgiving again and again, as long as there is evidence of repentance.

The Lord tells us to "forgive, if he repents," making restoration of relationship conditional on the response of the offender. Repentance is never merely saying, "I'm sorry." If that were the case, then repentance would be no different than penance, the performance of an act of contrition. True repentance, even if it is required seven times in a day, will be experienced by the abuser as a sorrow unto life, evidenced in a willingness to be humbled and an emerging hunger to deal with the consequences of sin. Anything less is not repentance; therefore, to receive the abuser's "I'm sorry" as sufficient evidence of change is a disrespectful disregard of what his soul is capable of offering through true repentance.

THE BATTLE CONTINUES

When a victim of sexual abuse pursues the path of love, she opens the door to the deepening of intimacy with others, and possibly with the abuser. Her choice to go the unusual route of maturity will increase her passion of sorrow and joy and in turn will strengthen her resolve to pursue the things of God. Her character will be transformed not because she is choosing to learn a new skill, but because the Holy Spirit will honor her heart's intention to follow Christ.

The battle continues. The growing man or woman will continue to drink deeply from the cup of honesty, repentance, and bold love. Each cycle in the process will strengthen conviction, weaken contempt, and deepen the hunger for more of God.

Some days the taste of life will be bitter. Other days it will be sweeter than any honey and more intoxicating than any wine. Drinking from the water that wells up to eternal life will satisfy the soul more deeply than words can express. The few rich tastes of God-given joy are worth the long, hard work of dealing with memories, rage, loneliness, and fear. In so doing we emulate Paul as a drink offering, poured out for the sake of our friends, family, and strangers, as we eagerly await Christ's return and the crown of righteousness well worth the battle fought and endured.

Epilogue:
Words to the Wise

The process of coming alive will be different for every man or woman who has been abused. The common elements of the process, however, will be honesty, repentance, and bold love.

My heart's desire is to relieve the unnecessary shame and contempt near the core of the awful struggle. Even more, I invite the victim to shed the harmful strategies of self-protection that rob her of joy and passion. I fear that she will contemptuously ingest the discussion of sin and self-protection and feel a greater burden on her heavy-laden soul. Instead, I pray she will taste God's compassion.

Although I have chosen to address the sexual abuse victim as the primary audience of this book, I hope it will be equally helpful for all those who are part of the abusive past and the restorative present. Before I have one last word with the victim, I would like to speak directly to those who have inflicted deep wounds—"players" in the actual abuse (perpetrator and nonoffending parents)—and those who are part of the healing process (abuser-surrogate, friends, pastors, and counselors).

WORDS TO THE PERPETRATOR

The grace of God extends to every sinner, including the one who violates the body and soul of a small child or impressionable adolescent. The path back to right relationship with God is not easy, however. It is not a matter of saying you're sorry, shedding tears, asking forgiveness, and then getting back to what you feel is a normal life. The Lord's stern rebuke ought to ring in your ears:

> "But if anyone causes one of these little ones who believe in me to sin, it would be better for him to have a large millstone hung around his neck and to be drowned in the depths of the sea." (Matthew 18:6)

Restitution does not heal the wound. Bowing your head in self-pitying contempt only adds more weight to the victim's load. The only route to restoration is through brokenness. Broken repentance will show in your willingness to submit yourself to the process of change through church discipline, counseling, interacting with other abusers, seeking wisdom and insight, and providing for the recuperative process of the victim. That can include offering to pay for counseling, career evaluation, and medical treatment.

Essentially, you must deal with the log in your own eye regarding the past abuse, current relational failures, and the potential issues of past abuse in your own life. Do not allow shame and contempt to circumvent the process of change in your life. Support the process of the abuse victim, without demanding or expecting warmth, closeness, or gratitude. Allow the victim time and space to take the process at his or her own pace.

In time, your joy will deepen as you choose a path of honesty, repentance, and bold love. The deep, deep sorrow of marring the beauty of a human soul will never be eradicated in this life, but the profound relief of brokenness will create a passionate desire for a day when all damage will be washed away. Your work of dealing with the damage is a death blow to our Adversary, the devouring lion.

WORDS TO THE NONOFFENDING PARENT(S)

Your sin is easiest to hide, behind the fact or the claim of ignorance. In most cases, the nonoffending parent feels either profound guilt (self-contempt) or vindictive anger (other-centered contempt) at the abuser or, even worse, at the victim for not sharing the data in the past or for bringing it out in the present. In either case, you are hindering the process of change for the victim.

If you missed or ignored the evidence in the past then you ought to ask yourself deep questions as to why your child was less important than what you were choosing to protect. I find that nonoffending parents tend to be unwilling to ask hard questions and deal with their failure to intervene. Don't let that happen. Stop protecting the abuser. It is not respecting or loving him to make excuses or to justify unjustifiable sin. It is also crucial to allow the abuse victim to express her anger toward you without fear that you will either crumble or abandon her.

In order to deal with all the issues that may be generated in you, I strongly recommend seeking a support group and personal counseling. Your commitment to change will be a wonderful encouragement to the abuse victim to continue on her own difficult path.

WORDS TO THE ABUSER-SURROGATE

Your role in the process of change is crucial. Your part is to provide a stable environment that neither pushes for change, nor defers involvement to a professional. In most cases, it is wise for the victim to seek counseling, but your willingness to join the process at appropriate moments, and even more to look at your own life in order to deprive the "fire" of a source of fuel, is imperative.

Separate the fact that you did not cause the problem from the likely fact that you have added salt to an already existing wound. It is important for you to gain knowledge about the issues of abuse. Read books, go to seminars, and listen, really listen, to your spouse. Don't push for discussion, but be willing to pursue it when she opens the door. Be aware that the process will be tumultuous. Your sex life may deteriorate, and the pleasant level of comfort you and she have gained through years of interaction may dissolve. Don't blame your spouse. Don't attack the process.

Be patient. Couples who are willing to deeply enter the process will come out stronger, with satisfying intimacy and more lively, passionate, and mutal sexual enjoyment.

Learn to experience righteous anger toward those who harmed your spouse; she wants your protection. Even more, learn to weep for your spouse; she wants your compassion. Whatever blocks you from being able to be righteously enraged and passionately moved will diminish trust and intimacy and hinder the process of change.

WORDS TO A FRIEND

You are the friend of someone who has been abused, and you are untrained, inexperienced, and scared. If I am accurate so far, then you have also seriously thought about backing out of the relationship with your abused friend. Not that you are going to treat her like a leper or avoid all contact, but the issue of abuse, the current struggles and fears, are off-limits.

My counsel to you is simple: Don't back off from the frightening terrain of a wounded heart. You may say the wrong things and even cause more harm, but the worst harm is to turn your back. Accept your limitations, but also acknowledge the fact that you are on the front lines of the battle. You may not like to hear it but the fact is, you are a foot soldier, an infantryman who is often the first to take the fire of the enemy.

As a therapist, I see your friend once, or maybe twice a week. You see her every day. I deal with significant issues in her soul, but you talk about the same issues, and even more. I may be necessary to the process, but you are even more so. Let me say it again: You are very important as a friend who will pray, talk, laugh, cry, read, embrace, shout, bake cookies, drive to Little League, and live life in intimate proximity. Don't allow your inexperience or your own personal past to keep you from loving well.

WORDS TO THE PASTOR

Your part in the process of change can be life giving. If you counsel, my thoughts for you are imbedded in my comments to the counselor (see next section). If your work is traditional pastoral preaching and teaching, then your role is more than crucial; it is culture changing. Among other things, the pulpit can serve as a platform for educating the sensibilities and altering the misconceptions of the Christian community. As I, a psychologist, address the issues of abuse, I can be easily written off. But when you admit that the problem exists and causes damage that is not immediately eradicated at conversion, you have allowed light into a dark, shameful room and touched the lives of countless people.

As a teacher-preacher, you can also challenge the inadequate conceptions of forgiveness promulgated among Christians, strengthen the survivor's resolve to continue dealing with the battle when it gets tough, and encourage the abuser-surrogate to persevere when quitting seems imminent. You may never spend much time in the counseling process, but your support and collaboration with a counselor will lend your faith, trust, and courage to the victim in her dark moments.

WORDS TO THE COUNSELOR

If you are like me, then you tenaciously hold to your own approach to the battle of abuse and restoration more dogmatically than you would like to admit. Likely, you have either an undealt-with history of abuse, or a history that has found solace in some "manageable" approach to change. If the approach has helped, then it is easy to assume that others need to walk the same path. But I encourage you never to uncritically accept any model of change merely on the basis of its effectiveness. Obviously, even satanic options for change work for a while.

If you are attempting to set forth a distinctively Christian approach to counseling, evaluate whether there is room in your model and technique for dealing with both human dignity and depravity. One of the divisive issues in our day involves our understanding of sin, its role in the structure of human personality, and its psychological symptoms.

Acknowledge the possible need for more training. Most professionals have never received specific training in dealing with the issues of sexual abuse. I went through two master's degrees and one A.P.A.-approved doctorate and never spent one minute on the unique issues of sexual abuse, let alone post-traumatic stress, multiple personality, and other secondary symptoms that are uniquely part of the personality structure of those who have suffered traumatic abuse. Pursue an understanding of the role of abuse in your own life, style of relating, countertransference, and choice of therapeutic modality.

Finally, make sure you are moral and honorable in word and touch. You should use caution and keen judgment in using touch even through handholding and hugging. The victim may interpret your touch to mean more than you imagine. It is not right to treat the abuse victim as a leper, avoiding all touch, but a conservative orientation is both circumspect and therapeutically wise.

WORDS TO THE ABUSE VICTIM

Listen to the words of a song written by Amy Grant and Tom Hemby:

Ask Me

I see her as a little girl hiding in her room.
She takes another bath,
And she sprays her momma's perfume —
To try and wipe away the scent he left behind,
But it haunts her mind.
You see she's his little rag —
Nothing more than just a waif —
And he's mopping up his need.
She is tired and afraid.
Maybe she'll find a way through these
Awful years — to disappear.

Ask me if I think there's a God up in the Heavens,
Where did He go in the middle of her shame?
Ask me if I think there's a God up in the Heavens.

I see no mercy, and no one down here's naming names,
Nobody's naming names.

Now she's looking in the mirror at a lovely woman face.
No more frightened little girl,
Like she's gone without a trace.
Still she leaves the light burning in the hall.
It's hard to sleep at all.
Til she crawls up in her bed
Acting quiet as a mouse,
Deep inside she's listening for a creaking in the house.
But no one's left to harm her,
She's finally safe and sound.
There's a peace she's found.

Ask her how she knows there's a God up in the Heavens,
Where did He go in the middle of her shame?
Ask her how she knows there's a God up in the Heavens.
She said His mercy is bringing her life again.

You have been damaged. But you have great hope. The mercy of God does not eradicate the damage, at least not in this life, but it soothes the soul and draws it forward to a hope that purifies and sets free. Allow the pain of the past and the travail of the change process to create fresh new life in you and to serve as a bridge over which another victim may walk from death to life. It is an honor beyond compare to be part of the birthing process of life and hope, and a joy deeper than words to see evil and its damage destroyed. I await that day and joy with you.

Notes

CHAPTER 2—THE ENEMY: SIN AND SHAME

1. C. S. Lewis, *The Great Divorce* (New York: Macmillan Publishing Co., Inc., 1978), pages 61-62.
2. A. W. Tozer, *The Pursuit of God* (Camp Hill, PA: Christian Publications, Inc., 1982), page 22.

CHAPTER 9—STYLE OF RELATING

1. I have left men out of this scheme for one reason: I am less certain about the patterns that are characteristic of male abuse survivors than I am of those common to female survivors. I do, however, have a few tentative thoughts regarding the typical relational styles of male victims of sexual abuse.

    Generally, males compensate for the damage they have experienced through the demonstration of physical or intellectual power. Many macho-tough and emotionally distant men mask their past abuse behind physical prowess or they use their keen intellect to intimidate others. This "macho boy" style of relating probably most closely resembles that of the Tough Girl.

    Another general pattern is reflected in the uninvolved,

withdrawn, and quietly hostile "nice guy." He is often tame, boring, and unassuming. I do not see him, however, as the exact male correlate to the Good Girl; he is too passive to be a guilt-driven people pleaser, though he is similar to the Good Girl in his commitment to conflict-free living. The nice guy often detaches from typical male interest in personal power through physique, sports, and cars. He is more likely to absorb himself in a hobby, club, or isolated activity.

The last parallel is to the Party Girl. The closest male counterpart, the "seductive boy," is far more predatory and less subtle in his commitment to conquer. Some would classify him as a modern-day "sexaholic." While a macho boy or a nice guy can be sexually addicted, the seductive boy continually and compulsively draws men and/or women into sexual talk, jokes, and activity. His preoccupation is sexual power. The correlation to the Party Girl is moderate. His sexual acting out is far less subtle and his commitment to others is almost nonexistent.

CHAPTER 10 — THE UNLIKELY ROUTE TO JOY

1. Annie Dillard, *Teaching a Stone to Talk* (New York: Harper & Row, 1982), page 65.

CHAPTER 13 — BOLD LOVE

1. John R. W. Stott, *The Cross of Christ* (Downers Grove, IL: Inter-Varsity Press, 1986), page 335.
2. Ellen Bass and Laura Davis, *The Courage to Heal* (New York: Harper & Row, 1988), page 348.
3. C. S. Lewis, *The Weight of Glory* (Grand Rapids, MI: W. B. Eerdmans Publishing Co., 1977), pages 14-15.
4. Stott, page 301.

Bibliography

SCHOLARLY BOOKS

Courtois, Christine A. *Healing the Incest Wound.* New York: W. W. Norton and Company, 1988.
> Courtois provides an excellent overview of the issues related to the dynamics of sexual abuse. She details the issues a therapist will face and a number of therapeutic intervention models for helping an adult who was abused as a child.

Finkelhor, David. *Child Sexual Abuse: New Theory and Research.* New York: The Free Press, 1984.
> Finkelhor reviews the current research and evaluates the methods used in the studies that underestimate the current number of sexual abuse cases. His book is an excellent blend of research, theory, and evaluation.

Finkelhor, David. *A Sourcebook on Child Sexual Abuse.* Beverly Hills, CA: Sage Publications, 1986.
> Finkelhor and associates deal with various topics of concern including: prevalence, abusers, initial and longterm effects. An excellent update on his past research.

Ganzarain, Ramon, and Bonnie Buchele. *Fugitives of Incest.*
Madison, CT: International Universities Press, 1988.
> An excellent book for those who have read other serious
> books on group counseling and want to expand their under-
> standing of the unique dimensions of working with incest
> victims in a group setting.

Haugaard, Jeffrey, and N. Dickon Reppucci. *The Sexual Abuse of
Children.* San Francisco, CA: Josey-Bass Publishers, Inc., 1988.
> A comprehensive overview of the issues and treatment
> strategy for intervention with young children and their
> families. A good primer for other reading in this impor-
> tant area.

Kaplan, Helen Singer. *Disorders of Sexual Desire.* New York:
Brunner/Mazel Publishers, Inc., 1979.
> A standard in the field of sex therapy. It does not directly
> address the issues of sexual abuse; however, the struggles of
> many abused people can be better understood after gaining
> a familiarity with Kaplan's concepts.

Maltz, Wendy, and Beverly Holman. *Incest and Sexuality: A
Guide to Understanding and Healing.* Lexington, MA: Lexington
Books, 1987.
> An excellent work for both an individual and a supportive
> spouse to read together and apply the concepts to their sex-
> ual struggles. It is written with both partners in mind and
> accomplishes a great deal in a relatively short book.

Ochberg, Frank. *Post-Traumatic Therapy and Victims of Violence.*
New York: Brunner/Mazel Publishers, Inc., 1988.
> An excellent introduction to the concept of Post-Traumatic
> Stress Disorder (PTSD), also known as the Vietnam Vet
> syndrome. The effects of sexual abuse are similar to the
> consequences of any highly traumatic stress event. An
> understanding of PTSD opens the door to a clearer perspec-
> tive on the effects of abuse.

Russell, Diana E. H. *The Secret Trauma: Incest in the Lives of Girls and Women.* New York: Basic Books, Inc., 1986.
> Russell's study of 930 women in San Francisco is the best-researched study available on the statistics of sexual abuse and incest. Her study covers almost every conceivable question that might be asked about the victims, perpetrators, and their families.

CHRISTIAN BOOKS ON SEXUAL ABUSE

Buhler, Rich. *Pain and Pretending.* Nashville: Thomas Nelson Publishers, Inc., 1988.
> Buhler is a passionate man who writes to change the lives of those who have been traumatized by past abuse. His commitment to remove the blinders of false trust, which denies the past harm and current pain, is laudatory.

Frank, Jan. *A Door of Hope.* San Bernadino, CA: Here's Life Publishers, 1987.
> This is an excellent book by a victim of incest. Frank details a ten-step process of recovery from the effects of sexual abuse with wisdom, sensitivity, and realism.

Hancock, Maxine, and Karen Burton Mains. *Child Sexual Abuse: A Hope for Healing.* Wheaton, IL: Harold Shaw Publishers, 1987.
> Hancock and Mains provide a thorough overview of the issues involved in sexual abuse. They emphasize the role of self-esteem and one's view of God. The details of the book are powerfully fleshed out by allowing the voices of a number of victims to speak about their pain.

Pellauer, Mary, Barbara Chester, and Jane Boyajian (eds.). *Sexual Assault and Abuse: A Handbook for Clergy and Religious Professionals.* San Francisco, CA: Harper & Row, 1987.
> This work is broadly religious and emphasizes a perspective that would make many evangelicals uncomfortable in their theological discussions. The work is helpful in its approach

to understanding how religious professionals are often part
of the problem and not the cure.

Peters, David. *A Betrayal of Innocence: What Everyone Should
Know About Child Sexual Abuse.* Waco, TX: Word Books, Inc.,
1986.
Peters deals with the signs and symptoms that every parent
should be aware of. His overview is helpful and biblically
reassuring that real change can occur.

Tanner, Vicki, and Lynda Elliott. *My Father's Child: Help and
Healing for the Victims of Emotional, Sexual, and Physical Abuse.*
Brentwood, TN: Wolgemuth and Hyatt, Publishers, Inc., 1988.
An excellent book for the victim of multiple abuse. The
tender and biblically sensitive portrayal of our relationship
with God will be a soothing comfort to many.

OTHER BOOKS

Crabb, Larry. *Inside Out.* Colorado Springs, CO: NavPress, 1988.
Inside Out is a courageous exposure of evangelical Christianity's shallow view of change. Change is more than
rearranging our externals; it is a radical change in our
definition of life. *Inside Out* looks at the courage needed
for change, the heart that needs to be changed, the central
direction of our heart, and the process involved in change.

Crabb, Larry. *Understanding People.* Grand Rapids, MI: Zonder-
van Corporation, 1987.
Understanding People provides an excellent picture of what it
means to be made in the image of God. The first part of the
book discusses how to go to the Bible to understand people;
the second part explains human nature in terms of our longings, thinking, choices, and feelings.

Stott, John R. W. *The Cross of Christ.* Downers Grove, IL: Inter-
Varsity Press, 1986.

A classic picture of the work of Jesus Christ on the cross and its implications for the Christian life and community. His section on suffering and dealing with evil is worth every penny the book may cost, and the rest of the book is equally compelling and life-changing.